ENGINEERING SOFTWARE PRODUCTS

An Introduction to Modern Software Engineering

Ian Sommerville

Pearson

Senior Vice President Courseware Portfolio Management: Engineering, Computer Science, Mathematics, Statistics, and Global Editions: *Marcia J. Horton*
Vice President, Portfolio Management: Engineering, Computer Science, and Global Editions: *Julian Partridge*
Executive Portfolio Manager: *Matt Goldstein*
Portfolio Management Assistant: *Meghan Jacoby*
Managing Producer, ECS and Mathematics: *Scott Disanno*
Senior Content Producer: *Erin Ault*
Project Manager: *Rose Kernan*
Manager, Rights and Permissions: *Ben Ferrini*
Operations Specialist: *Maura Zaldivar-Garcia*
Inventory Manager: *Bruce Boundy*
Product Marketing Manager: *Yvonne Vannatta*
Field Marketing Manager: *Demetrius Hall*
Marketing Assistant: *Jon Bryant*
Cover Design: *Black Horse Designs*
Cover Image: *Dmitrydesign/Shutterstock*
Composition: Pearson CSC
Cover Printer: *Phoenix Color/Hagerstown*
Printer/Binder: *Lake Side Communications, Inc. (LSC)*

Library of Congress Cataloging-in-Publication Data

Names: Sommerville, Ian, 1951–author.
Title: Engineering software products / Ian Sommerville.
Description: First edition. | Hoboken, NJ : Pearson, 2019. | Includes
     bibliographical references and indexes.
Identifiers: LCCN 2019004631 | ISBN 9780135210642
Subjects: LCSH: Software engineering. | Computer software—Development.
Classification: LCC QA76.758 .S67 2019 | DDC 005.1—dc23 LC record
available at https://lccn.loc.gov/2019004631

1   19

ISBN 10:   0-13-521064-X
ISBN 13: 978-0-13-521064-2

PREFACE

Software products, such as stand-alone programs, web apps and services, and mobile apps, have transformed our everyday life and work. There are tens of thousands of software product companies, and hundreds of thousands of software engineers are employed worldwide in software product development.

Contrary to what some people may think, engineering software products needs more than coding skills. So, I've written this book to introduce some of the software engineering activities that are important for the production of reliable and secure software products.

Who is the book for?

The book has been designed for students taking a first course in software engineering. People thinking about developing a product who don't have much software engineering experience may also find it useful.

Why do we need a software engineering book that's focused on software products?

Most software engineering texts focus on *project-based* software engineering, where a client develops a specification and the software is developed by another company. However, the software engineering methods and techniques that have been developed for large-scale projects are not suited to software product development.

Students often find it difficult to relate to large, custom software systems. I think that students find it easier to understand software engineering techniques when they are relevant to the type of software that they constantly use. Also, many product engineering techniques are more directly relevant to student projects than project-oriented techniques.

Is this a new edition of your other software engineering textbook?

No, this book takes a completely different approach and, apart from a couple of diagrams, does not reuse any material from *Software Engineering*, 10th edition.

What's in the book?

Ten chapters cover software products, agile software engineering, features, scenarios and user stories, software architecture, cloud-based software, microservices architecture, security and privacy, reliable programming, testing, and DevOps and code management.

I've designed the book so that it's suitable for a one-semester software engineering course.

How is this book different from other introductory texts on software engineering?

As I said, the focus is on *products* rather than *projects*. I cover techniques that most other SE texts don't cover, such as personas and scenarios, cloud computing, microservices, security, and DevOps. As product innovation doesn't come from university research, there are no citations or references to research and the book is written in an informal style.

What do I need to know to get value from the book?

I assume that you have programming experience with a modern object-oriented programming language such as Java or Python and that you are familiar with good programming practice, such as the use of meaningful names. You should also understand basic computing concepts, such as objects, classes, and databases. The program examples in the book are written in Python, but they are understandable by anyone with programming experience.

What extra material is available to help teachers and instructors?

1. An instructor's manual with solutions to exercises and quiz questions for all chapters

2. Suggestions how you can use the book in a one-semester software engineering course

3. Presentations for teaching (Keynote, PowerPoint, and PDF)

You can access this material at: https://www.pearsonhighered.com/sommerville

Additional material is available on the book's website
   https://iansommerville.com/engineering-software-products/

Where can I find out more?

I've written a couple of blog posts that are relevant to the book. These provide more information about my thoughts on teaching software engineering and my motivation for writing the book.

"Out with the UML (and other stuff too): reimagining introductory courses in software engineering"

https://iansommerville.com/systems-software-and-technology/what-should-we-teach-in-software-engineering-courses/

"Engineering Software Products"

https://iansommerville.com/systems-software-and-technology/engineering-software-products/

Acknowledgments

I'd like to thank the reviewers who made helpful and supportive suggestions when they reviewed the initial proposal for this book:

Paul Eggert—*UCLA Los Angeles*
Jeffrey Miller—*University of Southern California*
Harvey Siy—*University of Nebraska Omaha*
Edmund S. Yu—*Syracuse University*
Gregory Gay—*University of South Carolina*
Josh Delinger—*Towson University*
Rocky Slavin—*University of Texas San Antonio*
Bingyang Wei—*Midwestern State University*

Thanks also to Adam Barker from St. Andrews University for keeping me right on containers and to Rose Kernan who managed the production of the book.

Thanks, as ever, to my family for their help and support while I was writing the book. Particular thanks to my daughter Jane, who did a great job of reading and commenting on the text. She was a brutal editor! Her suggested changes significantly improved the quality of my prose.

Finally, special thanks to our newest family member, my beautiful grandson Cillian, who was born while I was writing this book. His bubbly personality and constant smiles were a very welcome distraction from the sometimes tedious job of book writing and editing.

Ian Sommerville

CONTENTS

1

Software Products

This book introduces software engineering techniques that are used to develop software products. Software products are generic software systems sold to governments, businesses, and consumers. They may be designed to support a business function, such as accounting; they may be productivity tools, such as note-taking systems; or they may be games or personal information systems. Software products range in size from millions of lines of code in large-scale business systems to a few hundred lines of code in a simple app for mobile phones.

We all use software products every day on our computers, tablets, and phones. I am using a software product—the Ulysses editor—to write this book. I'll use another editing product—Microsoft Word—to format the final version, and I'll use Dropbox to exchange the files with the publisher. On my phone, I use software products (apps) to read email, read and send tweets, check the weather, and so on.

The engineering techniques that are used for product development have evolved from the software engineering techniques developed in the 20th century to support custom software development. When software engineering emerged as a discipline in the 1970s, virtually all professional software was "one-off," custom software. Companies and governments wanted to automate their businesses, and they specified what they wanted their software to do. An in-house engineering team or an external software company then developed the software.

Examples of custom software that were developed around that time include:

- the U.S. Federal Aviation Administration's air traffic management system;
- accounting systems for all of the major banks;

- billing systems for utility companies such as electricity and gas suppliers;

- military command and control systems.

Software projects were set up to develop these one-off systems, with the software system based on a set of software requirements. The contract between the software customer and the software development company included a requirements document, which was a specification of the software that should be delivered. Customers defined their requirements and worked with the development team to specify, in detail, the software's functionality and its critical attributes.

This project-based approach dominated the software industry for more than 25 years. The methods and techniques that evolved to support project-based development came to define what was meant by "software engineering." The fundamental assumption was that successful software engineering required a lot of preparatory work before starting to write programs. For example, it was important to spend time getting the requirements "right" and to draw graphical models of the software. These models were created during the software design process and used to document the software.

As more and more companies automated their business, however, it became clear that most businesses didn't really need custom software. They could use generic software products that were designed for common business problems. The software product industry developed to meet this need. Project-based software engineering techniques were adapted to software product development.

Project-based techniques are not suited to product development because of fundamental differences between project-based and product-based software engineering. These differences are illustrated in Figures 1.1 and 1.2.

Software projects involve an external client or customer who decides on the functionality of the system and enters into a legal contract with the software development company. The customer's problem and current processes are used as a basis for creating the software requirements, which specify the software to be implemented. As the business changes, the supporting software has to change. The company using the software decides on and pays for the changes. Software often has a long lifetime, and the costs of changing large systems after delivery usually exceed the initial software development costs.

Software products are specified and developed in a different way. There is no external customer who creates requirements that define what the software

Figure 1.1 Project-based software engineering

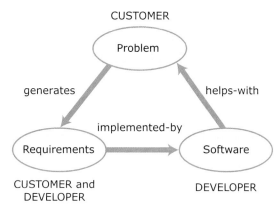

must do. The software developer decides on the features of the product, when new releases are to be made available, the platforms on which the software will be implemented, and so on. The needs of potential customers for the software are obviously considered, but customers can't insist that the software includes particular features or attributes. The development company chooses when changes will be made to the software and when they will be released to users.

As development costs are spread over a much larger customer base, product-based software is usually cheaper, for each customer, than custom software. However, buyers of the software have to adapt their ways of working to the software, since it has not been developed with their specific needs in mind. As the developer rather than the user is in control of changes, there

Figure 1.2 Product-based software engineering

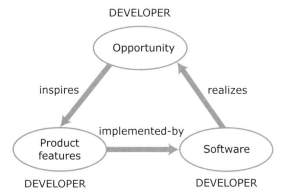

is a risk that the developer will stop supporting the software. Then the product customers will need to find an alternative product.

The starting point for product development is an opportunity that a company has identified to create a viable commercial product. This may be an original idea, such as Airbnb's idea for sharing accommodations; an improvement over existing systems, such as a cloud-based accounting system; or a generalization of a system that was developed for a specific customer, such as an asset management system.

Because the product developer is responsible for identifying the opportunity, they can decide on the features that will be included in the software product. These features are designed to appeal to potential customers so that there is a viable market for the software.

As well as the differences shown in Figures 1.1 and 1.2, there are two other important differences between project-based and product-based software engineering:

1. Product companies can decide when to change their product or take their product off the market. If a product is not selling well, the company can cut costs by stopping its development. Custom software developed in a software project usually has a long lifetime and has to be supported throughout that lifetime. The customer pays for the support and decides when and if it should end.

2. For most products, getting the product to customers quickly is critical. Excellent products often fail because an inferior product reaches the market first and customers buy that product. In practice, buyers are reluctant to change products after they have invested time and money in their initial choice.

Bringing the product to the market quickly is important for all types of products, from small-scale mobile apps to enterprise products such as Microsoft Word. This means that engineering techniques geared to rapid software development (agile methods) are universally used for product development. I explain agile methods and their role in product development in Chapter 2.

If you read about software products, you may come across two other terms: "software product lines" and "platforms" (Table 1.1). Software product lines are systems designed to be adaptable to meet the specific needs of customers by changing parts of the source code. Platforms provide a set of features that can be used to create new functionality. However, you always have to work within the constraints defined by the platform suppliers.

Table 1.1 Software product lines and platforms

Technology	Description
Software product line	A set of software products that share a common core. Each member of the product line includes customer-specific adaptations and additions. Software product lines may be used to implement a custom system for a customer with specific needs that can't be met by a generic product.
	For example, a company providing communication software to the emergency services may have a software product line where the core product includes basic communication services such as receive and log calls, initiate an emergency response, pass information to vehicles, and so on. However, each customer may use different radio equipment and their vehicles may be equipped in different ways. The core product has to be adapted for each customer to work with the equipment that they use.
Platform	A software (or software+hardware) product that includes functionality so that new applications can be built on it. An example of a platform that you probably use is Facebook. It provides an extensive set of product functionality but also provides support for creating "Facebook apps." These add new features that may be used by a business or a Facebook interest group.

When software products were first developed, they were delivered on a disk and installed by customers on their computers. The software ran on those computers and user data were stored on them. There was no communication between the users' computers and the vendor's computers. Now, customers can download products from either an app store or the vendor's website.

Some products are still based on a stand-alone execution model in which all computation is carried out on the product owner's computers. However, ubiquitous high-speed networking means that alternative execution models are now available. In these models, the product owner's computers act as a client, with some or all execution and data storage on the vendor's servers (Figure 1.3).

There are two alternatives to stand-alone software products:

1. *Hybrid products* Some functionality is implemented on the user's computer and some on the product vendor's servers that are accessed over the Internet. Many phone apps are hybrid products with computationally intensive processing offloaded to remote servers.

2. *Service-based products* Applications are accessed over the Internet from a web browser or an app. There may be some local processing using

Figure 1.3 Software execution models

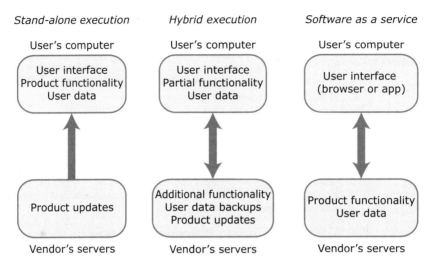

Javascript, but most computation is carried out on remote servers. More and more product companies are converting their products to services because it simplifies product updating and makes new business models, such as pay-as-you-go, feasible. I cover service-oriented systems in Chapters 5 and 6.

As I have said, the key characteristic of product development is that there is no external customer who generates software requirements and pays for the software. This is also true for some other types of software development:

1. *Student projects* As part of a computing or engineering course, students may be set assignments in which they work in groups to develop software. The group is responsible for deciding on the features of the system and how to work together to implement these features.

2. *Research software* Software is developed by a research team to support their work. For example, climate research depends on large-scale climate models that are designed by researchers and implemented in software. On a smaller scale, an engineering group may build software to model the characteristics of the material they are using.

3. *Internal tool development* A software development team may decide that it needs some specific tools to support their work. They specify and implement these tools as "internal" products.

You can use the product development techniques that I explain here for any type of software development that is not driven by external customer requirements.

There is a common view that software product engineering is simply advanced programming and that traditional software engineering is irrelevant. All you need to know is how to use a programming language plus the frameworks and libraries for that language. This is a misconception and I have written this book to explain the activities, apart from programming, that I believe are essential for developing high-quality software products.

If your product is to be a success, you need to think about issues other than programming. You must try to understand what your customers need and how potential users can work with your software. You need to design the overall structure of your software (software architecture) and know about technologies such as cloud computing and security engineering. You need to use professional techniques for verifying and testing your software and code management systems to keep track of a changing codebase.

You also need to think about the business case for your product. You must sell your product to survive. Creating a business case may involve market research, an analysis of competitors, and an understanding of the ways that target customers live and work. This book is about engineering, however, not business, so I don't cover business and commercial issues here.

1.1 The product vision

Your starting point for product development should be an informal "product vision." A product vision is a simple and succinct statement that defines the essence of the product that is being developed. It explains how the product differs from other competing products. This product vision is used as a basis for developing a more detailed description of the features and attributes of the product. As new features are proposed, you should check them against the vision to make sure they contribute to it.

The product vision should answer three fundamental questions:

1. *What* is the product that you propose to develop? What makes this product different from competing products?

2. *Who* are the target users and customers for the product?

3. *Why* should customers buy this product?

The need for the first question is obvious—before you start, you need to know what you are aiming for. The other questions concern the commercial viability of the product. Most products are intended for use by customers outside of the development team. You need to understand their background to create a viable product that these customers will find attractive and be willing to buy.

If you search the web for "product vision," you will find several variants of these questions and templates for expressing the product vision. Any of these templates can be used. The template that I like comes from the book *Crossing the Chasm* by Geoffrey Moore.[1] Moore suggests using a structured approach to writing the product vision based on keywords:

- FOR (target customer)
- WHO (statement of the need or opportunity)
- The (PRODUCT NAME) is a (product category)
- THAT (key benefit, compelling reason to buy)
- UNLIKE (primary competitive alternative)
- OUR PRODUCT (statement of primary differentiation)

On his blog *Joel on Software*, Joel Spolsky gives an example of a product described using this vision template:[2]

> *FOR a mid-sized company's marketing and sales departments WHO need basic CRM functionality, THE CRM-Innovator is a Web-based service THAT provides sales tracking, lead generation, and sales representative support features that improve customer relationships at critical touch points. UNLIKE other services or package software products, OUR product provides very capable services at a moderate cost.*

You can see how this vision answers the key questions that I identified above:

1. *What* A web-based service that provides sales tracking, lead generation, and sales representative support features. The information can be used to improve relationships with customers.

---

[1]Geoffrey Moore, *Crossing the Chasm: Marketing and selling technology products to mainstream customers* (Capstone Trade Press, 1998).

[2]J. Spolsky, Product Vision, 2002; http://www.joelonsoftware.com/articles/JimHighsmithonProductVisi.html

Table 1.2 Information sources for developing a product vision

Information source	Explanation
Domain experience	The product developers may work in a particular area (say, marketing and sales) and understand the software support that they need. They may be frustrated by the deficiencies in the software they use and see opportunities for an improved system.
Product experience	Users of existing software (such as word processing software) may see simpler and better ways of providing comparable functionality and propose a new system that implements this. New products can take advantage of recent technological developments such as speech interfaces.
Customer experience	The software developers may have extensive discussions with prospective customers of the product to understand the problems that they face; constraints, such as interoperability, that limit their flexibility to buy new software; and critical attributes of the software that they need.
Prototyping and "playing around"	Developers may have an idea for software but need to develop a better understanding of that idea and what might be involved in developing it into a product. They may develop a prototype system as an experiment and "play around" with ideas and variations using that prototype system as a platform.

2. *Who* The product is aimed at medium-sized companies that need standard customer relationship management software.

3. *Why* The most important product distinction is that it provides capable services at a moderate cost. It will be cheaper than alternative products.

A great deal of mythology surrounds software product visions. For successful consumer software products, the media like to present visions as if they emerge from a "Eureka moment" when the company founders have an "awesome idea" that changes the world. This view oversimplifies the effort and experimentation that are involved in refining a product idea. Product visions for successful products usually emerge after a lot of work and discussion. An initial idea is refined in stages as more information is collected and the development team discusses the practicalities of product implementation. Several different sources of information contribute to the product vision (Table 1.2).

Table 1.3 A vision statement for the iLearn system

FOR teachers and educators *WHO* need a way to help students use web-based learning resources and applications, *THE iLearn system* is an open learning environment *THAT* allows the set of resources used by classes and students to be easily configured for these students and classes by teachers themselves.
UNLIKE Virtual Learning Environments, such as Moodle, the focus of iLearn is the learning process rather than the administration and management of materials, assessments, and coursework. *OUR* product enables teachers to create subject and age-specific environments for their students using any web-based resources, such as videos, simulations, and written materials that are appropriate.

Schools and universities are the target customers for *the iLearn system* as it will significantly improve the learning experience of students at relatively low cost. It will collect and process learner analytics that will reduce the costs of progress tracking and reporting.

1.1.1   A vision example

As students, readers of this book may have used Virtual Learning Environments (VLEs), such as Blackboard and Moodle. Teachers use these VLEs to distribute class materials and assignments. Students can download the materials and upload completed assignments. Although the name suggests that VLEs are focused on learning, they are really geared to supporting learning administration rather than learning itself. They provide some features for students, but they are not open learning environments that can be tailored and adapted to a particular teacher's needs.

A few years ago, I worked on the development of a digital environment for learning support. This product was not just another VLE but was intended to provide flexible support for the process of learning. Our team looked at existing VLEs and talked to teachers and students who used them. We visited different types of school from kindergartens to colleges to examine how they used learning environments and how teachers were experimenting with software outside of these environments. We had extensive discussions with teachers about what they would like to be able to do with a digital learning environment. We finally arrived at the vision statement shown in Table 1.3.

In education, the teachers and students who use learning environments are not responsible for buying software. The purchaser is a school, university, or training center. The purchasing officer needs to know the benefits to the organization. Therefore, we added the final paragraph to the vision statement in Table 1.3 to make clear that there are benefits to organizations as well as individual learners.

1.2 Software product management

Software product management is a business activity focusing on the software products that are developed and sold by the business. Product managers (PMs) take overall responsibility for the product and are involved in planning, development, and marketing. They are the interface between the software development team, the broader organization, and the product's customers. PMs should be full members of the development team so that they can communicate business and customer requirements to the software developers.

Software product managers are involved at all stages of a product's life—from initial conception through vision development and implementation to marketing. Finally, they make decisions on when the product should be withdrawn from the market. Mid-size and large software companies may have dedicated PMs; in smaller software companies, the PM role is likely to be shared with other technical or business roles.

The job of the PM is to look outward to the customers and potential customers of the product rather than to focus on the software that is being developed. It is all too easy for a development team to get caught up in the details of "cool features" of the software, which most customers probably don't care about. For a product to be successful, the PM has to ensure that the development team implements features that deliver real value to customers, not just features that are technically interesting.

In a blog post, Martin Eriksson[3] explains that product managers have to be concerned with business, technology, and user experience issues. Figure 1.4, which I based on Martin's diagram, illustrates these multiple concerns.

Product managers have to be generalists, with both technical and communication skills. Business, technology, and customer issues are interdependent and PMs have to consider all of them:

1. *Business needs* PMs have to ensure that the software being developed meets the business goals and objectives of both the software product company and its customers. They must communicate the concerns and needs of the customers and the development team to the managers of the product business. They work with senior managers and with marketing staff to plan a release schedule for the product.

---

[3]Based on M. Erikkson, What, exactly, is a Product Manager, 2011; http://www.mindtheproduct.com/2011/10/what-exactly-is-a-product-manager/

Figure 1.4 Product management concerns

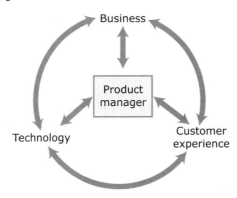

2. *Technology constraints* PMs must make developers aware of technology issues that are important to customers. These may affect the schedule, cost, and functionality of the product that is being developed.

3. *Customer experience* PMs should be in regular communication with customers to understand what they are looking for in a product, the types of user and their backgrounds, and the ways in which the product may be used. Their experience of customer capabilities is a critical input to the design of the product's user interface. PMs may also involve customers in alpha and beta product testing.

Because of the engineering focus of this book, I do not go into detail about the business role of product managers or their role in areas such as market research and financial planning. Rather, I concentrate on their interactions with the development team. PMs may interact with the development team in seven key areas (Figure 1.5).

1.2.1 Product vision management

Some writers say that the product manager should be responsible for developing the product vision. Large companies may adopt this approach, but it is often impractical in small software companies. In startups, the source of the product vision is often an original idea by the company founders. This vision is often developed long before anyone thinks about appointing a PM.

Obviously, it makes sense for PMs to take the lead in developing the product vision. They should be able to bring market and customer information to

Figure 1.5 Technical interactions of product managers

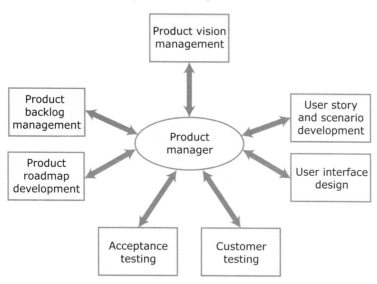

the process. However, I think all team members should be involved in vision development so that everyone can support what is finally agreed. When the team "owns" the vision, everyone is more likely to work coherently to realize that vision.

A key role of PMs is to manage the product vision. During the development process, changes are inevitably proposed by people from both inside and outside of the development team. PMs have to assess and evaluate these changes against the product vision. They must check that the changes don't contradict the ideas embodied in the product vision. PMs also have to ensure that there is no "vision drift," in which the vision is gradually extended to become broader and less focused.

1.2.2   Product roadmap development

A product roadmap is a plan for the development, release, and marketing of the software product. It sets out important product goals and milestones, such as the completion of critical features, the completion of the first version for user testing, and so on. It includes dates when these milestones should be reached and success criteria that help assess whether project goals have been attained. The roadmap should include a release schedule showing when different releases of the software will be available and the key features that will be included in each release.

The development of the product roadmap should be led by the product manager but must also involve the development team as well as company managers and marketing staff. Depending on the type of product, important deadlines may have to be met if the product is to be successful. For example, many large companies must make decisions on procurement toward the end of their financial year. If you want to sell a new product to such companies, you have to make it available before then.

1.2.3   User story and scenario development

User stories and scenarios are widely used to refine a product vision to identify features of the product. They are natural language descriptions of things that users might want to do with a product. Using them, the team can decide what features need to be included and how these features should work. I cover user stories and scenarios in Chapter 3.

The product manager's job is to understand the product's customers and potential customers. PMs should therefore lead the development of user scenarios and stories, which should be based on knowledge of the area and of the customer's business. PMs should also take scenarios and stories suggested by other team members back to customers to check that they reflect what the target users of the product might actually do.

1.2.4   Product backlog management

In product development, it is important for the process to be driven by a "product backlog." A product backlog is a to-do list that sets out what has to be done to complete the product development. The backlog is added to and refined incrementally during the development process. I explain how product backlogs are used in the Scrum method in Chapter 2.

The product manager plays a critical role as the authority on the product backlog items that should take priority for development. PMs also help to refine broad backlog items, such as "implement auto-save," in more detail at each project iteration. If suggestions for change are made, it is up to the PM to decide whether or not the product backlog should be rearranged to prioritize the suggested changes.

1.2.5   Acceptance testing

Acceptance testing is the process of verifying that a software release meets the goals set out in the product roadmap and that the product is efficient and reliable. Product managers should be involved in developing tests of the product features that reflect how customers use the product. They may work through usage scenarios to check that the product is ready to be released to customers.

Acceptance tests are refined as the product is developed, and products must pass these tests before being released to customers.

1.2.6   Customer testing

Customer testing involves taking a release of a product to existing and potential customers and getting feedback from them on the product's features, its usability, and the fit of the product to their business. Product managers are involved in selecting customers that might be interested in taking part in the customer testing process and working with them during that process. They have to ensure that the customer can use the product and that the customer testing process collects useful information for the development team.

1.2.7   User interface design

The user interface (UI) of a product is critical in the commercial acceptance of a software product. Technically excellent products are unlikely to be commercially successful if users find them difficult to use or if their UI is incompatible with other software that they use. UI design is challenging for small development teams because most users are less technically skilled than software developers. It is often difficult for developers to envision the problems that users may have with a software product.

Product managers should understand user limitations and act as surrogate users in their interactions with the development team. They should evaluate UI features as they are developed to check that these features are not unnecessarily complex or force users to work in an unnatural way. PMs may arrange for potential users to try out the software, comment on its UI, and assist with designing error messages and a help system.

1.3 Product prototyping

Product prototyping is the process of developing an early version of a product to test your ideas and to convince yourself and company funders that your product has real market potential. You use a product prototype to check that what you want to do is feasible and to demonstrate your software to potential customers and funders. Prototypes may also help you understand how to organize and structure the final version of your product.

You may be able to write an inspiring product vision, but your potential users can only really relate to your product when they see a working version of your software. They can point out what they like and don't like about it and make suggestions for new features. Venture capitalists, whom you may approach for funding, usually insist on seeing a product prototype before they commit to supporting a startup company. The prototype plays a critical role in convincing investors that your product has commercial potential.

A prototype may also help identify fundamental software components or services and test technology. You may find that the technology you planned to use is inadequate and that you have to revise your ideas on how to implement the software. For example, you may discover that the design you chose for the prototype cannot handle the expected load on the system, so you have to redesign the overall product architecture.

Building a prototype should be the first thing you do when developing a software product. Your goal should be to have a working version of your software that can be used to demonstrate its key features. A short development cycle is critical; you should aim to have a demonstrable system up and running in four to six weeks. Of course, you have to cut corners to do this, so you may choose to ignore issues such as reliability and performance and work with a rudimentary user interface.

Sometimes prototyping is a two-stage process:

1. *Feasibility demonstration* You create an executable system that demonstrates the new ideas in your product. The goals at this stage are to see whether your ideas actually work and to show funders and company management that your product features are better than those of competitors.

2. *Customer demonstration* You take an existing prototype created to demonstrate feasibility and extend it with your ideas for specific customer features and how these can be realized. Before you develop a customer prototype,

you need to do some user studies and have a clear idea of your potential users and scenarios of use. I explain how to develop user personas and usage scenarios in Chapter 3.

You should always use technology that you know and understand to develop a prototype so that you don't have to spend time learning a new language or framework. You don't need to design a robust software architecture. You may leave out security features and checking code to ensure software reliability. However, I recommend that, for prototypes, you should always use automated testing and code management. These are covered in Chapters 9 and 10.

If you are developing software without an external customer, such as software for a research group, it may be that a prototype system is all you need. You can develop and refine the prototype as your understanding of the problem develops. However, as soon as you have external users of your software, you should always think of your prototype as a "throw-away" system. The inevitable compromises and shortcuts you make to speed up development result in prototypes that become increasingly difficult to change and evolve to include new features. Adding security and reliability may be practically impossible.

KEY POINTS

- Software products are software systems that include general functionality that is likely to be useful to a wide range of customers.

- In product-based software engineering, the same company is responsible for deciding on both the features that should be part of the product and the implementation of these features.

- Software products may be delivered as stand-alone products running on the customer's computers, hybrid products, or service-based products. In hybrid products, some features are implemented locally and others are accessed from the Internet. All features are remotely accessed in service-based products.

- A product vision succinctly describes what is to be developed, who are the target customers for the product, and why customers should buy the product you are developing.

- Domain experience, product experience, customer experience, and an experimental software prototype may all contribute to the development of the product vision.

- Key responsibilities of product managers are to own the product vision, develop a product roadmap, create user stories and scenarios, manage the product backlog, conduct customer and acceptance testing, and design the user interface.

- Product managers work at the interface between the business, the software development team, and the product customers. They facilitate communication among these groups.

- You should always develop a product prototype to refine your own ideas and to demonstrate the planned product features to potential customers.

RECOMMENDED READING

"What is Product Line Engineering?" This article and the two linked articles provide an overview of software product line engineering and highlight the differences between product line engineering and software product development. (Biglever Software, 2013)

http://www.productlineengineering.com/overview/what-is-ple.html

"Building Software Products vs Platforms" This blog post briefly explains the differences between a software product and a software platform. (B. Algave, 2016)

https://blog.frogslayer.com/building-software-products-vs-platforms/

"Product Vision" This is an old article but an excellent summary of what is meant by a product vision and why it is important. (J. Spolsky, 2002)

http://www.joelonsoftware.com/articles/JimHighsmithonProductVisi.html

Agile Product Management with Scrum I generally avoid recommending books on product management as they are too detailed for most readers of this book. However, this book is worth looking at because of its focus on software and its integration with the Scrum agile method that I cover in Chapter 2. It's a short book that includes a succinct introduction to product management and discusses the creation of a product vision. (R. Pichler, 2010, Addison-Wesley)

The author's blog also has articles on product management.

http://www.romanpichler.com/blog/romans-product-management-framework/

"What, Exactly, is a Product Manager?" This excellent blog post explains why it's important that product managers work at the intersection of business, technology, and users. (M. Eriksson, 2011)

http://www.mindtheproduct.com/2011/10/what-exactly-is-a-product-manager/

PRESENTATIONS, VIDEOS, AND LINKS

https://iansommerville.com/engineering-software-products/software-products

EXERCISES

1.1. Briefly describe the fundamental differences between project-based and product-based software engineering.

1.2. What are three important differences between software products and software product lines.

1.3. Based on the example project vision for the iLearn system, identify the WHAT, WHO, and WHY for that software product.

1.4. Why do software product managers have to be generalists, with a range of skills, rather than simply technical specialists?

1.5. You are a software product manager for a company developing educational software products based on scientific simulations. Explain why it is important to develop a product roadmap so that final product releases are available in the first three months of the year.

1.6. Why should you implement a prototype before you start developing a new software product?

2

Agile Software Engineering

Bringing a software product to the market quickly is critically important. This is true for all types of products—from simple mobile apps to large-scale enterprise products. If a product is released later than planned, a competitor may have already captured the market or you may have missed a market window, such as the beginning of the holiday season. Once users have committed to a product, they are usually reluctant to change, even to a technically superior product.

Agile software engineering focuses on delivering functionality quickly, responding to changing product specifications, and minimizing development overheads. An "overhead" is any activity that doesn't contribute directly to rapid product delivery. Rapid development and delivery and the flexibility to make changes quickly are fundamental requirements for product development.

A large number of "agile methods" have been developed. Each has its adherents, who are often evangelical about the method's benefits. In practice, companies and individual development teams pick and choose agile techniques that work for them and that are most appropriate for their size and the type of product they are developing. There is no best agile method or technique. It depends on who is using the technique, the development team, and the type of product being developed.

2.1 Agile methods

In the 1980s and early 1990s, there was a widespread view that the best way to create good software was to use controlled and rigorous software development processes. The processes included detailed project planning, requirements specification and analysis, the use of analysis and design methods supported by software tools, and formal quality assurance. This view came from the software engineering community that was responsible for developing large, long-lived software systems such as aerospace and government systems. These were "one-off" systems, based on the customer requirements.

This approach is sometimes called plan-driven development. It evolved to support software engineering where large teams developed complex, long-lifetime systems. Teams were often geographically dispersed and worked on the software for long periods of time. An example of this type of software is a control system for a modern aircraft. Developing an avionic system might take five to ten years from initial specification to on-board deployment.

Plan-driven development involves significant overhead in planning, designing, and documenting the system. This overhead is justifiable for critical systems where the work of several development teams must be coordinated and different people may maintain and update the software during its lifetime. Detailed documents describing the software requirements and design are important when informal team communications are impossible.

If plan-driven development is used for small and medium-sized software products, however, the overhead involved is so large that it dominates the software development process. Too much time is spent writing documents that may never be read rather than writing code. The system is specified in detail before implementation begins. Specification errors, omissions, and misunderstandings are often discovered only after a significant chunk of the system has been implemented.

To fix these problems, developers have to redo work that they thought was complete. As a consequence, it is practically impossible to deliver software quickly and to respond rapidly to requests for changes to the delivered software.

Dissatisfaction with plan-driven software development led to the creation of agile methods in the 1990s. These methods allowed the development team to focus on the software itself, rather than on its design and documentation. Agile methods deliver working software quickly to customers, who can then propose new or different requirements for inclusion in later versions of the system. They reduce process bureaucracy by avoiding work that has dubious long-term value and eliminating documentation that will probably never be used.

The philosophy behind agile methods is reflected in the agile manifesto[1] that was agreed on by the leading developers of these methods. Table 2.1 shows the key message in the agile manifesto.

---

[1]Retrieved from http://agilemanifesto.org/. Used with permission.

Table 2.1 The agile manifesto

We are uncovering better ways of developing software by doing it and helping others to do it. Through this work, we have come to value:

- individuals and interactions over processes and tools;
- working software over comprehensive documentation;
- customer collaboration over contract negotiation;
- responding to change over following a plan.

While there is value on the items on the right, we value the items on the left more.

All agile methods are based on incremental development and delivery. The best way to understand incremental development is to think of a software product as a set of features. Each feature does something for the software user. There might be a feature that allows data to be entered, a feature to search the entered data, and a feature to format and display the data. Each software increment should implement a small number of product features.

With incremental development, you delay decisions until you really need to make them. You start by prioritizing the features so that the most important features are implemented first. You don't worry about the details of all the features—you define only the details of the feature that you plan to include in an increment. That feature is then implemented and delivered. Users or surrogate users can try it out and provide feedback to the development team. You then go on to define and implement the next feature of the system.

I show this process in Figure 2.1, and I describe incremental development activities in Table 2.2.

Figure 2.1 Incremental development

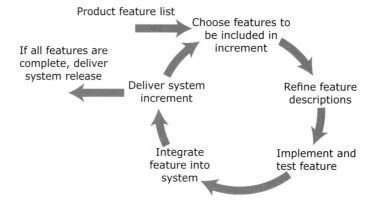

Table 2.2 Incremental development activities

Activity	Description
Choose features to be included in an increment	Using the list of features in the planned product, select those features that can be implemented in the next product increment.
Refine feature descriptions	Add detail to the feature descriptions so that the team members have a common understanding of each feature and there is sufficient detail to begin implementation.
Implement and test	Implement the feature and develop automated tests for that feature that show that its behavior is consistent with its description. I explain automated testing in Chapter 9.
Integrate feature and test	Integrate the developed feature with the existing system and test it to check that it works in conjunction with other features.
Deliver system increment	Deliver the system increment to the customer or product manager for checking and comments. If enough features have been implemented, release a version of the system for customer use.

Of course, reality doesn't always match this simple model of feature development. Sometimes an increment has to be devoted to developing an infrastructure service, such as a database service, that is used by several features; sometimes you need to plan the user interface so that you get a consistent interface across features; and sometimes an increment has to sort out problems, such as performance issues, that were discovered during system testing.

All agile methods share a set of principles based on the agile manifesto, so they have much in common. I summarize these agile principles in Table 2.3.

Almost all software products are now developed with an agile approach. Agile methods work for product engineering because software products are usually stand-alone systems rather than systems composed of independent subsystems. They are developed by co-located teams who can communicate informally. The product manager can easily interact with the development team. Consequently, there is no need for formal documents, meetings, and cross-team communication.

Table 2.3 Agile development principles

Principle	Description
Involve the customer	Involve customers closely with the software development team. Their role is to provide and prioritize new system requirements and to evaluate each increment of the system.
Embrace change	Expect the features of the product and the details of these features to change as the development team and the product manager learn more about the product. Adapt the software to cope with changes as they are made.
Develop and deliver incrementally	Always develop software products in increments. Test and evaluate each increment as it is developed and feed back required changes to the development team.
Maintain simplicity	Focus on simplicity in both the software being developed and the development process. Wherever possible, do what you can to eliminate complexity from the system.
Focus on people, not the development process	Trust the development team and do not expect everyone to always do things in the same way. Team members should be left to develop their own ways of working without being limited by prescriptive software processes.

2.2 Extreme Programming

The ideas underlying agile methods were developed by a number of different people in the 1990s. However, the most influential work that has changed the culture of software development was the development of Extreme Programming (XP). The name was coined by Kent Beck in 1998 because the approach pushed recognized good practice, such as iterative development, to "extreme" levels. For example, regular integration, in which the work of all programmers in a team is integrated and tested, is good software engineering practice. XP advocates that changed software should be integrated several times per day, as soon as the changes have been tested.

XP focused on new development techniques that were geared to rapid, incremental software development, change, and delivery. Figure 2.2 shows 10 fundamental practices, proposed by the developers of Extreme Programming, that characterize XP.

Figure 2.2 Extreme Programming practices

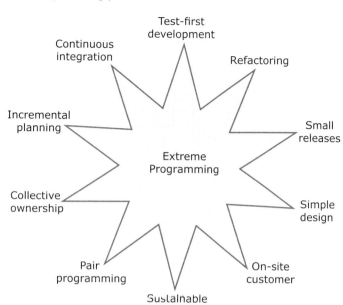

The developers of XP claim that it is a holistic approach. All of these practices are essential. In reality, however, development teams pick and choose the techniques that they find useful given their organizational culture and the type of software they are writing. Table 2.4 describes XP practices that have become part of mainstream software engineering, particularly for software product development. The other XP practices shown in Figure 2.2 have been less widely adopted but are used in some companies.

I cover these widely-used XP practices, in later chapters of the book. Incremental planning and user stories are covered in Chapter 3, refactoring in Chapter 8, test-driven development in Chapter 9, and continuous integration and small releases in Chapter 10.

You may be surprised that "Simple design" is not on the list of popular XP practices. The developers of XP suggested that the "YAGNI" (You Ain't Gonna Need It) principle should apply when designing software. You should include only functionality that is requested, and you should not add extra code to cope with situations anticipated by the developers. This sounds like a great idea.

Unfortunately, it ignores the fact that customers rarely understand system-wide issues such as security and reliability. You need to design and implement software to take these issues into account. This usually means including code to cope with situations that customers are unlikely to foresee and describe in user stories.

Table 2.4 Widely adopted XP practices

Practice	Description
Incremental planning/ user stories	There is no "grand plan" for the system. Instead, what needs to be implemented (the requirements) in each increment are established in discussions with a customer representative. The requirements are written as user stories. The stories to be included in a release are determined by the time available and their relative priority.
Small releases	The minimal useful set of functionality that provides business value is developed first. Releases of the system are frequent and incrementally add functionality to the previous release.
Test-driven development	Instead of writing code and then tests for that code, developers write the tests first. This helps clarify what the code should actually do and that there is always a "tested" version of the code available. An automated unit test framework is used to run the tests after every change. New code should not "break" code that has already been implemented.
Continuous integration	As soon as the work on a task is complete, it is integrated into the whole system and a new version of the system is created. All unit tests from all developers are run automatically and must be successful before the new version of the system is accepted.
Refactoring	Refactoring means improving the structure, readability, efficiency, and security of a program. All developers are expected to refactor the code as soon as potential code improvements are found. This keeps the code simple and maintainable.

Practices such as having an on-site customer and collective ownership of code are good ideas. An on-site customer works with the team, proposes stories and tests, and learns about the product. However, the reality is that customers and surrogate customers such as product managers have many other things to do. It is difficult for them to find the time to be fully embedded in a development team.

Collective ownership discourages the individual ownership of code, but it has proved to be impractical in many companies. Specialists are needed for some types of code. Some people may work part-time on a project and so cannot participate in its "ownership." Some team members may be psychologically unsuited to this way of working and have no wish to "own" someone else's code.

In pair programming two developers create each code unit. It was proposed by the inventors of XP because they believed the pair could learn from each other and catch each other's mistakes. They suggested that two people working together were more productive than two people working as individuals. However, there is no hard evidence that pair programming is more productive than individual work. Many managers consider pair programming to be unproductive because two people seem to be doing one job.

Working at a sustainable pace, with no overtime, is attractive in principle. Team members should be more productive if they are not tired and stressed. However, it is difficult to convince managers that this sustainable working will help meet tight delivery deadlines.

Extreme programming considers management to be a collective team activity; normally, there is no designated project manager responsible for communicating with management and planning the work of the team. In fact, software development is a business activity and so has to fit with broader business concerns of financing, costs, schedules, hiring and managing staff, and maintaining good customer relationships. This means that management issues cannot simply be left to the development team. There needs to be explicit management where a manager can take account of business needs and priorities as well as technical issues.

2.3 Scrum

In any software business, managers need to know what is going on and whether or not a software development project is likely to deliver the software on time and within its budget. Traditionally, this involves drawing up a project plan that shows a set of milestones (what will be achieved), deliverables (what will be delivered by the team), and deadlines (when a milestone will be reached). The "grand plan" for the project shows everything from start to finish. Progress is assessed by comparing that plan with what has been achieved.

The problem with up-front project planning is that it involves making detailed decisions about the software long before implementation begins. Inevitably things change. New requirements emerge, team members come and go, business priorities evolve, and so on. Almost from the day they are formulated, project plans have to change. Sometimes this means that "finished" work has to be redone. This is inefficient and often delays the final delivery of the software.

On this basis, the developers of agile methods argued that plan-based management is wasteful and unnecessary. It is better to plan incrementally so that the plan can change in response to changing circumstances. At the start of each development cycle, decisions are made on what features should be prioritized, how these should be developed and what each team member should do. Planning should be informal with minimal documentation and with no designated project manager.

Unfortunately, this informal approach to management does not meet the broader business need of progress tracking and assessment. Senior managers do not have the time to become involved in detailed discussions with team members. Managers want someone who can report on progress and take their concerns and priorities back to the development team. They need to know whether the software will be ready by the planned completion date, and they need information to update their business plan for the product.

This requirement for a more proactive approach to agile project management led to the development of Scrum. Unlike XP, Scrum is not based on a set of technical practices. Rather, it is designed to provide a framework for agile project organization with designated individuals (the ScrumMaster and the Product Owner) who act as the interface between the development team and the organization.

The developers of Scrum wanted to emphasize that these individuals were not "traditional" project managers who have the authority to direct the team. So they invented new Scrum terminology for both individuals and team activities (Table 2.5). You need to know this Scrum jargon to understand the Scrum method.

Two key roles in Scrum are not part of other methods:

1. The *Product Owner* is responsible for ensuring that the development team always focuses on the product they are building rather than diverted to technically interesting but less relevant work. In product development, the product manager should normally take on the Product Owner role.

2. The *ScrumMaster* is a Scrum expert whose job is to guide the team in the effective use of the Scrum method. The developers of Scrum emphasize that the ScrumMaster is not a conventional project manager but is a coach for the team. The ScrumMaster has the authority within the team on how Scrum is used. However, in many companies that use Scrum, the Scrum-Master also has some project management responsibilities.

Table 2.5 Scrum terminology

Scrum term	Explanation
Product	The software product that is being developed by the Scrum team.
Product Owner	A team member who is responsible for identifying product features and attributes. The Product Owner reviews work done and helps to test the product.
Product backlog	A to-do list of items such as bugs, features, and product improvements that the Scrum team has not yet completed.
Development team	A small self-organizing team of five to eight people who are responsible for developing the product.
Sprint	A short period, typically two to four weeks, when a product increment is developed.
Scrum	A daily team meeting where progress is reviewed and work to be done that day is discussed and agreed.
ScrumMaster	A team coach who guides the team in the effective use of Scrum.
Potentially shippable product increment	The output of a sprint that is of high enough quality to be deployed for customer use.
Velocity	An estimate of how much work a team can do in a single sprint.

The other Scrum term that may need explanation is "potentially shippable product increment." This means that the outcome of each sprint should be product-quality code. It should be completely tested, documented, and, if necessary, reviewed. Tests should be delivered with the code. There should always be a high-quality system available that can be demonstrated to management or potential customers.

The Scrum process or sprint cycle is shown in Figure 2.3. The fundamental idea underlying the Scrum process is that software should be developed in a series of "sprints." A sprint is a fixed-length (timeboxed) activity, with each sprint normally lasting two to four weeks. During a sprint, the team has daily meetings (Scrums) to review the work done so far and to agree on that day's activities. The "sprint backlog" is used to keep track of work that is to be done during that sprint.

Sprint planning is based on the product backlog, which is a list of all the activities that have to be completed to finish the product being developed. Before a new sprint starts, the product backlog is reviewed. The highest-priority

Figure 2.3 Scrum cycle

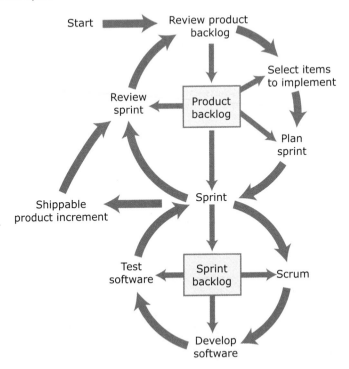

items are selected for implementation in the next sprint. Team members work together to plan the sprint by analyzing the selected items to create the sprint backlog. This is a list of activities to be completed during the sprint.

During implementation, the team implements as many of the sprint backlog items as they can in the fixed time period allowed for the sprint. Incomplete items are returned to the product backlog. Sprints are never extended to finish an incomplete item.

A sprint produces either a shippable product increment that can be delivered to customers or an internal deliverable. Internal deliverables, such as a product prototype or an architectural design, provide information for future sprints. If the sprint output is part of the final product, it should be complete. Unless the team has to change the software functionality, it should not have to do any more work on that software increment in future sprints.

On completion of a sprint, a review meeting is held involving all team members. The team discusses what went well during the sprint, what problems arose, and how the problems were tackled. Team members also reflect on the effectiveness of the tools and methods used. The aim of this meeting is for the team to learn from each other to avoid problems and to improve productivity in later sprints.

Figure 2.4 The top five benefits of using Scrum

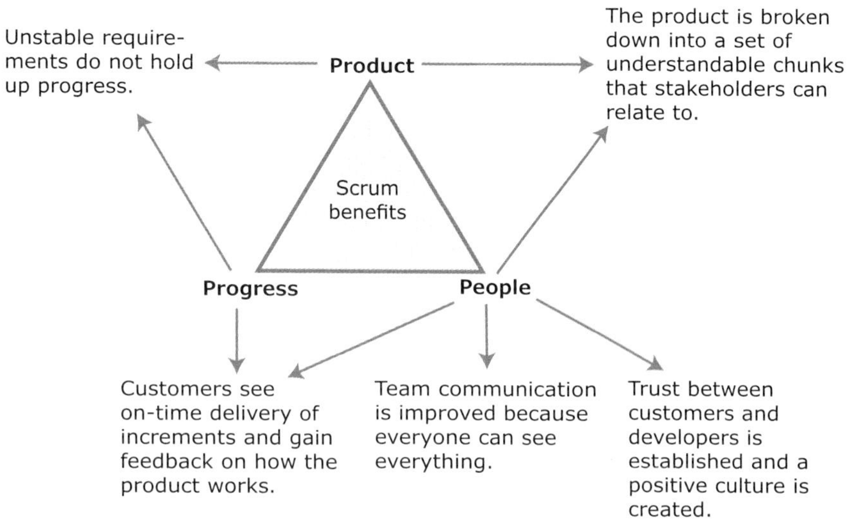

Unstable require-
ments do not hold
up progress.

Product

The product is broken
down into a set of
understandable chunks
that stakeholders can
relate to.

Scrum
benefits

Progress

People

Customers see
on-time delivery of
increments and gain
feedback on how the
product works.

Team communication
is improved because
everyone can see
everything.

Trust between
customers and
developers is
established and a
positive culture is
created.

The key benefits that come from using Scrum relate to the product being developed, the progress of the project, and the people involved (Figure 2.4).

Scrum has been very influential in the development of agile software engineering. It provides a framework for "doing" software engineering without prescribing the engineering techniques that should be used. However, Scrum is prescriptive in defining roles and the Scrum process. In *The Scrum Guide*[2], the "keepers" of the Scrum method state:

> *Scrum's roles, artefacts, events, and rules are immutable and although implementing only parts of Scrum is possible, the result is not Scrum. Scrum exists only in its entirety and functions well as a container for other techniques, methodologies, and practices.*

That is, they believe you should not pick and choose a subset of Scrum practices. Rather, you should take the whole of the method on board. It seems to me that this inflexibility contradicts the fundamental agile principle that individuals and interactions should be preferred over processes and tools. This principle suggests that individuals should be able to adapt and modify Scrum to suit their circumstances.

In some circumstances, I think it makes sense to use some of the ideas from Scrum without strictly following the method or defining the roles as exactly envisaged in Scrum. In general, "pure Scrum" with its various roles can't

---

[2]*The Scrum Guide* This definitive guide to the Scrum method defines all the Scrum roles and activities. (K. Schwaber and J. Sutherland, 2013).

Table 2.6 Examples of product backlog items

1. As a teacher, I want to be able to configure the group of tools that are available to individual classes. (feature)
2. As a parent, I want to be able to view my children's work and the assessments made by their teachers. (feature)
3. As a teacher of young children, I want a pictorial interface for children with limited reading ability. (user request)
4. Establish criteria for the assessment of open source software that might be used as a basis for parts of this system. (development activity)
5. Refactor user interface code to improve understandability and performance. (engineering improvement)
6. Implement encryption for all personal user data. (engineering improvement)

be used by teams with fewer than five people. So, if you are working with a smaller development team, you have to modify the method.

Small software development teams are the norm in startups, where the whole company may be the development team. They are also common in educational and research settings, where teams develop software as part of their learning, and in larger manufacturing companies, where software development is part of a broader product development process.

I think that motivated teams should make their own decisions about how to use Scrum or a Scrum-like process. However, I recommend that three important features of Scrum should be part of any product development process: product backlogs, timeboxed sprints, and self-organizing teams.

2.3.1 Product backlogs

The product backlog is a list of what needs to be done to complete the development of the product. The items on this list are called product backlog items (PBIs). The product backlog may include a variety of different items such as product features to be implemented, user requests, essential development activities, and desirable engineering improvements. The product backlog should always be prioritized so that the items that will be implemented first are at the top of the list.

Product backlog items are initially described in broad terms without much detail. For example, the items shown in Table 2.6 might be included in the product backlog for a version of the iLearn system, which I introduced in Chapter 1. In Chapter 3 I explain how system features can be identified from a product vision. These then become PBIs. I also explain how user stories can be used to identify PBIs.

Table 2.7 Product backlog item states

Heading	Description
Ready for consideration	These are high-level ideas and feature descriptions that will be considered for inclusion in the product. They are tentative so may radically change or may not be included in the final product.
Ready for refinement	The team has agreed that this is an important item that should be implemented as part of the current development. There is a reasonably clear definition of what is required. However, work is needed to understand and refine the item.
Ready for implementation	The PBI has enough detail for the team to estimate the effort involved and to implement the item. Dependencies on other items have been identified.

Table 2.6 shows different types of product backlog items. The first three items are user stories that are related to features of the product that have to be implemented. The fourth item is a team activity. The team must spend time deciding how to select open-source software that may be used in later increments. This type of activity should be specifically accounted for as a PBI rather than taken as an implicit activity that takes up team members' time. The last two items are concerned with engineering improvements to the software. These don't lead to new software functionality.

PBIs may be specified at a high level and the team decides how to implement these items. For example, the development team is best placed to decide how to refactor code for efficiency and understandability. It does not make sense to refine this item in more detail at the start of a sprint. However, high-level feature definitions usually need refinement so that team members have a clear idea of what is required and can estimate the work involved.

Items in the product backlog are considered to be in one of three states, as shown in Table 2.7. The product backlog is continually changed and extended during the project as new items are added and items in one state are analyzed and moved to a more refined state.

A critical part of the Scrum agile process is the product backlog review, which should be the first item in the sprint planning process. In this review, the product backlog is analyzed and backlog items are prioritized and refined. Backlog reviews may also take place during sprints as the team learns more about the system. Team members may modify or refine existing backlog items or add new items to be implemented in a later sprint. During a product backlog review, items may be moved from one state to another.

Figure 2.5 Product backlog activities

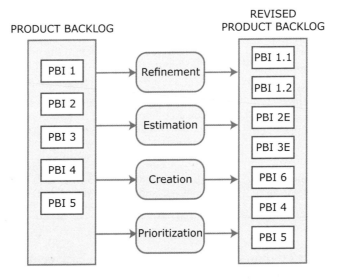

Figure 2.5 shows the four operations that may modify the product backlog. In this example, backlog item 1 has been split into two items, items 2 and 3 have been estimated, items 4 and 5 have been re-prioritized, and item 6 has been added. Notice that the new item 6 has a higher priority than existing items 4 and 5.

The Scrum community sometimes uses the term "backlog grooming" to cover these four activities:

1. *Refinement* Existing PBIs are analyzed and refined to create more detailed PBIs. This may also lead to the creation of new backlog items.

2. *Estimation* The team estimates the amount of work required to implement a PBI and adds this assessment to each analyzed PBI.

3. *Creation* New items are added to the backlog. These may be new features suggested by the product manager, required feature changes, engineering improvements, or process activities such as the assessment of development tools that might be used.

4. *Prioritization* The PBIs are reordered to take new information and changed circumstances into account.

Backlog prioritization is a whole-team activity in which decisions are made on which items to work on during a sprint. Input from product managers is essential because they should know about customer needs and priorities. The highest-priority items are refined by the development team to create a "sprint backlog," which is a list of more detailed implementation items. In situations such as speculative product development or research system development, where there is no specified product owner, the team should collectively prioritize the items.

Items that are ready for implementation should always have an associated estimate of how much effort is needed to implement them. Estimates are essential for sprint planning because a team uses them to decide how much work they can take on for an individual sprint. This effort estimate is an input to the prioritization activity. Sometimes it makes sense to place a higher priority on the items that deliver the most value for the least effort.

PBI estimates provide an indication of the effort required to complete each item. Two metrics are commonly used:

1. *Effort required* The amount of effort may be expressed in person-hours or person-days—that is, the number of hours or days it would take one person to implement that PBI. This is not the same as calendar time. Several people may work on an item, which may shorten the calendar time required. Alternatively, a developer may have other responsibilities that prevent full-time work on a project. Then the calendar time required is longer than the effort estimate.

2. *Story points* Story points are an arbitrary estimate of the effort involved in implementing a PBI, taking into account the size of the task, its complexity, the technology that may be required, and the "unknown" characteristics of the work. Story points were derived originally by comparing user stories, but they can be used for estimating any kind of PBI. Story points are estimated relatively. The team agrees on the story points for a baseline task. Other tasks are then estimated by comparison with this baseline—for example, more or less complex, larger or smaller, and so on. The advantage of story points is that they are more abstract than effort required because all story points should be the same, irrespective of individual abilities.

Effort estimation is hard, especially at the beginning of a project when a team has little or no previous experience with this type of work or when technologies new to the team are used. Estimates are based on the subjective judgment of the team members, and initial estimates are inevitably wrong. Estimates usually improve, however, as the team gains experience with the product and its development process.

The Scrum method recommends a team-based estimation approach called "Planning Poker," which I don't go into here. The rationale is that teams should be able to make better estimates than individuals. However, there is no convincing empirical evidence showing that collective estimation is better than estimates made by experienced, individual developers.

After a number of sprints have been completed, it becomes possible for a team to estimate its "velocity." Simplistically, a team's velocity is the sum of the size estimates of the items that have been completed during a fixed-time sprint. For example, assume that PBIs are estimated in story points and, in consecutive sprints, the team implements 17, 14, 16, and 19 story points. The team's velocity is therefore between 16 and 17 story points per sprint.

Velocity is used to decide how many PBIs a team can realistically commit to in each sprint. In the above example, the team should commit to about 17 story points. Velocity may also be used as a measure of productivity. Teams should try to refine how they work so that their velocity improves over the course of a project.

The product backlog is a shared, "living" document that is regularly updated during product development. It is usually too large to fit on a whiteboard, so it makes sense to maintain it as a shared digital document. Several specialized tools that support Scrum include facilities to share and revise product backlogs. Some companies may decide to buy these tools for their software developers.

Small companies or groups with limited resources can use a shared document system such as Office 365 or Google docs. These low-cost systems don't require new software to be bought and installed. If you are starting out using product backlogs in your development process, I recommend this general approach to gain experience before you decide whether you need specialized tools for backlog management.

2.3.2 Timeboxed sprints

A Scrum concept that is useful in any agile development process is timeboxed sprints. Timeboxing means that a fixed time is allocated for completing an activity. At the end of the timebox, work on the activity stops whether or not the planned work has been completed. Sprints are short activities (one to four weeks) and take place between defined start and end dates. During a sprint, the team works on the items from the product backlog. The product is therefore developed in a series of sprints, each of which delivers an increment of the product or supporting software.

Figure 2.6 Benefits of using timeboxed sprints

There is a tangible output (usually a software
demonstrator) that can be delivered at the
end of every sprint.

Demonstrable progress

Time-
boxing
benefits

Problem discovery   **Work planning**

If errors and omissions are   The team develops an under-
discovered, the rework   standing of how much work
required is limited to the   they can do in a fixed time
duration of a sprint.   period.

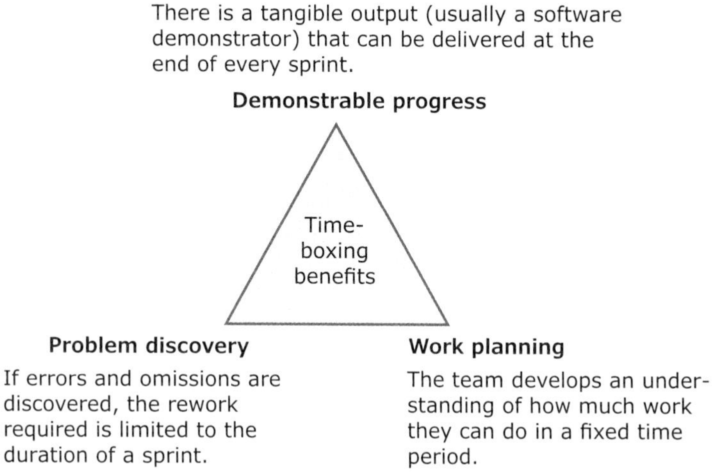

Incremental development is a fundamental part of all agile methods, and I
think Scrum has got it right in insisting that the time spent on each increment
should be the same. In Figure 2.6, I show three important benefits that arise
from using timeboxed sprints.

Every sprint involves three fundamental activities:

1. *Sprint planning* Work items to be completed during that sprint are selected
   and, if necessary, refined to create a sprint backlog. This should not last
   more than a day at the beginning of the sprint.

2. *Sprint execution* The team works to implement the sprint backlog items
   that have been chosen for that sprint. If it is impossible to complete all of
   the sprint backlog items, the time for the sprint is not extended. Rather,
   the unfinished items are returned to the product backlog and queued for
   a future sprint.

3. *Sprint reviewing* The work done during the sprint is reviewed by the team
   and (possibly) external stakeholders. The team reflects on what went well
   and what went wrong during the sprint, with a view to improving the
   work process.

Figure 2.7 shows the cycle of these activities and a more detailed breakdown of sprint execution. The sprint backlog is created during the planning
process and drives the development activities when the sprint is executed.

Figure 2.7 Sprint activities

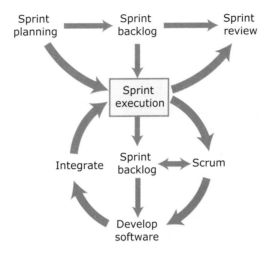

Each sprint should start with a planning meeting at which team members collectively decide on the PBIs to be implemented during the sprint. The inputs to this activity are the product backlog items that are ready for implementation and information from the Product Owner about which of these PBIs has the highest priority.

When planning a sprint, the team do three things:

- agree on a sprint goal;

- decide on the list of items from the product backlog that should be implemented;

- create a sprint backlog, a more detailed version of the product backlog that records the work to be done during the sprint.

The sprint goal is a succinct statement of what the team plans to achieve during a sprint. It could be the implementation of a product feature, the development of some essential product infrastructure, or the improvement of some product attribute, such as its performance. It should be possible to decide objectively whether or not the goal has been achieved by the end of the sprint. Figure 2.8 shows the three types of sprint goals and gives an example of each type.

Functional sprint goals relate to the implementation of system features for end-users. Performance and reliability goals relate to improvements in the performance, efficiency, reliability, and security of the system. Support goals cover ancillary activities such as developing infrastructure software or designing the system architecture.

Figure 2.8 Sprint goals

Implement user roles so that users can select
their role when they log in to the system.

Functional

Sprint
goals

Support
Develop analytics that
maintain information about
the time users spend using
each feature of the system.

Performance and reliability
Ensure that the login response time is
less than 10 seconds for all users where
there are up to 2000 simultaneous login
connections.

You should always consider the highest-priority items on the product backlog when deciding on a sprint goal. The team chooses these items for implementation at the same time as the sprint goal is being set. It makes sense to choose
a coherent set of high-priority items that are consistent with the sprint goal.
Sometimes items of lower priority in the product backlog are chosen because
they are closely related to other items that are part of the overall sprint goal.

As a general rule, the sprint goal should not be changed during the sprint.
Sometimes, however, the sprint goal has to be changed if unexpected problems are discovered or if the team finds a way to implement a feature more
quickly than originally estimated. In these cases, the scope of the goal may
be reduced or extended.

Once a sprint goal has been established, the team should discuss and decide
on a sprint plan. As I explained, PBIs should have an associated effort estimate,
which is a critical input to the sprint planning process. It's important that a team
does not try to implement too many items during the sprint. Overcommitment
may make it impossible to achieve the sprint goal.

The velocity of the team is another important input to the sprint planning
process. The velocity reflects how much work the team can normally cover
in a sprint. You may estimate story points as I have explained, where the
team's velocity is the number of story points it can normally implement in
a two-week or four-week sprint. This approach obviously makes sense for a
team that has a stable velocity.

A team's velocity might be unstable, however, which means that the
number of PBIs completed varies from one sprint to another. Velocity may

Table 2.8 Scrums

A scrum is a short, daily meeting that is usually held at the beginning of the day. During a scrum, all team members share information, describe their progress since the previous day's scrum, and present problems that have arisen and plans for the coming day. This means that everyone on the team knows what is going on and, if problems arise, can re-plan short-term work to cope with them.

Scrum meetings should be short and focused. To dissuade team members from getting involved in long discussions, scrums are sometimes organized as "stand-up" meetings where there are no chairs in the meeting room.

During a scrum, the sprint backlog is reviewed. Completed items are removed from it. New items may be added to the backlog as new information emerges. The team then decides who should work on sprint backlog items that day.

be unstable if the team membership changes, if easier items are assigned a higher priority than items that are harder to implement, or if a team includes inexperienced members who improve as the project progresses. If a team's velocity is unstable or unknown, then you have to take a more intuitive approach to choosing the number of PBIs to be implemented during a sprint.

The sprint backlog is a list of work items to be completed during the sprint. Sometimes, a PBI can be transferred directly to the sprint backlog. However, the team normally breaks down each PBI into smaller tasks that are added to the sprint backlog. All team members then discuss how these tasks will be allocated. Each task should have a relatively short duration—one or two days at most—so that the team can assess its progress during the daily sprint meeting. The sprint backlog should be much shorter than the product backlog, so it can be maintained on a shared whiteboard. The whole team can see what items are to be implemented and what items have been completed.

The focus of a sprint is the development of product features or infrastructure and the team works to create the planned software increment. To facilitate cooperation, team members coordinate their work every day in a short meeting called a scrum (Table 2.8). The Scrum method is named after these meetings, which are an essential part of the method. They are a way for teams to communicate—nothing like scrums in the game of rugby.

The Scrum method does not include specific technical development practices; the team may use any agile practices they think are appropriate. Some teams like pair programming; others prefer that members work individually. However, I recommend that two practices always be used in code development sprints:

Table 2.9 Code completeness checklist

State	Description
Reviewed	The code has been reviewed by another team member who has checked that it meets agreed coding standards, is understandable, includes appropriate comments, and has been refactored if necessary.
Unit tested	All unit tests have been run automatically and all tests have executed successfully.
Integrated	The code has been integrated with the project codebase and no integration errors have been reported.
Integration tested	All integration tests have been run automatically and all tests have been executed successfully.
Accepted	Acceptance tests have been run if appropriate and the Product Owner or the development team has confirmed that the product backlog item has been completed.

1. *Test automation* As far as possible, product testing should be automated. You should develop a suite of executable tests that can be run at any time. I explain how to do this in Chapter 9.

2. *Continuous integration* Whenever anyone makes changes to the software components they are developing, these components should be immediately integrated with other components to create a system. This system should then be tested to check for unanticipated component interaction problems. I explain continuous integration in Chapter 10.

The aim of a sprint is to develop a "potentially shippable product increment." Of course, the software will not necessarily be released to customers, but it should not require further work before it can be released. This means different things for different types of software, so it is important that a team establish a "definition of done," which specifies what has to be completed for code that is developed during a sprint.

For example, for a software product that is being developed for external customers, the team may create a checklist that applies to all the software that is being developed. Table 2.9 is an example of a checklist that can be used to judge the completeness of an implemented feature.

If it is not possible to complete all items on this checklist during a sprint, the unfinished items should be added to the product backlog for future implementation. The sprint should never be extended to complete unfinished items.

At the end of each sprint, there is a review meeting that involves the whole team. This meeting has three purposes. First, it reviews whether or not the sprint has met its goal. Second, it sets out any new problems and issues that have emerged during the sprint. Finally, it is a way for a team to reflect on how they can improve the way they work. Members discuss what has gone well, what has gone badly, and what improvements could be made.

The review may involve external stakeholders as well as the development team. The team should be honest about what has and hasn't been achieved during the sprint so that the output of the review is a definitive assessment of the state of the product being developed. If items are unfinished or if new items have been identified, these should be added to the product backlog. The Product Owner has the ultimate authority to decide whether or not the goal of the sprint has been achieved. They should confirm that the implementation of the selected product backlog items is complete.

An important part of a sprint review is a process review, in which the team reflects on its own way of working and how Scrum has been used. The aim of a process review is to identify ways to improve and to discuss how to use Scrum more productively. Over the course of a development process, a Scrum team should try to continually improve its effectiveness.

During the review, the team may discuss communication breakdowns, good and bad experiences with tools and the development environment, technical practices that have been adopted, reusable software and libraries that have been discovered, and other issues. If problems have been identified, the team should discuss how they should be addressed in future sprints. For example, a decision may be made to investigate alternative tools to those being used by the team. If aspects of the work have been successful, the team may explicitly schedule time so that experience can be shared and good practice adopted across the team.

2.3.3 Self-organizing teams

A fundamental principle of all agile development methods is that the software development team should be self-organizing. Self-organizing teams don't have a project manager who assigns tasks and makes decisions for the team. Rather, as shown in Figure 2.9, they make their own decisions. Self-organizing teams work by discussing issues and making decisions by consensus.

Figure 2.9 Self-organizing teams

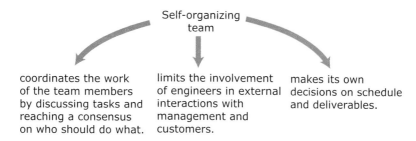

The ideal Scrum team size is between five and eight people—large enough to be diverse yet small enough to communicate informally and effectively and to agree on the priorities of the team. Because teams have to tackle diverse tasks, it's important to have a range of expertise in a Scrum team such as networking, user experience, database design and so on.

In reality, it may not be possible to form *ideal* teams. In a non-commercial setting such as a university, teams are smaller and made up of people who have largely the same skill set. There is a worldwide shortage of software engineers, so it is sometimes impossible to find people with the right mix of skills and experience. A team may change during a project as people leave and new members are hired. Some team members may work part-time or from home.

The advantage of an effective self-organizing team is that it can be cohesive and can adapt to change. Because the team rather than individuals takes responsibility for the work, the team can cope with people leaving and joining the group. Good team communication means that team members inevitably learn something about each other's areas. They can therefore compensate, to some extent, when people leave the team.

In a managed team, the project manager coordinates the work. Managers look at the work to be done and assign tasks to team members. Project managers have to arrange things so that work is not delayed because one team member is waiting for others to finish their work. They have to tell all team members about problems and other factors that may delay the work. Team members are not encouraged to take responsibility for coordination and communication.

In a self-organizing team, the team itself has to put in place ways to coordinate the work and communicate issues to all team members. The developers of Scrum assumed that team members are co-located. They work in the same office and can communicate informally. If one team member needs to know something about what another has done, they simply talk to each other to find out. There is no need for people to document their work for others to read. Daily scrums mean that the team members know what's been done and what others are doing.

The Scrum approach embodies the essentials for coordination in a self-managed team—namely, good informal communication and regular meetings to ensure that everyone is up to speed. Team members explain their work and are aware of team progress and possible risks that may affect the team. However, there are practical reasons why informal verbal communication may not always work:

1. Scrum assumes that the team is made up of full-time workers who share a workspace. In reality, team members may be part-time and may work in different places. For a student project, team members may take different classes at different times, so it may be difficult to find a time slot where all team members can meet.

2. Scrum assumes that all team members can attend a morning meeting to coordinate the work for the day. This does not take into account that team members may work flexible hours (for example, because of child care responsibilities) or may work part-time on several projects. They are, therefore, not available every morning.

If co-located working with daily meetings is impractical, then the team must work out other ways to communicate. Messaging systems, such as Slack, can be effective for informal communications. The benefit of messaging is that all messages are recorded so that people can catch up on conversations that they missed. Messaging does not have the immediacy of face-to-face communication, but it is better than email or shared documents for coordination.

Talking to each other is the best way for team members to coordinate work and to communicate what has gone well and what problems have arisen. Daily meetings may be impossible, but agile teams really have to schedule progress meetings regularly even if all members can't attend or have to attend virtually using teleconferencing. Members who can't attend should submit a short summary of their own progress so that the team can assess how well the work is going.

All development teams, even those working in small startups or non-commercial developments, have some external interactions. Some interactions will help the team understand what customers require from the software

Figure 2.10 Managing external interactions

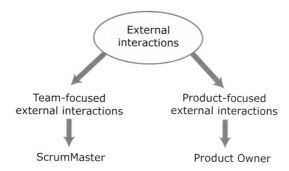

product being developed. Others will be with company management and other parts of the company, such as human resources and marketing.

In a Scrum project, the ScrumMaster and the Product Owner should be jointly responsible for managing interactions with people outside the team (Figure 2.10).

Product Owners are responsible for interactions with current and potential customers as well as the company's sales and marketing staff. Their job is to understand what customers are looking for in a software product and to identify possible barriers to the adoption and use of the product being developed. They should understand the innovative features of the product to establish how customers can benefit from them. Product Owners use this knowledge to help develop the product backlog and to prioritize backlog items for implementation.

The ScrumMaster role has a dual function. Part of the role is to work closely with the team, coaching them in the use of Scrum and working on the development of the product backlog. *The Scrum Guide* states that the ScrumMaster should also work with people outside of the team to "remove impediments"; that is, they should deal with external problems and queries and represent the team to the wider organization. The intention is for the team to be able to work on software development without external interference or distractions.

Whether or not a team is using Scrum or some other agile approach, you need to pay attention to these issues. In small teams, it may be impossible to have different people take care of interactions with customers and interactions with managers. The best approach may be for one person to take on both of these roles and to work part-time on software development. The key requirement for "external communicators" is good communication and people skills

Figure 2.11 Project management responsibilities

so that they can talk about the team's work in a way that people outside the team can understand and relate to.

The ScrumMaster is not a conventional project manager. The job is to help team members use the Scrum method effectively and to ensure that they are not distracted by external considerations. However, in all commercial projects, someone has to take on essential project management responsibilities (Figure 2.11).

The Scrum Guide and many Scrum books (although not Rubin's book that I've included in Recommended Reading) simply ignore these issues. But they are a reality of working in all but the smallest companies. A self-organizing team has to appoint a team member to take on management tasks. Because of the need to maintain continuity of communication with people outside of the group, sharing the management tasks among team members is not a viable approach.

In response to this issue, Rubin suggests that it may sometimes be appropriate for a project manager outside of the team to act for several Scrum teams. I think this idea is unworkable for three reasons:

1. Small companies may not have the resources to support dedicated project managers.

2. Many project management tasks require detailed knowledge of a team's work. If a project manager is working across several teams, it may be impossible to know the work of each team in detail.

3. Self-organizing teams are cohesive and tend to resent being told what to do by people outside of the team. Members are liable to obstruct, rather than support, an external project manager.

In my opinion it is unrealistic for the ScrumMaster role to exclude project management responsibilities. ScrumMasters know the work going on and are in by far the best position to provide accurate information and project plans and progress.

KEY POINTS

- The best way to develop software products is to use agile software engineering methods that are geared to rapid product development and delivery.

- Agile methods are based on iterative development and the minimization of overheads during the development process.

- Extreme Programming (XP) is an influential agile method that introduced agile development practices such as user stories, test-first development, and continuous integration. These are now mainstream software development activities.

- Scrum is an agile method that focuses on agile planning and management. Unlike XP, it does not define the engineering practices to be used. The development team may use any technical practices they consider appropriate for the product being developed.

- In Scrum, work to be done is maintained in a product backlog, a list of work items to be completed. Each increment of the software implements some of the work items from the product backlog.

- Sprints are fixed-time activities (usually two to four weeks) in which a product increment is developed. Increments should be potentially shippable; that is, they should not need further work before they are delivered.

- A self-organizing team is a development team that organizes the work to be done by discussion and agreement among team members.

- Scrum practices, such as the product backlog, sprints, and self-organizing teams, can be used in any agile development process, even if other aspects of Scrum are not used.

RECOMMENDED READING

Extreme Programming Explained This was the first book on XP and I think it's still the best one. It explains the approach from the perspective of one of its inventors, and his enthusiasm comes through very clearly in the book. (K. Beck and C. Andres, Addison-Wesley, 2004)

Essential Scrum: A practical guide to the most popular agile process This is a comprehensive and readable description of the 2011 version of the Scrum method. The diagrams are sometimes overcomplicated and a bit difficult to understand, but it is the best book on Scrum I have seen. (K. S. Rubin, Addison-Wesley, 2012)

The Scrum Guide This definitive guide to the Scrum method defines all the Scrum roles and activities. (K. Schwaber and J. Sutherland, 2013)

http://www.scrumguides.org/docs/scrumguide/v1/scrum-guide-us.pdf

"The Agile Mindset" This blog post argues for a flexible, pick-and-mix approach to Scrum practices rather than the inflexible model proposed in *The Scrum Guide*. I generally agree with what the author is saying here. (D. Thomas, 2014)

http://blog.scottlogic.com/2014/09/18/the-agile-mindset.html

"The Advantages and Disadvantages of Agile Scrum Software Development" An article by a project management expert rather than a Scrum evangelist presents a balanced picture of the advantages and disadvantages of Scrum. (S. de Sousa, undated)

http://www.my-project-management-expert.com/the-advantages-and-disadvantages-of-agile-scrum-software-development.html

"A Criticism of Scrum" This tongue-in-cheek blog post sets out what the author really doesn't like about Scrum. I agree with some of his points; others I think are exaggerated. (A. Gray, 2015)

https://www.aaron-gray.com/a-criticism-of-scrum/

PRESENTATIONS, VIDEOS, AND LINKS

https://iansommerville.com/engineering-software-products/agile-software-engineering

EXERCISES

2.1. Explain why it is important that software products are developed and delivered quickly. Why is it sometimes sensible to deliver an unfinished product and then issue new versions of that product after delivery?

2.2. Explain why the fundamental objectives of agile software engineering are consistent with the accelerated development and delivery of software products.

2.3. Give three reasons why Extreme Programming, as envisaged by its developers, is not widely used.

2.4. You are developing a software product to help manage student admissions at a university. Your agile development team suggests that they create a number of small releases that potential customers can try and then provide feedback. Comment on this idea and suggest why it may not be acceptable to the system's users.

2.5. Explain why the Product Owner plays an essential role in a Scrum development team. How might a development team that is working in an environment where there are no external customers (e.g., a student project team) reproduce this Product Owner role?

2.6. Why is it is important that each sprint normally produces a potentially shippable product increment? When might the team relax this rule and produce something that is not ready to ship?

2.7. Explain why estimating the effort required to complete a product backlog item using person-hours or person-days may lead to significant variations between the estimated effort and the actual effort.

2.8. Why are daily scrums likely to reduce the time that is normally required for new team members to become productive?

2.9. One problem with self-organizing teams is that more experienced team members tend to dominate discussions and therefore influence the team's way of working. Suggest ways to counteract this problem.

2.10. Scrum is designed for use by a team of five to eight people working together to develop a software product. What problems might arise if you try to use Scrum for student team projects in which members work together to develop a program? What parts of Scrum could be used in this situation?

3

Features, Scenarios, and Stories

Some software products are inspired. The developers of these products have a vision of the software that they want to create. They don't have a product manager, they don't do user surveys, they don't collect and document requirements or model how users will interact with the system. They simply get on with developing a prototype system. Some of the most successful software products, such as Facebook, started like this.

However, the vast majority of software products that are solely based on a developer's inspiration are commercial failures. These products either don't meet a real user need or don't fit with the ways in which users really work. Inspiration is important but most successful products are based on an understanding of business and user problems and user interaction. Even when inspiration leads to many users adopting a product, continuing use depends on its developers understanding how the software is used and new features that users may want.

Apart from inspiration, there are three factors that drive the design of software products:

1. *Business and consumer needs that are not met by current products* For example, book and magazine publishers are moving to both online and paper publication, yet few software products allow seamless conversion from one medium to another.

2. *Dissatisfaction with existing business or consumer software products* For example, many current software products are bloated with features that are rarely used. New companies may decide to produce simpler products in the same area that meet the needs of most users.

3. *Changes in technology that make completely new types of products possible* For example, as virtual reality (VR) technology matures and the hardware gets cheaper, new products may exploit this opportunity.

As I explained in Chapter 1, software products are not developed to meet the requirements of a specific client. Consequently, techniques that have been developed for eliciting, documenting, and managing software requirements aren't used for product engineering. You don't need to have a complete and detailed requirements document as part of a software development contract. There is no need for prolonged consultations when requirements change. Product development is incremental and agile, so you can use less formal ways of defining your product.

In the early stage of product development, rather than understanding the requirements of a specific client, you are trying to understand what product features will be useful to users and what they like and dislike about the products that they use. Briefly, a feature is a fragment of functionality, such as a Print feature, a Change Background feature, a New Document feature, and so on. Before you start programming a product, you should create a list of features to be included in your product. This is your starting point for product design and development.

It makes sense in any product development to spend time trying to understand the potential users and customers of your product. A range of techniques have been developed for understanding the ways that people work and use software. These include user interviews, surveys, ethnography, and task analysis.[1] Some of these techniques are expensive and unrealistic for small companies. However, informal user analysis and discussions, which simply involve asking users about their work, the software that they use, and its strengths and weaknesses, are inexpensive and very valuable.

One problem with informal user studies for business products is that the users simply may not want new software. For business products, the business buys the product, but its employees are the users. These users may be hostile to new products because they have to change their familiar way of working or perhaps because increased automation may reduce the number of jobs available. Business managers may suggest what they want from a new software product, but this does not always reflect the needs or wishes of the product's users.

---

[1] I discuss techniques of user analysis to discover software requirements in my general software engineering textbook, *Software Engineering*, 10th edition (Pearson Education, 2015).

Figure 3.1 From personas to features

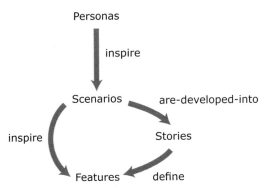

In this chapter, I assume that informal user consultations are possible. I explain ways of representing users (personas) and communicating with them and other product stakeholders. I focus on how short, natural language descriptions (scenarios and stories) can be used to visualize and document how users might interact with a software product.

Figure 3.1 shows that personas, scenarios, and user stories lead to features that might be implemented in a software product.

If you look on the web, you can find a range of definitions of a "product feature," but I think of a feature as a fragment of functionality that implements some user or system need. You access features through the user interface of a product. For example, the editor that I used to write this book includes a feature to create a "New Group," in which a group is a set of documents that is accessed as a pull-down menu.

A feature is something that the user needs or wants. You can write a user story to make this explicit:

As an author I need a way to organize the text of the book that I'm writing into chapters and sections.

Using the New Group feature, you create a group for each chapter, and the documents within that group are the sections of that chapter. This feature can be described using a short, narrative, feature description:

The "New Group" command, activated by a menu choice or keyboard shortcut, creates a named container for a set of documents and groups.

Alternatively, you can use a standard template where you define the feature by its input, its functionality, its output, and how it is activated. Figure 3.2

Figure 3.2 Feature description

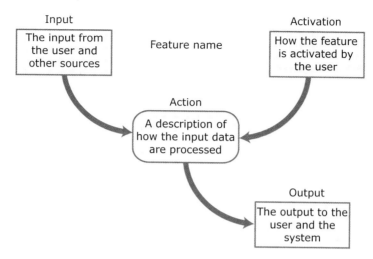

shows the elements of the standard template, and Figure 3.3 shows how the New Group feature can be defined using this template.

Features can be defined using the input/action/output model that I have shown. However, system developers often need only a short feature description; then they fill in the feature details. This is especially true when the

Figure 3.3 The New Group feature description

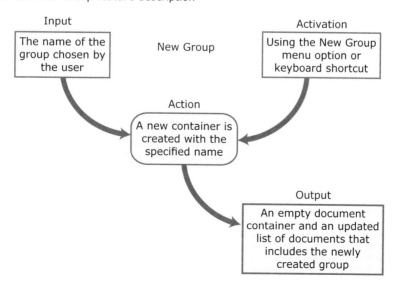

feature is a "utility" feature that is commonly available in other products. For example, the Cut and Paste feature is well known, so might be defined as:

Cut and Paste – any selected object can be cut or copied, then inserted elsewhere into the document.

Sometimes all you need to say is that a Cut and Paste feature should be included and then rely on the developer's general understanding to implement this.

Features are the fundamental elements of an agile method called Feature-Driven Development (FDD). I have no experience with this method and have not met anyone who uses it for product development, so I can't comment on it directly. One aspect of this approach that I have used, however, is its template for feature description:

<action> **the** *<result>* **<by|for|of|to>** *<object>*

So, the New Group feature above could be described as:

Create **the** *container* **for** *documents or groups*

I show another example of this simple approach to feature description in Section 3.4.2.

I return to the topic of features in Section 3.4 after I have described scenarios and user stories. You can use both of these narrative techniques for deriving the list of features to be included in a system.

3.1 Personas

One of the first questions you should ask when developing a software product is "Who are the target users for my product?" You need to have some understanding of your potential users in order to design features that they are likely to find useful and to design a user interface that is suited to them.

Sometimes you know the users. If you are a software engineer developing software tools for other engineers, then you understand, to some extent at least, what they are likely to want. If you are designing a phone or tablet app for general use, you may talk to friends and family to understand what potential users may like or dislike. In those circumstances, you may be able to design using an

Table 3.1 A persona for a primary school teacher

Jack, a primary school teacher

Jack, age 32, is a primary school (elementary school) teacher in Ullapool, a large coastal village in the Scottish Highlands. He teaches children from ages 9 to 12. He was born in a fishing community north of Ullapool, where his father runs a marine fuels supply business and his mother is a community nurse. He has a degree in English from Glasgow University and retrained as a teacher after several years working as a web content author for a large leisure group.

Jack's experience as a web developer means that he is confident in all aspects of digital technology. He passionately believes that the effective use of digital technologies, blended with face-to-face teaching, can enhance the learning experience for children. He is particularly interested in using the iLearn system for project-based teaching, where students work together across subject areas on a challenging topic.

intuitive idea of who the users are and what they can do. However, you should be aware that your users are diverse and your own experience may not provide a complete picture of what they might want and how they might work.

For some types of software products, you may not know much about the background, skills, and experience of potential users. Individuals on the development team may have their own ideas about the product users and their capabilities. This can lead to product inconsistencies as these different views are reflected in the software implementation. Ideally, the team should have a shared vision of users, their skills, and their motivations for using the software. Personas are one way of representing this shared vision.

Personas are about "imagined users," character portraits of types of user that you think might adopt your product. For example, if your product is aimed at managing appointments for dentists, you might create a dentist persona, a receptionist persona, and a patient persona. Personas of different types of users help you imagine what these users may want to do with your software and how they might use it. They also help you envisage difficulties that users might have in understanding and using product features.

A persona should paint a picture of a type of product user. You should describe the users' backgrounds and why they might want to use your product. You should also say something about their education and technical skills. This helps you assess whether or not a software feature is likely to be useful and understandable by typical product users.

An example of a persona that I wrote when designing the iLearn system, described in Chapter 1, is shown in Table 3.1. This is the persona of a teacher who is committed to digital learning and who believes that using digital devices can enhance the overall learning process.

Figure 3.4 Persona descriptions

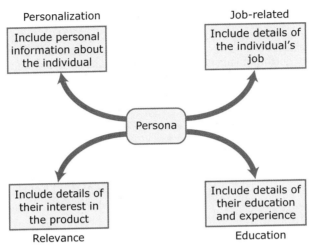

Personalization

Include personal information about the individual

Job-related

Include details of the individual's job

Persona

Include details of their interest in the product

Relevance

Include details of their education and experience

Education

There is no standard way of representing a persona; if you search the web, you will find a number of different recommendations. Common features of these suggestions are shown in Figure 3.4. The recommended aspects of a persona description—namely, personalization, relevance, education, and job-related—are explained in Table 3.2.

Many recommendations about what should be included in a persona suggest describing the individual's goals. I disagree because it's impossible to pin down what is meant by "goals." Goals are a broad concept. Some people have goals of self-improvement and learning; others have work-oriented goals of career progression and promotion. For some people, goals are not related to work. Their goals are simply to get through the day and earn enough so that they can do the things outside of work that give them pleasure and satisfaction.

My experience is that trying to define "user goals" is not helpful. I have found that most people don't have clearly defined goals when they use software. They may have been told to use the software as part of their job, they may see the software as a way to do their work more effectively, or they may find the software useful in organizing their life. Rather than try to set out goals, I think it's better to try to explain why the software might be useful and to give examples of what potential users may want to do with it.

If your product is targeted at a specific group of users, you may need only one or two personas to represent potential system users. For some products, however, the user group may be very broad and you may think that a large number of personas are needed. In fact, using many personas can make it more difficult to design a coherent system because they inevitably overlap.

Table 3.2 Aspects of persona descriptions

Aspect	Description
Personalization	You should give them a name and say something about their personal circumstances. It is sometimes helpful to use an appropriate stock photograph to represent the person in the persona. Some studies suggest that this helps project teams use personas more effectively.
Job-related	If your product is targeted at business, you should say something about their job and (if necessary) what that job involves. For some jobs, such as a teacher where readers are likely to be familiar with the job, this may not be necessary.
Education	You should describe their educational background and their level of technical skills and experience. This is important, especially for interface design.
Relevance	If you can, you should say why they might be interested in using the product and what they might want to do with it.

In general, you don't need more than five personas to help identify the key features of a system.

Personas should be relatively short and easy to read. For the iLearn system, we developed personas that we described in two or three paragraphs of text. We found that these had enough information to be useful. Two of the personas that we created are shown in Tables 3.3 and 3.4.

The persona in Table 3.3 represents users who do not have a technical background. They simply want a system to provide support for administration.

Table 3.3 A persona for a history teacher

Emma, a history teacher

Emma, age 41, is a history teacher in a secondary school (high school) in Edinburgh. She teaches students from ages 12 to 18. She was born in Cardiff in Wales, where both her father and her mother were teachers. After completing a degree in history from Newcastle University, she moved to Edinburgh to be with her partner and trained as a teacher. She has two children, aged 6 and 8, who both attend the local primary school. She likes to get home as early as she can to see her children, so often does lesson preparation, administration, and marking from home.

Emma uses social media and the usual productivity applications to prepare her lessons, but is not particularly interested in digital technologies. She hates the virtual learning environment that is currently used in her school and avoids using it if she can. She believes that face-to-face teaching is most effective. She might use the iLearn system for administration and access to historical films and documents. However, she is not interested in a blended digital/face-to-face approach to teaching.

Table 3.4 A persona for an IT technician

Elena, a school IT technician

Elena, age 28, is a senior IT technician in a large secondary school (high school) in Glasgow with over 2000 students. Originally from Poland, she has a diploma in electronics from Potsdam University. She moved to Scotland in 2011 after being unemployed for a year after graduation. She has a Scottish partner, no children, and hopes to develop her career in Scotland. She was originally appointed as a junior technician but was promoted, in 2014, to a senior post responsible for all the school computers.

Although not involved directly in teaching, Elena is often called on to help in computer science classes. She is a competent Python programmer and is a "power user" of digital technologies. She has a long-term career goal of becoming a technical expert in digital learning technologies and being involved in their development. She wants to become an expert in the iLearn system and sees it as an experimental platform for supporting new uses for digital learning.

Elena's persona in Table 3.4 represents technically skilled support staff who may be responsible for setting up and configuring the iLearn software.

I haven't included personas for the students who were intended to be the ultimate end-users of the iLearn system. The reason is that we saw the iLearn system as a platform product that should be configured to suit the preferences and needs of individual schools and teachers. Students would use iLearn to access tools. However, they would not use the configuration features that make iLearn a unique system. Although we planned to include a standard set of applications with the system, we were driven by the belief that the best people to create learning systems were teachers, supported by local technical staff.

Ideally, software development teams should be diverse, with people of different ages and genders. However, the reality is that software product developers are still, overwhelmingly, young men with a high level of technical skill. Software users are more diverse, with varying levels of technical skill. Some developers find it hard to appreciate the problems that users may have with the software. An important benefit of personas is that they help the development team members empathize with potential users of the software. Personas are a tool that allows team members to "step into the users' shoes." Instead of thinking about what they would do in a particular situation, they can imagine how a persona would behave and react.

So, when you have an idea for a feature, you can ask "Would this persona be interested in this feature?" and "How would that persona access and use the feature?". Personas can help you check your ideas to make sure that you are not including product features that aren't really needed. They help you to avoid making unwarranted assumptions, based on your own knowledge, and designing an overcomplicated or irrelevant product.

Personas should be based on an understanding of the potential product users: their jobs, their backgrounds, and their aspirations. You should study and survey potential users to understand what they want and how they might use the product. From these data, you can abstract the essential information about the different types of product users and then use this as a basis for creating personas. These personas should then be cross-checked against the user data to make sure that they reflect typical product users.

It may be possible to study the users when your product is a development of an existing product. For new products, however, you may find it impractical to carry out detailed user surveys. You may not have easy access to potential users. You may not have the resources to carry out user surveys, and you may want to keep your product confidential until it is ready to launch.

If you know nothing about an area, you can't develop reliable personas, so you need to do some user research before you start. This does not have to be a formal or prolonged process. You may know people working in an area and they might be able to help you meet their colleagues to discuss your ideas. For example, my daughter is a teacher and she helped arrange lunch with a group of her colleagues to discuss how they use digital technologies. This helped with both persona and scenario development.

Personas that are developed on the basis of limited user information are called proto-personas. Proto-personas may be created as a collective team exercise using whatever information is available about potential product users. They can never be as accurate as personas developed from detailed user studies, but they are better than nothing. They represent the product users as seen by the development team, and they allow the developers to build a common understanding of the potential product users.

3.2 Scenarios

As a product developer, your aim should be to discover the product features that will tempt users to adopt your product rather than competing software. There is no easy way to define the "best" set of product features. You have to use your own judgement about what to include in your product. To help select and design features, I recommend that you invent scenarios to imagine how users could interact with the product that you are designing.

A scenario is a narrative that describes a situation in which a user is using your product's features to do something that they want to do. The scenario should briefly explain the user's problem and present an imagined way that

Table 3.5 Jack's scenario: Using the iLearn system for class projects

Fishing in Ullapool
Jack is a primary school teacher in Ullapool, teaching P6 pupils. He has decided that a class project should be focused around the fishing industry in the area, looking at the history, development, and economic impact of fishing.
As part of this, students are asked to gather and share reminiscences from relatives, use newspaper archives, and collect old photographs related to fishing and fishing communities in the area. Pupils use an iLearn wiki to gather together fishing stories and SCRAN (a history archive site) to access newspaper archives and photographs. However, Jack also needs a photo-sharing site as he wants students to take and comment on each others' photos and to upload scans of old photographs that they may have in their families. He needs to be able to moderate posts with photos before they are shared, because pre-teen children can't understand copyright and privacy issues.
Jack sends an email to a primary school teachers' group to see if anyone can recommend an appropriate system. Two teachers reply and both suggest that he use KidsTakePics, a photo-sharing site that allows teachers to check and moderate content. As KidsTakePics is not integrated with the iLearn authentication service, he sets up a teacher and a class account with KidsTakePics.
He uses the the iLearn setup service to add KidsTakePics to the services seen by the students in his class so that, when they log in, they can immediately use the system to upload photos from their phones and class computers.

the problem might be solved. There is no need to include everything in the scenario; it isn't a detailed system specification.

Table 3.5 is an example scenario that shows how Jack, whose persona I described in Section 3.2, might use the iLearn system.

From this description of how iLearn might be used for class projects, you can see some of the key elements of a scenario (Figure 3.5) that may be included to help you think about the product features that you need.

The most important elements of a scenario are:

1. A brief statement of the overall objective. In Jack's scenario, shown in Table 3.5, this is to support a class project on the fishing industry.

2. References to the persona involved (Jack) so that you can get information about the capabilities and motivation of that user.

3. Information about what is involved in doing the activity. For example, in Jack's scenario, this involves gathering reminiscences from relatives, accessing newspaper archives, and so on.

4. If appropriate, an explanation of problems that can't be readily addressed using the existing system. Young children don't understand

Figure 3.5 Elements of a scenario description

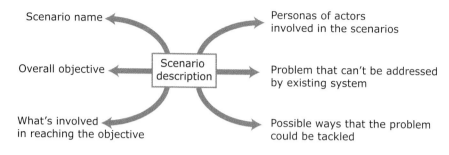

Scenario name

Personas of actors
involved in the scenarios

Overall objective

Scenario
description

Problem that can't be addressed
by existing system

What's involved
in reaching the objective

Possible ways that the problem
could be tackled

issues such as copyright and privacy, so photo sharing requires a site
that a teacher can moderate to make sure that published images are legal
and acceptable.

5. A description of one way that the identified problem might be addressed.
    This may not always be included especially if technical knowledge is
    needed to solve the problem. In Jack's scenario, the preferred approach
    is to use an external tool designed for school students.

The idea of using scenarios to support software engineering has been
around since the 1980s. Different types of scenarios have been proposed,
ranging from high-level scenarios like this one about Jack to more detailed
and specific scenarios that set out the steps involved in a user's interaction
with a system. They are the basis for both use cases, which are extensively
used in object-oriented methods, and user stories, which are used in agile
methods. Scenarios are used in the design of requirements and system features, in system testing, and in user interface design.

Narrative, high-level scenarios, like Jack's scenario, are primarily a means
of facilitating communication and stimulating design creativity. They are
effective in communication because they are understandable and accessible
to users and to people responsible for funding and buying the system.[2] Like
personas, they help developers to gain a shared understanding of the system
that they are creating. You should always be aware, however, that scenarios
are not specifications. They lack detail, they may be incomplete, and they may
not represent all types of user interactions.

---

[2]I presented some of the scenarios for the iLearn system to a government minister for education. He commented that this was the first time he had ever attended a meeting on an IT system
where he actually understood what the system was supposed to do.

Some people recommend that scenarios should be structured with different fields such as what the user sees at the beginning of a scenario, a description of the normal flow of events, a description of what might go wrong, and so on. If you are using scenarios to elicit detailed requirements, the benefit of structure is that you have a consistent presentation, which means you are less likely to forget to include elements that relate to critical system requirements. Engineers usually like this structured approach. However, my experience is that system users, who read and check the scenarios, find structured scenarios to be intimidating and hard to understand.

Consequently, when you are using scenarios at the early stages of product design, I recommend narrative rather than structured scenarios. These scenarios may range from two or three paragraphs of text, like Jack's scenario in Table 3.5, to longer descriptions. You may need to write longer descriptions when your software will be used in existing processes and must interoperate with other software. Your scenarios may then have to include descriptions of interactions with other processes and software systems.

Emma's scenario (shown in Table 3.6) is an example of a longer scenario. In it, she uses the iLearn system to help her with the administration involved in setting up a class trip.

Emma's scenario is different from Jack's scenario because it describes a common and well-understood process rather than something new. The scenario discusses how parts of the process (setting up an email group and web page) are automated by the iLearn system. Remember that Emma is an e-learning skeptic; she is not interested in innovative applications. She wants a system that will make her life easier and reduce the amount of routine administration that she has to do.

In this type of scenario, you are much more likely to include specific details of what might be in the system. For example, it explains that Emma logs in to the system with her Google credentials. This means she doesn't have to remember a separate login name and password. I discuss this approach to authentication in Chapter 7.

When you see this kind of information in a scenario, you need to check whether this is what the user really needs or whether it represents a more general requirement. The statement that the software has to support login using Google credentials might actually reflect a more general need—to provide a login mechanism in which users don't have to remember yet another set of credentials. You may decide on an alternative approach to authentication, such as fingerprint or face recognition on a mobile phone, that avoids the need for system-specific login credentials.

Table 3.6 Using the iLearn system for administration

Emma is teaching the history of World War I to a class of 14-year-olds (S3). A group of S3 students are visiting the historic World War I battlefields in northern France. She wants to set up a "battlefields group" where the students who are attending the trip can share their research about the places they are visiting as well as their pictures and thoughts about the visit.

From home, she logs onto the iLearn system using her Google account credentials. Emma has two iLearn accounts—her teacher account and a parent account associated with the local primary school. The system recognizes that she is a multiple account owner and asks her to select the account to be used. She chooses the teacher account and the system generates her personal welcome screen. As well as her selected applications, this also shows management apps that help teachers create and manage student groups.

Emma selects the "group management" app, which recognizes her role and school from her identity information and creates a new group. The system prompts for the class year (S3) and subject (history) and automatically populates the new group with all S3 students who are studying history. She selects those students going on the trip and adds her teacher colleagues, Jamie and Claire, to the group.

She names the group and confirms that it should be created. The app sets up an icon on her iLearn screen to represent the group, creates an email alias for the group, and asks Emma if she wishes to share the group. She shares access with everyone in the group, which means that they also see the icon on their screen. To avoid getting too many emails from students, she restricts sharing of the email alias to Jamie and Claire.

The group management app then asks Emma if she wishes to set up a group web page, wiki, and blog. Emma confirms that a web page should be created and she types some text to be included on that page.

She then accesses Flickr using the icon on her screen, logs in, and creates a private group to share trip photos that students and teachers have taken. She uploads some of her own photos from previous trips and emails an invitation to join the photo-sharing group to the battlefields email list. Emma uploads material from her own laptop that she has written about the trip to iLearn and shares this with the battlefields group. This action adds her documents to the web page and generates an alert to group members that new material is available.

3.2.1 Writing scenarios

Your starting point for scenario writing should be the personas you have created. You should normally try to imagine several scenarios for each persona. Remember that these scenarios are intended to stimulate thinking rather than provide a complete description of the system. You don't need to cover everything you think users might do with your product.

Scenarios should always be written from the user's perspective and should be based on identified personas or real users. Some writers suggest that scenarios should focus on goals—what the user wants to do—rather than the mechanisms they use to do this. They argue that scenarios should not include specific details of an interaction as these limit the freedom of feature designers. I disagree. As you can see from Emma's scenario, it sometimes makes sense to talk about mechanisms, such as login with Google, that both product users and developers understand.

Furthermore, writing scenarios in a general way that doesn't make assumptions about implementation can be potentially confusing for both users and developers. For example, I think that "X cuts paragraphs from the newspaper archive and pastes them into the project wiki" is easier to read and understand than "X uses an information transfer mechanism to move paragraphs from the newspaper archive to the project wiki."

Sometimes there may be a specific requirement to include a particular feature in the system because that feature is widely used. For example, Jack's scenario in Table 3.5 discusses the use of an iLearn wiki. Many teachers currently use wikis to support group writing and they specifically want to have wikis in the new system. Such user requirements might be even more specific. For example, when designing the iLearn system, we discovered that teachers wanted Wordpress blogs, not just a general blogging facility. So, you should include specific details in a scenario when they reflect reality.

Scenario writing is not a systematic process and different teams approach it in different ways. I recommend that each team member be given individual responsibility for creating a small number of scenarios and work individually to do this. Obviously, members may discuss the scenarios with users and other experts, but this is not essential. The team then discusses the proposed scenarios. Each scenario is refined based on that discussion.

Because it is easy for anyone to read and understand scenarios, it is possible to get users involved in their development. For the iLearn system, we found that the best approach was to develop an imaginary scenario based on our understanding of how the system might be used and then ask users to tell us what we got wrong. Users could ask about things they did not understand, such as "Why can't a photo-sharing site like Flickr be used in Jack's scenario?" They could suggest how the scenario could be extended and made more realistic.

We tried an experiment in which we asked a group of users to write their own scenarios about how they might use the system. This was not a success. The scenarios they created were simply based on how they worked at the moment. They were far too detailed and the writers couldn't easily generalize their experience. Their scenarios were not useful because we wanted something to help us generate ideas rather than replicate the systems that they already used.

Scenarios are not software specifications but are ways of helping people think about what a software system should do. There is no simple answer

Table 3.7 Elena's scenario: Configuring the iLearn system

Elena has been asked by David, the head of the art department in her school, to help set up an iLearn environment for his department. David wants an environment that includes tools for making and sharing art, access to external websites to study artworks, and "exhibition" facilities so that the students' work can be displayed.

Elena starts by talking to art teachers to discover the tools that they recommend and the art sites that they use for studies. She also discovers that the tools they use and the sites they access vary according to the age of their students. Consequently, different student groups should be presented with a toolset that is appropriate for their age and experience.

Once she has established what is required, Elena logs into the iLearn system as an administrator and starts configuring the art environment using the iLearn setup service. She creates sub-environments for three age groups plus a shared environment that includes tools and sites that may be used by all students.

She drags and drops tools that are available locally and the URLs of external websites into each of these environments. For each of the sub-environments, she assigns an art teacher as its administrator so that they can't refine the tool and website selection that has been set up. She publishes the environments in "review mode" and makes them available to the teachers in the art department.

After discussing the environments with the teachers, Elena shows them how to refine and extend the environments. Once they have agreed that the art environment is useful, it is released to all students in the school.

to the question "How many scenarios do I need?" In the iLearn system, 22 scenarios were developed to cover different aspects of system use. There was quite a lot of overlap among these scenarios, so it was probably more than we really needed. Generally, I recommend developing three or four scenarios per persona to get a useful set of information.

Although scenarios certainly don't have to describe every possible use of a system, it is important that you look at the roles of each of the personas that you have developed and write scenarios that cover the main responsibilities for that role. Jack's scenario and Emma's scenario are based on using the iLearn system to support teaching.

Like other system products designed for use in an organization, however, iLearn needs to be configured for use. While some of this configuration can be done by tech-savvy teachers, in many schools it is technical support staff who have this responsibility. Elena's scenario, shown in Table 3.7, describes how she might configure the iLearn software.

Writing scenarios always gives you ideas for the features that you can include in the system. You may then develop these ideas in more detail by analyzing the text of the scenario, as I explain in the next section.

3.3 User stories

I explained in Section 3.2 that scenarios are descriptions of situations in which a user is trying to do something with a software system. Scenarios are high-level stories of system use. They should describe a sequence of interactions with the system but should not include details of these interactions.

User stories are finer-grain narratives that set out in a more detailed and structured way a single thing that a user wants from a software system. I presented a user story at the beginning of the chapter:

> *As an author I need a way to organize the book that I'm writing into chapters and sections.*

This story reflects what has become the standard format of a user story:

> *As a <role>, I <want / need> to <do something>*

Another example of a user story taken from Emma's scenario might be:

> *As a teacher, I want to tell all members of my group when new information is available.*

A variant of this standard format adds a justification for the action:

> *As a <role> I <want / need> to <do something> so that <reason>*

For example:

> *As a teacher, I need to be able to report who is attending a class trip so that the school maintains the required health and safety records.*

Some people argue that a rationale or justification should always be part of a user story. I think this is unnecessary if the story makes sense on its own. Knowing one reason why this might be useful doesn't help the product developers. However, in situations where some developers are unfamiliar with what users do, a rationale can help those developers understand why the story has been included. A rationale may also help trigger ideas about alternative ways of providing what the user wants.

An important use of user stories is in planning, and many users of the Scrum method represent the product backlog as a set of user stories. For this purpose, user stories should focus on a clearly defined system feature or

Figure 3.6 User stories from Emma's scenario

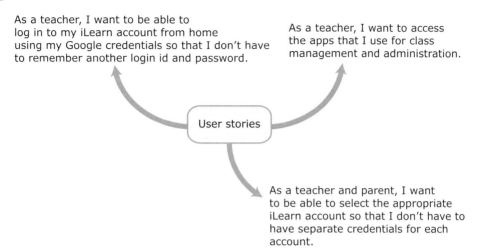

As a teacher, I want to be able to log in to my iLearn account from home using my Google credentials so that I don't have to remember another login id and password.

As a teacher, I want to access the apps that I use for class management and administration.

User stories

As a teacher and parent, I want to be able to select the appropriate iLearn account so that I don't have to have separate credentials for each account.

aspect of a feature that can be implemented within a single sprint. If the story is about a more complex feature that might take several sprints to implement, then it is called an "epic." An example of an epic might be:

> *As a system manager, I need a way to back up the system and restore individual applications, files, directories, or the whole system.*

A lot of functionality is associated with this user story. For implementation, it should be broken down into simpler stories, with each story focusing on a single aspect of the backup system.

When you are thinking about product features, user stories are not intended for planning but for helping with feature identification. Therefore, you don't need to be overly concerned about whether your stories are simple stories or epics. You should aim to develop stories that are helpful in one of two ways:

■ as a way of extending and adding detail to a scenario;

■ as part of the description of the system feature that you have identified.

As an example of scenario refinement, the initial actions in Emma's scenario shown in Figure 3.6 can be represented by three user stories. Recall that the scenario says:

> From home, she logs onto the iLearn system using her Google account credentials. Emma has two iLearn accounts—her teacher account and

Figure 3.7 User stories describing the Groups feature

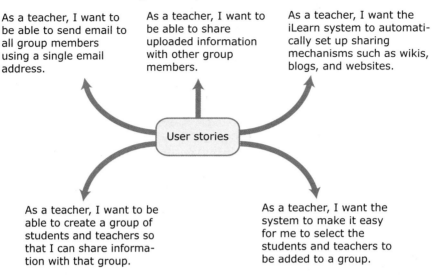

As a teacher, I want to be able to send email to all group members using a single email address.

As a teacher, I want to be able to share uploaded information with other group members.

As a teacher, I want the iLearn system to automatically set up sharing mechanisms such as wikis, blogs, and websites.

User stories

As a teacher, I want to be able to create a group of students and teachers so that I can share information with that group.

As a teacher, I want the system to make it easy for me to select the students and teachers to be added to a group.

a parent account associated with the local primary school. The system recognizes that she is a multiple account owner and asks her to select the account to be used. She chooses the teacher account and the system generates her personal welcome screen. As well as her selected applications, this also shows management apps that help teachers create and manage student groups.

You can create user stories from this account, as I show in Figure 3.6.

You can see from the stories in Figure 3.6 that I have included a rationale in the story that explains why Emma wants to work in the way specified in the scenario. It is best not to include rationale in a scenario, as it tends to disrupt the flow of the description and make it more difficult to read and understand.

When you define user stories from a scenario, you provide more information to developers to help them design the product's features. We can see an example of this in the stories shown in Figure 3.6. Emma wants an easy way to authenticate herself to the system, either as a teacher or as a parent. She doesn't want to have to remember more login credentials, and she doesn't want to have two accounts with different credentials.

As an example of how stories can be used to describe the features of a system, Emma's scenario discusses how a group can be created and explains system actions that take place on group creation. The user stories shown in Figure 3.7 can be derived from the scenario to describe the Groups feature in the iLearn system.

The set of stories shown in Figure 3.7 is not a complete description of the Groups feature. No stories are concerned with deleting or changing a group, restricting access, and other tasks. You start by deriving stories from a scenario, but you then have to think about what other stories might be needed for a complete description of a feature's functionality.

A question that is sometimes asked about user stories is whether you should write "negative stories" that describe what a user doesn't want. For example, you might write this negative story:

As a user, I don't want the system to log and transmit my information to any external servers.

If you are writing stories to be part of a product backlog, you should avoid negative stories. It is impossible to write system tests that demonstrate a negative. In the early stages of product design, however, it may be helpful to write negative stories if they define an absolute constraint on the system. Alternatively, you can sometimes reframe negative stories in a positive way. For example, instead of the above story, you could write:

As a user, I want to be able to control the information that is logged and transmitted by the system to external servers so that I can ensure that my personal information is not shared.

Some of the user stories that you develop will be sufficiently detailed that you can use them directly in planning. You can include them in a product backlog. Sometimes, however, to use stories in planning, you have to refine the stories to relate them more directly to the implementation of the system.

It is possible to express all of the functionality described in a scenario as user stories. So, an obvious question that you might ask is "Why not just develop user stories and forget about scenarios?" Some agile methods rely exclusively on user stories, but I think that scenarios are more natural and are helpful for the following reasons:

1. Scenarios read more naturally because they describe what a user of a system is actually doing with that system. People often find it easier to relate to this specific information rather than to the statement of wants or needs set out in a set of user stories.

2. When you are interviewing real users or checking a scenario with real users, they don't talk in the stylized way that is used in user stories. People relate better to the more natural narrative in scenarios.

3. Scenarios often provide more context—information about what users are trying to do and their normal ways of working. You can do this in user stories, but it means that they are no longer simple statements about the use of a system feature.

Scenarios and stories are helpful in both choosing and designing system features. However, you should think of scenarios and user stories as "tools for thinking" about a system rather than a system specification. Scenarios and stories that are used to stimulate thinking don't have to be complete or consistent, and there are no rules about how many of each you need.

3.4 Feature identification

As I said in the chapter introduction, your aim at this early stage of product design is to create a list of features that define your software product. A feature is a way of allowing users to access and use your product's functionality so that the feature list defines the overall functionality of the system. In this section, I explain how scenarios and stories can be used to help identify product features.

You should, ideally, identify product features that are independent, coherent and relevant:

1. *Independence* A feature should not depend on how other system features are implemented and should not be affected by the order of activation of other features.

2. *Coherence* Features should be linked to a single item of functionality. They should not do more than one thing, and they should never have side effects.

3. *Relevance* System features should reflect the way users normally carry out some task. They should not offer obscure functionality that is rarely required.

There is no definitive method for feature selection and design. Rather, the four important knowledge sources shown in Figure 3.8 can help with this.

Table 3.8 explains these knowledge sources in more detail. Of course, these are not all of equal importance for all products. For example, domain knowledge is very important for business products but less important for generic consumer products. You therefore need to think carefully about the knowledge required for your specific product.

Figure 3.8 Feature design

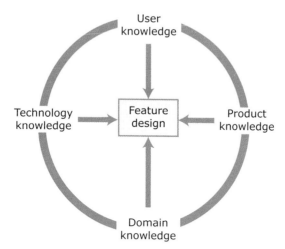

Innovation often stems from a combination of domain and technology knowledge. A good example is the Git system for code management that I cover in Chapter 10. Git works in a completely different way from previous code management systems. These older systems were based on a technology model in which storage was expensive, so they focused on limiting storage use and delivering information to users as required. The developer of Git realized

Table 3.8 Knowledge required for feature design

Knowledge	Description
User knowledge	You can use user scenarios and user stories to inform the team of what users want and how they might use the software features.
Product knowledge	You may have experience of existing products or decide to research what these products do as part of your development process. Sometimes your features have to replicate existing features in these products because they provide fundamental functionality that is always required.
Domain knowledge	This is knowledge of the domain or work area (e.g., finance, event booking) that your product aims to support. By understanding the domain, you can think of new innovative ways of helping users do what they want to do.
Technology knowledge	New products often emerge to take advantage of technological developments since their competitors were launched. If you understand the latest technology, you can design features to make use of it.

Figure 3.9 Factors in feature set design

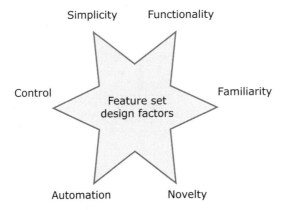

that storage had become much cheaper, so it was possible for all users to have a complete copy of all information. This allowed for a new approach that dramatically simplified software development by distributed teams.

When you are designing a product feature set and deciding how features should work, you have to consider the six factors shown in Figure 3.9.

Unfortunately, it is impossible to design a feature set in which all of these factors are optimized, so you have to make some trade-offs:

1. *Simplicity and functionality* Everyone says they want software to be as simple as possible to use. At the same time, they demand functionality that helps them do what they want to do. You need to find a balance between providing a simple, easy-to-use system and including enough functionality to attract users with a variety of needs.

2. *Familiarity and novelty* Users prefer that new software should support the familiar everyday tasks that are part of their work or life. However, if you simply replicate the features of a product that they already use, there is no real motivation for them to change. To encourage users to adopt your system, you need to include new features that will convince users that your product can do more than its competitors.

3. *Automation and control* You may decide that your product can automatically do things for users that other products can't. However, users inevitably do things differently from one another. Some may like automation, where the software does things for them. Others prefer to have control. You therefore have to think carefully about what can be automated, how it is automated, and how users can configure the automation so that the system can be tailored to their preferences.

Your choices have a major influence on the features to be included in your product, how they integrate, and the functionality they provide. You may make a specific choice—for example, to focus on simplicity—that will drive the design of your product.

One problem that product developers should be aware of and try to avoid is "feature creep." Feature creep means that the number of features in a product creeps up as new potential uses of the product are envisaged.

The size and complexity of many large software products such as Microsoft Office and Adobe Photoshop are a consequence of feature creep. Most users use only a relatively small subset of the features of these products. Rather than stepping back and simplifying things, developers continually added new features to the software.

Feature creep adds to the complexity of a product, which means that you are likely to introduce bugs and security vulnerabilities into the software. It also usually makes the user interface more complex. A large feature set often means that you have to bundle vaguely related features together and provide access to these through a higher-level menu. This can be confusing, especially for less experienced users.

Feature creep happens for three reasons:

1. Product managers and marketing executives discuss the functionality they need with a range of different product users. Different users have slightly different needs or may do the same thing but in slightly different ways. There is a natural reluctance to say no to important users, so functionality to meet all of the users' demands ends up in the product.

2. Competitive products are introduced with slightly different functionality to your product. There is marketing pressure to include comparable functionality so that market share is not lost to these competitors. This can lead to "feature wars," where competing products become more and more bloated as they replicate the features of their competitors.

3. The product tries to support both experienced and inexperienced users. Easy ways of implementing common actions are added for inexperienced users and the more complex features to accomplish the same thing are retained because experienced users prefer to work that way.

To avoid feature creep, the product manager and the development team should review all feature proposals and compare new proposals to features that have already been accepted for implementation. The questions shown in Figure 3.10 may be used to help identify unnecessary features.

Figure 3.10 Avoiding feature creep

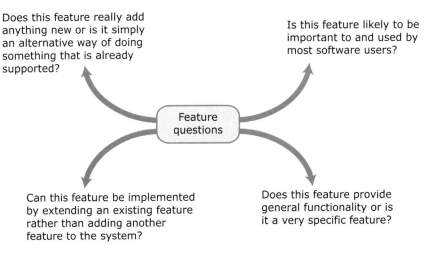

Does this feature really add anything new or is it simply an alternative way of doing something that is already supported?

Is this feature likely to be important to and used by most software users?

Can this feature be implemented by extending an existing feature rather than adding another feature to the system?

Does this feature provide general functionality or is it a very specific feature?

Feature questions

3.4.1 Feature derivation

When you start with a product vision or writing scenarios based on that vision, product features immediately come to mind. I discussed the iLearn system vision in Chapter 1 and I repeat it in Table 3.9.

I have highlighted phrases in this vision suggesting features that should be part of the product, including:

▪ a feature that allows users to access and use existing web-based resources;

▪ a feature that allows the system to exist in multiple different configurations;

▪ a feature that allows user configuration of the system to create a specific environment.

These features distinguish the iLearn system from existing VLEs and are the central features of the product.

Table 3.9 The iLearn system vision

FOR teachers and educators WHO need a way to *help students use web-based learning resources and applications,* THE iLearn system is an open learning environment THAT *allows the set of resources used by classes and students to be easily configured for these students and classes by teachers themselves.*

UNLIKE Virtual Learning Environments, such as Moodle, the focus of iLearn is the learning process rather than the administration and management of materials, assessments, and coursework. OUR product *enables teachers to create subject and age-specific environments for their students* using any web-based resources, such as videos, simulations, and written materials that are appropriate

Table 3.10 Jack's scenario with highlighted phrases

Jack is a primary school teacher in Ullapool, teaching P6 pupils. He has decided that a class project should be focused around the fishing industry in the area, looking at the history, development, and economic impact of fishing.

As part of this, students are asked to gather and share reminiscences from relatives, use newspaper archives, and collect old photographs related to fishing and fishing communities in the area. *Students use an iLearn wiki* to gather together fishing stories and *SCRAN (a history archive) to access newspaper archives and photographs.* However, Jack also needs a photo-sharing site as he wants *pupils to take and comment on each others' photos and to upload scans of old photographs* that they may have in their families. He needs to be able to moderate posts with photos before they are shared, because pre-teen children can't understand copyright and privacy issues.

Jack *sends an email to a primary school teachers' group* to see if anyone can recommend an appropriate system. Two teachers reply and both suggest that he use KidsTakePics, a photo-sharing site that allows teachers to check and moderate content. As KidsTakePics *is not integrated with the iLearn authentication service,* he sets up a teacher and a class account with KidsTakePics.

He uses the the iLearn setup service to add KidsTakePics to the services seen by the students in his class so that when they log in, they can immediately use the system to upload photos from their phones and class computers.

This approach of highlighting phrases in a narrative description can be used when analyzing scenarios to find system features. You read through the scenarios, look for user actions (usually denoted by active verbs, such as "use," "choose," "send," "update," and so on), and highlight the phrases where these are mentioned. You then think about the product features that can support these actions and how they might be implemented.

In Table 3.10, I have done this with Jack's scenario (see Table 3.5), in which he sets up a system for his students' project work.

The highlighted text identifies features and feature characteristics that should be part of the iLearn system:

- a wiki for group writing;

- access to the SCRAN history archive, which is a shared national resource that provides access to historical newspaper and magazine articles for schools and universities;

- the ability to set up and access an email group;

- the ability to integrate some applications with the iLearn authentication service.

It also confirms the need for the configuration feature that has already been identified from the product vision.

Feature identification should be a team activity, and as features are identified, the team should discuss them and generate ideas about related features. Jack's scenario suggests that there is a need for groups to write together. You should therefore think about age-appropriate ways to design features for:

■ collaborative writing, where several people can work simultaneously on the same document;

■ blogs and web pages as a way of sharing information.

You can also think about generalizing the features suggested by the scenario. The scenario identifies the need for access to an external archive (SCRAN). However, perhaps the feature that you add to the software should support access to any external archive and allow students to transfer information to the iLearn system.

You can go through a similar process of highlighting phrases in all of the scenarios that you have developed and using them to identify and then generalize a set of product features. If you have developed user stories to refine your scenarios, these may immediately suggest a product feature or feature characteristic. For example, this story was derived from Emma's scenario (see Table 3.6):

As a teacher and a parent, I want to be able to select the appropriate iLearn account so that I don't have to have separate credentials for each account.

This story states that the account feature of the iLearn system has to accommodate the idea that a single user may have multiple accounts. Each account is associated with a particular role the user may adopt when using the system. When logging in, users should be able to select the account they wish to use.

3.4.2 The feature list

The output of the feature identification process should be a list of features that you use for designing and implementing your product. There is no need to go into a lot of detail about the features at this stage. You add detail when you are implementing the feature.

You may describe the features on the list using the input/action/output model that I showed in Figure 3.2. Alternatively, you can use a standard template, which includes a narrative description of the feature, constraints that have to be considered, and other relevant comments.

Figure 3.11 The iLearn authentication feature

Description
Authentication is used to identify users to the system and is currently based on a login id/password system. Users may authenticate themselves using their national user id and a personal password or may use their Google or Facebook credentials.

iLearn authentication

Constraints
All users must have a national user id and system password that they use for initial system authentication. They may then link their account with their Google or Facebook account for future authentication sessions.

Comments
Future authentication mechanisms may be based on biometrics and this should be considered in the design of the system.

Figure 3.11 is an example of this feature template that is used to describe the system authentication feature in the iLearn system.

The descriptions associated with the feature can sometimes be very simple. For example, a Print feature might be described using the simple feature template that I introduced at the beginning of the chapter:

Print **the** *document* **to** *a selected printer* **or to** *PDF.*

Alternatively, you can describe a feature from one or more user stories. Descriptions based on user stories are particularly useful if you intend to use Scrum and story-based planning when developing the software.

Table 3.11 shows how you can describe the configuration feature of the iLearn system using user stories and the feature template shown in Figure 3.11. In this example, I have used an alternative text-based form of the feature template. This is useful when you have relatively long feature descriptions. Notice that the table includes user stories from the system manager and a teacher.

The product development team should meet to discuss the scenarios and stories, and it makes sense to set out the initial list of features on a whiteboard. This can be done using a web-based discussion, but these are less effective than a face-to-face meeting. The feature list should then be recorded in a

Table 3.11 Feature description using user stories

iLearn system configuration
Description   As a system manager, I want to create and configure an iLearn environment by adding and removing services to/from that environment so that I can create environments for specific purposes.   As a system manager, I want to set up sub-environments that include a subset of services that are included in another environment.   As a system manager, I want to assign administrators to created environments.   As a system manager, I want to limit the rights of environment administrators so that they cannot accidentally or deliberately disrupt the operation of key services.   As a teacher, I want to be able to add services that are not integrated with the iLearn authentication system.
Constraints   The use of some tools may be limited for license reasons so there may be a need to access license management tools during configuration.
Comments   Based on Elena's and Jack's scenarios

shared document such as a wiki, a Google Sheet, or an issue-tracking system such as JIRA. Feature descriptions may then be updated and shared as new information about the features emerges.

When you have developed an initial list of feature ideas, you should either extend your existing prototype or create a prototype system to demonstrate these features. As I said in Chapter 1, the aim of software prototyping is to test and clarify product ideas and to demonstrate your product to management, funders, and potential customers. You should focus on the novel and critical features of your system. You don't need to implement or demonstrate routine features such as Cut and Paste or Print.

When you have a prototype and have experimented with it, you will inevitably discover problems, omissions, and inconsistencies in your initial list of features. You then update and change this list before moving on to the development of your software product.

I think that scenarios and user stories should always be your starting point for identifying product features. However, the problem with basing product designs on user modeling and research is that it locks in existing ways of working. Scenarios tell you how users work at the moment; they don't show how they might change their ways of working if they had the right software to support them.

User research, on its own, rarely helps you innovate and invent new ways of working. Famously, Nokia, then the world leader in mobile (cell) phones, did extensive user research and produced better and better conventional phones. Then Apple invented the smartphone without user research, and Nokia is now a minor player in the phone business.

As I said, stories and scenarios are tools for thinking; the most important benefit of using them is that you gain an understanding of how your software might be used. It makes sense to start by identifying a feature set from stories and scenarios. However, you should also think creatively about alternative or additional features that help users to work more efficiently or to do things differently.

KEY POINTS

- A software product feature is a fragment of functionality that implements something a user may need or want when using the product.

- The first stage of product development is to identify the list of product features in which you name each feature and give a brief description of its functionality.

- Personas are "imagined users"— character portraits of types of users you think might use your product.

- A persona description should paint a picture of a typical product user. It should describe the user's educational background, technology experience, and why they might want to use your product.

- A scenario is a narrative that describes a situation where a user is accessing product features to do something that they want to do.

- Scenarios should always be written from the user's perspective and should be based on identified personas or real users.

- User stories are finer-grain narratives that set out, in a structured way, something that a user wants from a software system.

- User stories may be used to extend and add detail to a scenario or as part of the description of system features.

- The key influences in feature identification and design are user research, domain knowledge, product knowledge, and technology knowledge.

- You can identify features from scenarios and stories by highlighting user actions in these narratives and thinking about the features that you need to support these actions.

RECOMMENDED READING

"An Introduction to Feature-Driven Development" This article is an introduction to this agile method that focuses on features, a key element of software products. (S. Palmer, 2009)

https://dzone.com/articles/introduction-feature-driven

"A Closer Look at Personas: What they are and how they work" This excellent article on personas explains how they can be used in different situations. Lots of links to relevant associated articles. (S. Golz, 2014)

https://www.smashingmagazine.com/2014/08/a-closer-look-at-personas-part-1/

"How User Scenarios Help to Improve Your UX" Scenarios are often used in designing the user experience for a system. However, the advice here is just as relevant for scenarios intended to help discover system features. (S. Idler, 2011)

https://usabilla.com/blog/how-user-scenarios-help-to-improve-your-ux/

"10 Tips for Writing Good User Stories" Sound advice on story writing is presented by an author who takes a pragmatic view of the value of user stories. (R. Pichler, 2016)

http://www.romanpichler.com/blog/10-tips-writing-good-user-stories/

"What Is a Feature? A qualitative study of features in industrial software product lines" This academic paper discusses a study of features in four different systems and tries to establish what a "good" feature is. It concludes that good features should describe customer-related functionality precisely. (T. Berger et al., 2015)

https://people.csail.mit.edu/mjulia/publications/What_Is_A_Feature_2015.pdf

PRESENTATIONS, VIDEOS, AND LINKS

https://iansommerville.com/engineering-software-products/features-scenarios-and-stories

EXERCISES

3.1. Using the input/action/output template that I introduced at the beginning of this chapter, describe two features of software that you commonly use, such as an editor or a presentation system.

3.2. Explain why it is helpful to develop a number of personas representing types of system user before you move on to write scenarios of how the system will be used.

3.3. Based on your own experience of school and teachers, write a persona for a high school science teacher who is interested in building simple electronic systems and using them in class teaching.

3.4. Extend Jack's scenario, shown in Table 3.5, to include a section in which students record audio reminiscences from their older friends and relatives and include them in the iLearn system.

3.5. What do you think are the weaknesses of scenarios as a way of envisaging how users might interact with a software system?

3.6. Starting with Jack's scenario (Table 3.5), derive four user stories about the use of the iLearn system by both students and teachers.

3.7. What do you think are the weaknesses of user stories when used to identify system features and how they work?

3.8. Explain why domain knowledge is important when identifying and designing product features.

3.9. Suggest how a development team might avoid feature creep when "it is" to be in agreement with "a team" faced with many different suggestions for new features to be added to a product.

3.10. Based on Elena's scenario, shown in Table 3.7, use the method of highlighting phrases in the scenario to identify four features that might be included in the iLearn system.

4
Software Architecture

The focus of this book is software products—individual applications that run on servers, personal computers, or mobile devices. To create a reliable, secure, and efficient product, you need to pay attention to its overall organization, how the software is decomposed into components, the server organization, and the technologies used to build the software. In short, you need to design the software architecture.

The architecture of a software product affects its performance, usability, security, reliability, and maintainability. Architectural issues are so important that three chapters in this book are devoted to them. In this chapter I discuss the decomposition of software into components, client–server architecture, and technology issues that affect the software architecture. In Chapter 5 I cover architectural issues and choices you have to make when implementing your software on the cloud. In Chapter 6 I cover microservices architecture, which is particularly important for cloud-based products.

If you google "software architecture definition," you find many different interpretations of the term. Some focus on "architecture" as a noun, the structure of a system; others consider "architecture" as a verb, the process of defining these structures. Rather than try to invent yet another definition, I use a definition of software architecture that is included in an IEEE standard,[1] shown in Table 4.1.

An important term in this definition is "components." Here it is used in a very general way, so a component can be anything from a program (large

---

[1] IEEE standard 1471. This has now been superseded by a later standard that has revised the definition. In my opinion, the revised definition is not an improvement and it is harder to explain and understand. https://en.wikipedia.org/wiki/IEEE_1471

Table 4.1 The IEEE definition of software architecture

Software architecture

Architecture is the fundamental organization of a software system embodied in its components, their relationships to each other and to the environment, and the principles guiding its design and evolution.

scale) to an object (small scale). A component is an element that implements a coherent set of functionality or features. When designing software architecture, you don't have to decide how an architectural element or component is to be implemented. Rather, you design the component interface and leave the implementation of that interface to a later stage of the development process.

The best way to think of a software component is as a collection of one or more services that may be used by other components (Figure 4.1). A service is a coherent fragment of functionality. It can range from a large-scale service, such as a database service, to a microservice, which does one very specific thing. For example, a microservice might simply check the validity of a URL. Services can be implemented directly, as I discuss in Chapter 6, which covers microservice architecture. Alternatively, services can be part of modules or objects and accessed through a defined component interface or an application programming interface (API).

The initial enthusiasts for agile development invented slogans such as "You Ain't Gonna Need It" (YAGNI) and "Big Design Up Front" (BDUF), where YAGNI is good and BDUF is bad. They suggested that developers should not plan for change in their systems because change can't be predicted and might never happen. Many people think this means that agile developers believed there was no need to design the architecture of a software system

Figure 4.1 Access to services provided by software components

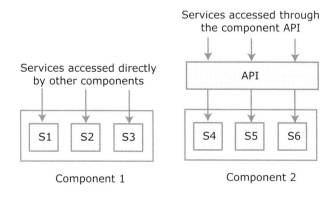

before implementation. Rather, when issues emerged during development, they should simply be tackled by refactoring—changing and reorganizing the software.

The inventors of agile methods are good engineers, and I don't think they intended that software architecture should not be designed. A principle of agile methods is that system planning and documentation should be minimized. However, this does not mean that you can't plan and describe the overall structure of your system. Agile methods now recognize the importance of architectural design and suggest that this should be an early activity in the development process. You can do this in a Scrum sprint where the outcome of the sprint is an informal architectural design.

Some people think it is best to have a single software architect. This person should be an experienced engineer who uses background knowledge and expertise to create a coherent architecture. However, the problems with this "single architect" model is that the team may not understand the architectural decisions that were made. To make sure that your whole team understands the architecture, I think everyone should be involved, in some way, in the architectural design process. This helps less experienced team members learn and understand why decisions are made. Furthermore, new team members may have knowledge and insights into new or unfamiliar technologies that can be used in the design and implementation of the software.

A development team should design and discuss the software product architecture before starting the final product implementation. They should agree on priorities and understand the trade-offs that they are making in these architectural decisions. They should create a description of the product architecture that sets out the fundamental structure of the software and serves as a reference for its implementation.

4.1 Why is architecture important?

I suggested in Chapter 1 that you should always develop a product prototype. The aim of a prototype is to help you understand more about the product that you are developing, and so you should aim to develop this as quickly as possible. Issues such as security, usability, and long-term maintainability are not important at this stage.

When you are developing a final product, however, "non-functional" attributes are critically important (Table 4.2). It is these attributes, rather than

Table 4.2 Non-functional system quality attributes

Attribute	Key issue
Responsiveness	Does the system return results to users in a reasonable time?
Reliability	Do the system features behave as expected by both developers and users?
Availability	Can the system deliver its services when requested by users?
Security	Does the system protect itself and users' data from unauthorized attacks and intrusions?
Usability	Can system users access the features that they need and use them quickly and without errors?
Maintainability	Can the system be readily updated and new features added without undue costs?
Resilience	Can the system continue to deliver user services in the event of partial failure or external attack?

product features, that influence user judgements about the quality of your software. If your product is unreliable, insecure, or difficult to use, then it is almost bound to be a failure. Product development takes much longer than prototyping because of the time and effort that are needed to ensure that your product is reliable, maintainable, secure, and so on.

Architecture is important because the architecture of a system has a fundamental influence on these non-functional properties. Table 4.3 is a

Table 4.3 The influence of architecture on system security

A centralized security architecture

In the *Star Wars* prequel *Rogue One* (https://en.wikipedia.org/wiki/Rogue_One), the evil Empire has stored the plans for all of their equipment in a single, highly secure, well-guarded, remote location. This is called a centralized security architecture. It is based on the principle that if you maintain all of your information in one place, then you can apply lots of resources to protect that information and ensure that intruders can't get it.

Unfortunately (for the Empire), the rebels managed to breach their security. They stole the plans for the Death Star, an event that underpins the whole *Star Wars* saga. In trying to stop them, the Empire destroyed their entire archive of system documentation with who knows what resultant costs. Had the Empire chosen a distributed security architecture, with different parts of the Death Star plans stored in different locations, then stealing the plans would have been more difficult. The rebels would have had to breach security in all locations to steal the complete Death Star blueprints.

Figure 4.2 Shared database architecture

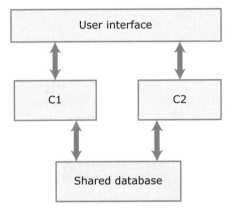

non-computing example of how architectural choices affect system properties. It is taken from the film *Rogue One*, part of the *Star Wars* saga.

Rogue One is science fiction, but it demonstrates that architectural decisions have fundamental consequences. The benefits of a centralized security
architecture are that it is easy to design and build protection and the protected
information can be accessed efficiently. However, if your security is breached,
you lose everything. If you distribute information, it takes longer to access all
of the information and costs more to protect it. If security is breached in one
location, however, you lose only the information that you have stored there.

Figures 4.2 and 4.3 illustrate a situation where the system architecture
affects the maintainability and performance of a system. Figure 4.2 shows
a system with two components (C1 and C2) that share a common database.
This is a common architecture for web-based systems. Let's assume that C1
runs slowly because it has to reorganize the information in the database before
using it. The only way to make C1 faster might be to change the database.
This means that C2 also has to be changed, which may potentially affect its
response time.

Figure 4.3 shows a different architecture where each component has its
own copy of the parts of the database that it needs. Each of these components
can therefore use a different database structure, and so operate efficiently.
If one component needs to change the database organization, this does not
affect the other component. Also, the system can continue to provide a partial
service in the event of a database failure. This is impossible in a centralized
database architecture.

However, the distributed database architecture may run more slowly and
may cost more to implement and change. There needs to be a mechanism

Figure 4.3 Multiple database architecture

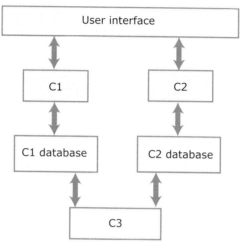

Database reconciliation

(shown here as component C3) to ensure that the data shared by C1 and C2 are kept consistent when changes are made. This takes time and it is possible that users will occasionally see inconsistent information. Furthermore, additional storage costs are associated with the distributed database architecture and higher costs of change if a new component that requires its own database has to be added to the system.

It is impossible to optimize all of the non-functional attributes in the same system. Optimizing one attribute, such as security, inevitably affects other attributes, such as system usability and efficiency. You have to think about these issues and the software architecture before you start programming. Otherwise, it is almost inevitable that your product will have undesirable characteristics and will be difficult to change.

Another reason why architecture is important is that the software architecture you choose affects the complexity of your product. The more complex a system, the more difficult and expensive it is to understand and change. Programmers are more likely to make mistakes and introduce bugs and security vulnerabilities when they are modifying or extending a complex system. Therefore, minimizing complexity should be an important goal for architectural design.

The organization of a system has a profound effect on its complexity, and it is very important to pay attention to this when designing the software architecture. I explain architectural complexity in Section 4.3, and I cover general issues of program complexity in Chapter 8.

Figure 4.4 Issues that influence architectural decisions

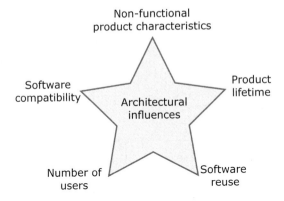

4.2 Architectural design

Architectural design involves understanding the issues that affect the architecture of your particular product and creating a description of the architecture that shows the critical components and some of their relationships. The architectural issues that are most important for software product development are shown in Figure 4.4 and Table 4.4.

Other human and organizational factors also affect architectural design decisions. These include the planned schedule to bring the product to market, the capabilities of your development team, and the software development budget. If you choose an architecture that requires your team to learn unfamiliar technologies, then this may delay the delivery of your system. There is no point in creating a "perfect" architecture that is delivered late if this means that a competing product captures the market.

Architectural design involves considering these issues and deciding on essential compromises that allow you to create a system that is "good enough" and can be delivered on time and on budget. Because it is impossible to optimize everything, you have to make a series of trade-offs when choosing an architecture for your system. Some examples are:

■ maintainability vs. performance;

■ security vs. usability;

■ availability vs. time to market and cost.

Table 4.4 The importance of architectural design issues

Issue	Architectural importance
Non-functional product characteristics	Non-functional product characteristics such as security and performance affect all users. If you get these wrong, your product is unlikely to be a commercial success. Unfortunately, some characteristics are opposing, so you can optimize only the most important.
Product lifetime	If you anticipate a long product lifetime, you need to create regular product revisions. You therefore need an architecture that can evolve, so that it can be adapted to accommodate new features and technology.
Software reuse	You can save a lot of time and effort if you can reuse large components from other products or open-source software. However, this constrains your architectural choices because you must fit your design around the software that is being reused.
Number of users	If you are developing consumer software delivered over the Internet, the number of users can change very quickly. This can lead to serious performance degradation unless you design your architecture so that your system can be quickly scaled up and down.
Software compatibility	For some products, it is important to maintain compatibility with other software so that users can adopt your product and use data prepared using a different system. This may limit architectural choices, such as the database software that you can use.

System maintainability is an attribute that reflects how difficult and expensive it is to make changes to a system after it has been released to customers. In general, you improve maintainability by building a system from small self-contained parts, each of which can be replaced or enhanced if changes are required. Wherever possible, you should avoid shared data structures and you should make sure that, when data are processed, separate components are used to "produce" and to "consume" data.

In architectural terms, this means that the system should be decomposed into fine-grain components, each of which does one thing and one thing only. More general functionality emerges by creating networks of these components that communicate and exchange information. Microservice architectures, explained in Chapter 6, are an example of this type of architecture.

However, it takes time for components to communicate with each other. Consequently, if many components are involved in implementing a product feature,

Figure 4.5 Authentication layers

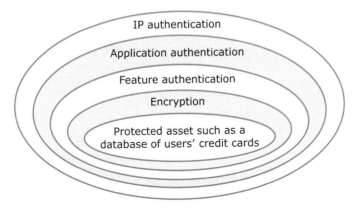

the software will be slower. Avoiding shared data structures also has an impact on performance. There may be delays involved in transferring data from one component to another and in ensuring that duplicated data are kept consistent.

The constant and increasing risk of cybercrime means that all product developers have to design security into their software. Security is so important for product development that I devote a separate chapter (Chapter 7) to this topic. You can achieve security by designing the system protection as a series of layers (Figure 4.5). An attacker has to penetrate all of those layers before the system is compromised. Layers might include system authentication layers, a separate critical feature authentication layer, an encryption layer, and so on. Architecturally, you can implement each of these layers as separate components so that if an attacker compromises one of these components, then the other layers remain intact.

Unfortunately, there are drawbacks to using multiple authentication layers. A layered approach to security affects the usability of the software. Users have to remember information, like passwords, that is needed to penetrate a security layer. Their interaction with the system is inevitably slowed by its security features. Many users find this irritating and often look for work-arounds so that they do not have to re-authenticate to access system features or data.

Many security breaches arise because users behave in an insecure way, such as choosing passwords that are easy to guess, sharing passwords, and leaving systems logged on. They do this because they are frustrated by system security features that are difficult to use or that slow down their access to the system and its data. To avoid this, you need an architecture that doesn't have too many security layers, that doesn't enforce unnecessary security, and that provides, where possible, helper components that reduce the load on users.

The availability of a system is a measure of the amount of uptime of that system. It is normally expressed as a percentage of the time that a system is available to deliver user services. Therefore, an availability of 99.9% in a system that is intended to be constantly available means that the system should be available for 86,313 seconds out of the 86,400 seconds in a day. Availability is particularly important in enterprise products, such as products for the finance industry, where 24/7 operation is expected.

Architecturally, you improve availability by having redundant components in a system. To make use of redundancy, you include sensor components that detect failure and switching components that switch operation to a redundant component when a failure is detected. The problem here is that implementing these extra components takes time and increases the cost of system development. It adds complexity to the system and therefore increases the chances of introducing bugs and vulnerabilities. For this reason, most product software does not use component-switching in the event of system failure. As I explain in Chapter 8, you can use reliable programming techniques to reduce the changes of system failure.

Once you have decided on the most important quality attributes for your software, you have to consider three questions about the architectural design of your product:

1. How should the system be organized as a set of architectural components, where each of these components provides a subset of the overall system functionality? The organization should deliver the system security, reliability, and performance that you need.

2. How should these architectural components be distributed and communicate with each other?

3. What technologies should be used in building the system, and what components should be reused?

I cover these three questions in the remaining sections of this chapter.

Architectural descriptions in product development provide a basis for the development team to discuss the organization of the system. An important secondary role is to document a shared understanding of what needs to be developed and what assumptions have been made in designing the software. The final system may differ from the original architectural model, so it is not a reliable way of documenting delivered software.

I think informal diagrams based around icons to represent entities, lines to represent relationships, and text are the best way to describe and share information about software product architectures. Everyone can participate in the design process. You can draw and change informal diagrams quickly without using special software tools. Informal notations are flexible so that you can make unanticipated changes easily. New people joining a team can understand them without specialist knowledge.

The main problems with informal models are that they are ambiguous and they can't be checked automatically for omissions and inconsistencies. If you use more formal approaches, based on architectural description languages (ADLs) or the Unified Modeling Language (UML), you reduce ambiguity and can use checking tools. However, my experience is that formal notations get in the way of the creative design process. They constrain expressiveness and require everyone to understand them before they can participate in the design process.

4.3 System decomposition

The idea of abstraction is fundamental to all software design. Abstraction in software design means that you focus on the essential elements of a system or software component without concern for its details. At the architectural level, your concern should be on large-scale architectural components. Decomposition involves analyzing these large-scale components and representing them as a set of finer-grain components.

For example, Figure 4.6 is a diagram of the architecture of a product that I was involved with some years ago. This system was designed for use in libraries and gave users access to documents that were stored in a number of private databases, such as legal and patent databases. Payment was required for access to these documents. The system had to manage the rights to these documents and collect and account for access payments.

In this diagram, each layer in the system includes a number of logically related components. Informal layered models, like Figure 4.6, are widely used to show how a system is decomposed into components, with each component providing significant system functionality.

Web-based and mobile systems are event-based systems. An event in the user interface, such as a mouse click, triggers the actions to implement the user's choice. This means that the flow of control in a layered system is top-down. User events in the higher layers trigger actions in that layer that, in turn, trigger events in lower layers. By contrast, most information flows in the

Figure 4.6 An architectural model of a document retrieval system

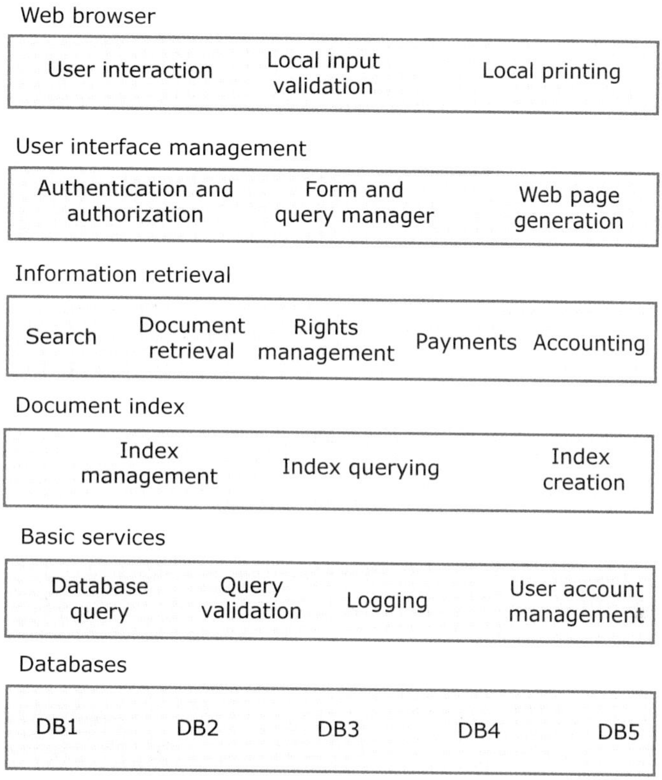

Web browser

User interaction	Local input validation	Local printing

User interface management

Authentication and authorization	Form and query manager	Web page generation

Information retrieval

Search	Document retrieval	Rights management	Payments	Accounting

Document index

Index management	Index querying	Index creation

Basic services

Database query	Query validation	Logging	User account management

Databases

DB1	DB2	DB3	DB4	DB5

system are bottom-up. Information is created at lower layers, is transformed in the intermediate layers, and is finally delivered to users at the top level.

There is often confusion about architectural terminology, words such as "service," "component," and "module." There are no standard, widely accepted definitions of these terms, but I try to use them consistently in this chapter and elsewhere in the book:

1. A *service* is a coherent unit of functionality. This may mean different things at different levels of the system. For example, a system may offer an email service and this email service may itself include services for creating, sending, reading, and storing email.

2. A *component* is a named software unit that offers one or more services to other software components or to the end-users of the software. When used by other components, these services are accessed through an API. Components may use several other components to implement their services.

Figure 4.7 Examples of component relationships

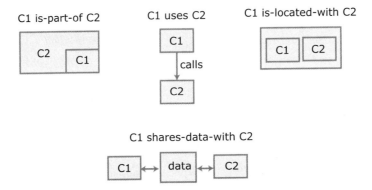

3. A *module* is a named set of components. The components in a module should have something in common. For example, they may provide a set of related services.

Complexity in a system architecture arises because of the number and the nature of the relationships among components in that system. I discuss this in more detail in Chapter 8. When you change a program, you have to understand these relationships to know how changes to one component affect other components. When decomposing a system into components, you should try to avoid introducing unnecessary complexity into the software.

Components have different types of relationships with other components (Figure 4.7). Because of these relationships, when you make a change to one component, you often need to make changes to several other components.

Figure 4.7 shows four types of component relationship:

1. *Part-of* One component is part of another component. For example, a function or method may be part of an object.

2. *Uses* One component uses the functionality provided by another component.

3. *Is-located-with* One component is defined in the same module or object as another component.

4. *Shares-data-with* A component shares data with another component.

As the number of components increases, the number of relationships tends to increase at a faster rate. This is the reason large systems are more complex than small systems. It is impossible to avoid complexity increasing with the

Figure 4.8 Architectural design guidelines

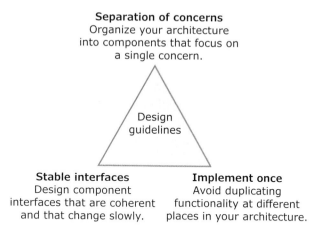

size of the software. However, you can control architectural complexity by doing two things:

1. *Localize relationships* If there are relationships between components A and B (say), they are easier to understand if A and B are defined in the same module. You should identify logical component groupings (such as the layers in a layered architecture) with relationships mostly within a component group.

2. *Reduce shared dependencies* Where components A and B depend on some other component or data, complexity increases because changes to the shared component mean you have to understand how these changes affect both A and B. It is always preferable to use local data wherever possible and to avoid sharing data if you can.

Three general design guidelines help to control complexity, as shown in Figure 4.8.

The *separation of concerns* guideline suggests that you should identify relevant architectural concerns in groupings of related functionality. Examples of architectural concerns are user interaction, authentication, system monitoring, and database management. Ideally, you should be able to identify the components or groupings of components in your architecture that are related to each concern. At a lower level, separation of concerns means that components should, ideally, do only one thing. I cover separation of concerns in more detail in Chapter 8.

The *implement once* guideline suggests that you should not duplicate functionality in your software architecture. This is important, as duplication can cause problems when changes are made. If you find that more than one architectural component needs or provides the same or a similar service, you should reorganize your architecture to avoid duplication.

You should never design and implement software where components know of and rely on the implementation of other components. Implementation dependencies mean that if a component is changed, then the components that rely on its implementation also have to be changed. Implementation details should be hidden behind a component interface (API).

The *stable interfaces* guideline is important so that components that use an interface do not have to be changed because the interface has changed.

Layered architectures, such as the document retrieval system architecture shown in Figure 4.6, are based on these general design guidelines:

1. Each layer is an area of concern and is considered separately from other layers. The top layer is concerned with user interaction, the next layer down with user interface management, the third layer with information retrieval, and so on.

2. Within each layer, the components are independent and do not overlap in functionality. The lower layers include components that provide general functionality, so there is no need to replicate this in the components in a higher level.

3. The architectural model is a high-level model that does not include implementation information. Ideally, components at level X (say) should only interact with the APIs of the components in level X-1; that is, interactions should be between layers and not across layers. In practice, however, this is often impossible without code duplication. The lower levels of the stack of layers provide basic services that may be required by components that are not in the immediate level above them. It makes no sense to add additional components in a higher layer if these are used only to access lower-level components.

Layered models are informal and are easy to draw and understand. They can be drawn on a whiteboard so that the whole team can see how the system is decomposed. In a layered model, components in lower layers should never depend on higher-level components. All dependencies should be on lower-level components. This means that if you change a component at level X in the stack, you should not have to make changes to components at lower levels in the stack. You only have to consider the effects of the change on components at higher levels.

Figure 4.9 Cross-cutting concerns

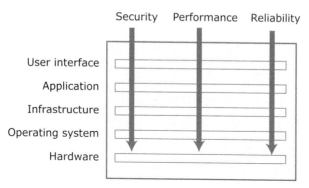

The layers in the architectural model are not components or modules but are simply logical groupings of components. They are relevant when you are designing the system, but you can't normally identify these layers in the system implementation.

The general idea of controlling complexity by localizing concerns within a single layer of an architecture is a compelling one. If you can do this, you don't have to change components in other layers when components in any one layer are modified. Unfortunately, there are two reasons why localizing concerns may not always be possible:

1. For practical reasons of usability and efficiency, it may be necessary to divide functionality so that it is implemented in different layers.

2. Some concerns are cross-cutting concerns and have to be considered at every layer in the stack.

You can see an example of the problem of practical separation of concerns in Figure 4.6. The top layer includes "Local input validation" and the fifth layer in the stack includes "Query validation." The "validation concern" is not implemented in a single lower-level server component because this is likely to generate too much network traffic.

If user data validation is a server rather than a browser operation, this requires a network transaction for every field in a form. Obviously, this slows the system down. Therefore, it makes sense to implement some local input checking, such as date checking, in the user's browser or mobile app. Some checking, however, may require knowledge of database structure or a user's permissions, and this can be carried out only when all of the form has been completed. As I explain in Chapter 7, the checking of security-critical fields should also be a server-side operation.

Cross-cutting concerns are systemic concerns; that is, they affect the whole system. In a layered architecture, cross-cutting concerns affect all layers in the system as well as the way in which people use the system. Figure 4.9 shows

Table 4.5 Security as a cross-cutting concern

Security architecture
Different technologies are used in different layers, such as an SQL database or a Firefox browser. Attackers can try to use vulnerabilities in these technologies to gain access. Consequently, you need protection from attacks at each layer as well as protection at lower layers in the system from successful attacks that have occurred at higher-level layers.
If there is only a single security component in a system, this represents a critical system vulnerability. If all security checking goes through that component and it stops working properly or is compromised in an attack, then you have no reliable security in your system. By distributing security across the layers, your system is more resilient to attacks and software failure (remember the *Rogue One* example earlier in the chapter).

three cross-cutting concerns—security, performance and reliability—that are important for software products.

Cross-cutting concerns are completely different from the functional concerns represented by layers in a software architecture. Every layer has to take them into account, and there are inevitably interactions between the layers because of these concerns. These cross-cutting concerns make it difficult to improve system security after it has been designed. Table 4.5 explains why security cannot be localized in a single component or layer.

Let's assume that you are a software architect and you want to organize your system into a series of layers to help control complexity. You are then faced with the general question "Where do I start?". Fortunately, many software products that are delivered over the web have a common layered structure that you can use as a starting point for your design. This common structure is shown in Figure 4.10. The functionality of the layers in this generic layered architecture is explained in Table 4.6.

For web-based applications, the layers shown in Figure 4.10 can be the starting point for your decomposition process. The first stage is to think about whether this five-layer model is the right one or whether you need more or fewer layers. Your aim should be for layers to be logically coherent, so that all components in a layer have something in common. This may mean that you need one or more additional layers for your application-specific functionality. Sometimes you may wish to have authentication in a separate layer, and sometimes it makes sense to integrate shared services with the database management layer.

Figure 4.10 A generic layered architecture for a web-based application

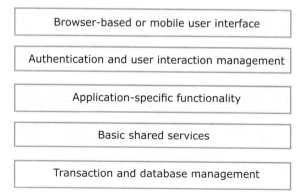

Once you have figured out how many layers to include in your system, you can start to populate these layers. In my experience, the best way to do this is to involve the whole team and try out various decompositions to help understand their advantages and disadvantages. This is a trial-and-error process; you stop when you have what seems to be a workable decomposition architecture.

Table 4.6 Layer functionality in a web-based application

Layer	Explanation
Browser-based or mobile user interface	A web browser system interface in which HTML forms are often used to collect user input. Javascript components for local actions, such as input validation, should also be included at this level. Alternatively, a mobile interface may be implemented as an app.
Authentication and UI management	A user interface management layer that may include components for user authentication and web page generation.
Application-specific functionality	An "application" layer that provides functionality of the application. Sometimes this may be expanded into more than one layer.
Basic shared services	A shared services layer that includes components that provide services used by the application layer components.
Database and transaction management	A database layer that provides services such as transaction management and recovery. If your application does not use a database, then this may not be required.

Table 4.7 iLearn architectural design principles

Principle	Explanation
Replaceability	It should be possible for users to replace applications in the system with alternatives and to add new applications. Consequently, the list of applications included should not be hard-wired into the system.
Extensibility	It should be possible for users or system administrators to create their own versions of the system, which may extend or limit the "standard" system.
Age-appropriate	Alternative user interfaces should be supported so that age-appropriate interfaces for students at different levels can be created.
Programmability	It should be easy for users to create their own applications by linking existing applications in the system.
Minimum work	Users who do not wish to change the system should not have to do extra work so that other users can make changes.

The discussion about system decomposition may be driven by fundamental principles that should apply to the design of your application system. These set out goals that you wish to achieve. You can then evaluate architectural design decisions against these goals. For example, Table 4.7 shows the principles that we thought were most important when designing the iLearn system architecture.

Our goal in designing the iLearn system was to create an adaptable, universal system that could be updated easily as new learning tools became available. This means it must be possible to change and replace components and services in the system (principles 1 and 2). Because the potential system users ranged in age from 3 to 18, we needed to provide age-appropriate user interfaces and make it easy to choose an interface (principle 3). Principle 4 also contributes to system adaptability, and principle 5 was included to ensure that this adaptability did not adversely affect users who did not require it.

Unfortunately, principle 1 may sometimes conflict with principle 4. If you allow users to create new functionality by combining applications, then these combined applications may not work if one or more of the constituent applications are replaced. You often have to address this kind of conflict in architectural design.

These principles led us to an architectural design decision that the iLearn system should be service-oriented. Every component in the system is a service. Any service is potentially replaceable, and new services can be created by combining existing services. Different services that deliver comparable functionality can be provided for students of different ages.

Using services means that the potential conflict I identified above is mostly avoidable. If a new service is created by using an existing service and, subsequently, other users want to introduce an alternative, they may do so. The older service can be retained in the system, so that users of that service don't have to do more work because a newer service has been introduced.

We assumed that only a minority of users would be interested in programming their own system versions. Therefore, we decided to provide a standard set of application services that had some degree of integration with other services. We anticipated that most users would rely on these and would not wish to replace them. Integrated application services, such as blogging and wiki services, could be designed to share information and make use of common shared services. Some users may wish to introduce other services into their environment, so we also allowed for services that were not tightly integrated with other system services.

We decided to support three types of application service integration:

1. *Full integration* Services are aware of and can communicate with other services through their APIs. Services may share system services and one or more databases. An example of a fully integrated service is a specially written authentication service that checks the credentials of system users.

2. *Partial integration* Services may share service components and databases, but they are not aware of and cannot communicate directly with other application services. An example of a partially integrated service is a Wordpress service in which the Wordpress system was changed to use the standard authentication and storage services in the system. Office 365, which can be integrated with local authentication systems, is another example of a partially integrated service that we included in the iLearn system.

3. *Independent* These services do not use any shared system services or databases, and they are unaware of any other services in the system. They can be replaced by any other comparable service. An example of an independent service is a photo management system that maintains its own data.

The layered model for the iLearn system that we designed is shown in Figure 4.11. To support application "replaceability", we did not base the system around a shared database. However, we assumed that fully-integrated applications would use shared services such as storage and authentication.

Figure 4.11 A layered architectural model of the iLearn system

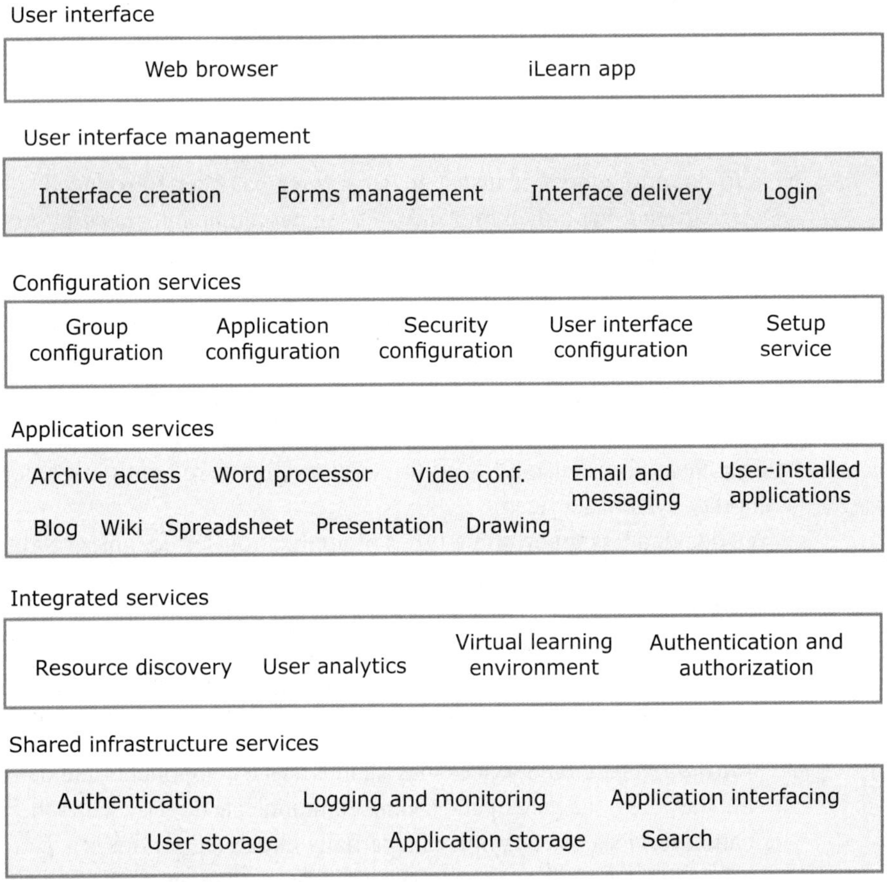

User interface

Web browser	iLearn app

User interface management

Interface creation	Forms management	Interface delivery	Login

Configuration services

Group configuration	Application configuration	Security configuration	User interface configuration	Setup service

Application services

Archive access	Word processor	Video conf.	Email and messaging	User-installed applications
Blog Wiki Spreadsheet Presentation Drawing				

Integrated services

Resource discovery	User analytics	Virtual learning environment	Authentication and authorization

Shared infrastructure services

Authentication	Logging and monitoring	Application interfacing
User storage	Application storage	Search

To support the requirement that users should be able to configure their own version of an iLearn system, we introduced an additional layer into the system, above the application layer. This layer includes several components that incorporate knowledge of the installed applications and provide configuration functionality to end-users.

The system has a set of pre-installed application services. Additional application services can be added or existing services replaced by using the application configuration facilities. Most of these application services are independent and manage their own data. Some services are partially integrated, however, which simplifies information sharing and allows more detailed user information to be collected.

The fully integrated services have to be specially written or adapted from open-source software. They require knowledge of how the system is used and access to user data in the storage system. They may make use of other services at the same level. For example, the user analytics service provides information about how individual students use the system and can highlight problems to teachers. It needs to be able to access both log information and student records from the virtual learning environment.

System decomposition has to be done in conjunction with choosing technologies for your system (see Section 4.5). The reason for this is that the choice of technology used in a particular layer affects the components in the layers above. For example, you may decide to use a relational database technology as the lowest layer in your system. This makes sense if you are dealing with well-structured data. However, your decision affects the components to be included in the services layer because you need to be able to communicate with the database. You may have to include components to adapt the data passed to and from the database.

Another important technology-related decision is the interface technologies that you will use. This choice depends on whether you will be supporting browser interfaces only (often the case with business systems) or you also want to provide interfaces on mobile devices. If you are supporting mobile devices, you need to include components to interface with the relevant iOS and Android UI development toolkits.

4.4 Distribution architecture

The majority of software products are now web-based products, so they have a client–server architecture. In this architecture, the user interface is implemented on the user's own computer or mobile device. Functionality is distributed between the client and one or more server computers. During the architectural design process, you have to decide on the "distribution architecture" of the system. This defines the servers in the system and the allocation of components to these servers.

Client–server architectures are a type of distribution architecture that is suited to applications in which clients access a shared database and business logic operations on those data. Figure 4.12 shows a logical view of a client–server architecture that is widely used in web-based and mobile software products. These applications include several servers, such as web servers and database servers. Access to the server set is usually mediated by a load balancer, which distributes requests to servers. It is designed to ensure that the computing load is evenly shared by the set of servers.

Figure 4.12 Client–server architecture

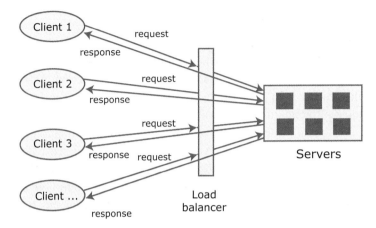

The client is responsible for user interaction, based on data passed to and from the server. When this architecture was originally devised, clients were character terminals with hardly any local processing capability. The server was a mainframe computer. All processing was carried out on the server, with the client handling only user interaction. Now clients are computers or mobile devices with lots of processing power, so most applications are designed to include significant client-side processing.

Client–server interaction is usually organized using what is called the Model-View-Controller (MVC) pattern. This architectural pattern is used so that client interfaces can be updated when data on the server change (Figure 4.13).

The term "model" is used to mean the system data and the associated business logic. The model is always shared and maintained on the server. Each client has its own view of the data, with views responsible for HTML page generation and forms management. There may be several views on each client in which the data are presented in different ways. Each view registers with the model so that when the model changes, all views are updated. Changing the information in one view leads to all other views of the same information being updated.

User inputs that change the model are handled by the controller. The controller sends update requests to the model on the server. It may also be responsible for local input processing, such as data validation.

The MVC pattern has many variants. In some, all communication between the view and the model goes through the controller. In others, views can also handle user inputs. However, the essence of all of these variants is that the model is decoupled from its presentation. It can, therefore, be presented in different ways and each presentation can be independently updated when changes to the data are made.

Figure 4.13 The Model-View-Controller pattern

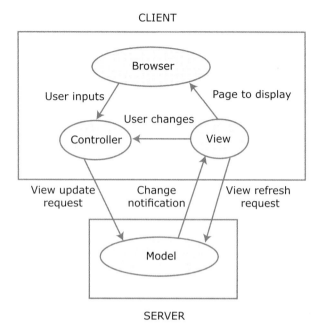

For web-based products, Javascript is mostly used for client-side programming. Mobile apps are mostly developed in Java (Android) and Swift (iOS). I don't have experience in mobile app development, so I focus here on web-based products. However, the underlying principles of interaction are the same.

Client–server communication normally uses the HTTP protocol, which is a text-based request/response protocol. The client sends a message to the server that includes an instruction such as GET or POST along with the identifier of a resource (usually a URL) on which that instruction should operate. The message may also include additional information, such as information collected from a form. So, a database update may be encoded as a POST instruction, an identifier for the information to be updated plus the changed information input by the user. Servers do not send requests to clients, and clients always wait for a response from the server.[2]

HTTP is a text-only protocol, so structured data must be represented as text. Two ways of representing these data are widely used—namely, XML and JSON. XML is a markup language with tags used to identify each data item. JSON is

---

[2]This is not strictly true if a technology such as Node.js is used to build server-side applications. This allows both clients and servers to generate requests and responses. However, the general client–server model still applies.

Program 4.1 An example of JSON information representation

```
{
"book": [
{
"title":    "Software Engineering",
"author": "Ian Sommerville",
"publisher": "Pearson Higher Education",
"place": "Hoboken, NJ",
 "year": "2015",
"edition": "10th",
 "ISBN": "978-0-13-394303-0"
},
 ]
}
```

a simpler representation based on the representation of objects in the Javascript language. Usually JSON representations are more compact and faster to parse than XML text. I recommend that you use JSON for data representation.

As well as being faster to process than XML, JSON is easier for people to read. Program 4.1 shows the JSON representation of cataloging information about a software engineering textbook.

There are good JSON tutorials available on the web, so I don't go into more detail about this notation.

Many web-based applications use a multi-tier architecture with several communicating servers, each with its own responsibilities. Figure 4.14 illustrates the distributed components in a multi-tier web-based system architecture. For simplicity, I assume there is only a single instance of each of these servers and so a load balancer is not required. Web-based applications usually include three types of server:

1. A web server that communicates with clients using the HTTP protocol. It delivers web pages to the browser for rendering and processes HTTP requests from the client.

2. An application server that is responsible for application-specific operations. For example, in a booking system for a theater, the application server provides information about the shows as well as basic functionality that allows a theatergoer to book seats for shows.

3. A database server that manages the system data and transfers these data to and from the system database.

Figure 4.14 Multi-tier client–server architecture

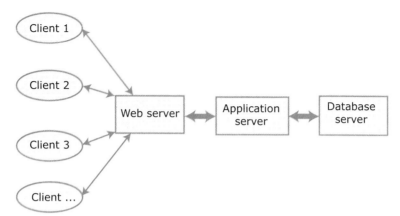

Sometimes a multi-tier architecture may use additional specialized servers. For example, in a theater booking system, the user's payments may be handled by a credit card payment server provided by a company that specializes in credit card payments. This makes sense for most e-commerce applications, as a high cost is involved in developing a trusted payment system. Another type of specialized server that is commonly used is an authentication server. This checks users' credentials when they log in to the system.

An alternative to a multi-tier client–server architecture is a service-oriented architecture (Figure 4.15) where many servers may be involved in providing services. Services in a service-oriented architecture are stateless components, which means that they can be replicated and can migrate from one computer to another. A service-oriented architecture is usually easier to scale as demand increases and is resilient to failure.

The services shown in Figure 4.15 are services that support features in the system. These are the services provided by the application layer and layers above this in the decomposition stack. To keep the diagram simple, I do not show interactions between services or infrastructure services that provide functionality from lower levels in the decomposition. Service-oriented architectures are increasingly used, and I discuss them in more detail in Chapter 6.

We chose a service-oriented distribution architecture for the iLearn system, with each of the components shown in Figure 4.11 implemented as a separate service. We chose this architecture because we wanted to make it easy to update the system with new functionality. It also simplified the problem of adding new, unforeseen services to the system.

Figure 4.15 Service-oriented architecture

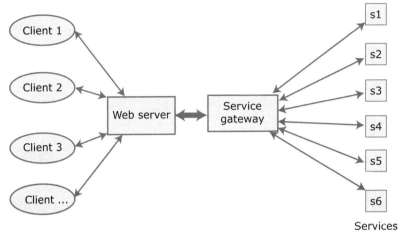

Multi-tier and service-oriented architectures are the main types of distribution architecture for web-based and mobile systems. You have to decide which of these to choose for your software product. The issues that you must consider are:

1. *Data type and data updates* If you are mostly using structured data that may be updated by different system features, it is usually best to have a single shared database that provides locking and transaction management. If data are distributed across services, you need a way to keep them consistent, and this adds overhead to your system.

2. *Frequency of change* If you anticipate that system components will regularly be changed or replaced, then isolating these components as separate services simplifies those changes.

3. *The system execution platform* If you plan to run your system on the cloud with users accessing it over the Internet, it is usually best to implement it as a service-oriented architecture because scaling the system is simpler. However, if your product is a business system that runs on local servers, a multi-tier architecture may be more appropriate.

When I wrote this book in 2018, the distribution architecture of most business software products was a multi-tier client–server architecture with user interaction implemented using the MVC pattern. However, these products are increasingly being updated to use service-oriented architectures, running on public cloud platforms. I think that, over time, this type of architecture will become the norm for web-based software products.

Table 4.8 Technology choices

Technology	Design decision
Database	Should you use a relational SQL database or an unstructured NoSQL database?
Platform	Should you deliver your product on a mobile app and/or a web platform?
Server	Should you use dedicated in-house servers or design your system to run on a public cloud? If a public cloud, should you use Amazon, Google, Microsoft, or some other option?
Open source	Are there suitable open-source components that you could incorporate into your products?
Development tools	Do your development tools embed architectural assumptions about the software being developed that limit your architectural choices?

4.5 Technology issues

An important part of the process of designing software architecture is to make decisions about the technologies you will use in your product. The technologies that you choose affect and constrain the overall architecture of your system. It is difficult and expensive to change these during development, so it is important that you carefully consider your technology choices.

An advantage of product development compared to enterprise system development is that you are less likely to be affected by legacy technology issues. Legacy technologies are technologies that have been used in old systems and are still operational. For example, some old enterprise systems still rely on 1970s database technology. Modern systems may have to interact with these and this limits their design.

Unless you have to interoperate with other software products sold by your company, your choice of technology for product development is fairly flexible. Table 4.8 shows some of the important technology choices you may have to make at an early stage of product development.

4.5.1 Database

Most software products rely on a database system of some kind. Two kinds of database are now commonly used: relational databases, in which the data are organized into structured tables, and NoSQL databases, in which the data have a more flexible, user-defined organization. The database has a huge influence on how your system is implemented, so which type of database to use is an important technology choice.

Relational databases, such as MySQL, are particularly suitable for situations where you need transaction management and the data structures are predictable and fairly simple. Relational databases support ACID transactions. Transactions guarantee that the database will always remain consistent even if a transaction fails, that updates will be serialized, and that recovery to a consistent state is always possible. This is really important for financial information where inconsistencies are unacceptable. So, if your product deals with financial information, or any information where consistency is critical, you should choose a relational database.

However, there are lots of situations where data are not well structured and where most database operations are concerned with reading and analyzing data rather than writing to the database. NoSQL databases, such as MongoDB, are more flexible and potentially more efficient than relational databases for this type of application. NoSQL databases allow data to be organized hierarchically rather than as flat tables, and this allows for more efficient concurrent processing of "big data."

Some applications need a mixture of both transactions and big data processing, and more of this kind of application will likely be developed in the future. Database vendors are now starting to integrate these approaches. It is likely that, during the lifetime of this book, efficient integrated database systems will become available.

4.5.2 Delivery platform

Globally, more people access the web using smartphones and tablets rather than browsers on a laptop or desktop. Most business systems are still browser-based, but as the workforce becomes more mobile, there is increasing demand for mobile access to business systems.

In addition to the obvious difference in screen size and keyboard availability, there are other important differences between developing software for a mobile device and developing software that runs on a client computer. On a phone or tablet, several factors have to be considered:

1. *Intermittent connectivity* You must be able to provide a limited service without network connectivity.

2. *Processor power* Mobile devices have less powerful processors, so you need to minimize computationally intensive operations.

3. *Power management* Mobile battery life is limited, so you should try to minimize the power used by your application.

4. *On-screen keyboard* On-screen keyboards are slow and error prone. You should minimize input using the screen keyboard to reduce user frustration.

To deal with these differences, you usually need separate browser-based and mobile versions of your product front-end. You may need a completely different decomposition architecture in these different versions to ensure that performance and other characteristics are maintained.

As a product developer, you have to decide early in the process whether you will focus on a mobile or a desktop version of your software. For consumer products, you may decide to focus on mobile delivery, but for business systems, you have to make a choice about which should be your priority. Trying to develop mobile and browser-based versions of a product at the same time is an expensive process.

4.5.3 Server

Cloud computing is now ubiquitous so a key decision you have to make is whether to design your system to run on individual servers or on the cloud. Of course, it is possible to rent a server from Amazon or some other provider, but this does not really take full advantage of the cloud. To develop for the cloud, you need to design your architecture as a service-oriented system and use the platform APIs provided by the cloud vendor to implement your software. These allow for automatic scalability and system resilience.

For consumer products that are not simply mobile apps, I think it almost always makes sense to develop for the cloud. The decision is more difficult for business products. Some businesses are concerned about cloud security and prefer to run their systems on in-house servers. They may have a predictable pattern of system usage, so there is less need to design the software to cope with large changes in demand.

If you decide to develop for the cloud, the next decision is to choose a cloud provider. The major providers are Amazon, Google, and Microsoft, but unfortunately their APIs are not compatible. This means you can't easily move a product from one to the other. The majority of consumer products probably run on Amazon's or Google's cloud, but businesses often prefer Microsoft's Azure system because of its compatibility with their existing .NET software. Alternatively, there are other cloud providers, such as IBM, that specialize in business services.

4.5.4 Open source

Open-source software is software that is freely available and you can change and modify it as you wish. The obvious advantage is that you can reuse rather than implement new software, thereby reducing development costs and time to market. The disadvantages of open-source software are that you are constrained by that software and have no control over its evolution. It may be impossible to change that software to give your product a "competitive edge" over competitors that use the same software. There are also license issues that must be considered. They may limit your freedom to incorporate the open-source software into your product.

The decision about open-source software also depends on the availability, maturity, and continuing support of open-source components. Using an open-source database system such as MySQL or MongoDB is cheaper than using a proprietary database such as Oracle's database system. These are mature systems with a large number of contributing developers. You would normally only choose a proprietary database if your product is aimed at businesses that already use that kind of database. At higher levels in the architecture, depending on the type of product you are developing, fewer open-source components may be available, they may be buggy, and their continuing development may depend on a relatively small support community.

Your choice of open-source software should depend on the type of product you are developing, your target market, and the expertise of your development team. There's often a mismatch between the "ideal" open-source software and the expertise that you have available. The ideal software may be better in the long term but could delay your product launch as your team becomes familiar with it. You have to decide whether the long-term benefits justify that delay. There is no point in building a better system if your company runs out of money before that system is delivered.

4.5.5 Development technology

Development technologies, such as a mobile development toolkit or a web application framework, influence the architecture of your software. These technologies have built-in assumptions about system architectures, and you have to conform to these assumptions to use the development system. For example, many web development frameworks are designed to create applications that use the model-view-controller architectural pattern.

The development technology that you use may also have an indirect influence on the system architecture. Developers usually favor architectural choices that use familiar technologies that they understand. For example, if your team has a lot of experience with relational databases, they may argue for this instead of a NoSQL database. This can make sense, as it means the team does not have to spend time learning about a new system. It can have long-term negative consequences, however, if the familiar technology is not the right one for your software.

KEY POINTS

- Software architecture is the fundamental organization of a system embodied in its components, their relationships to each other and to the environment, and the principles guiding its design and evolution.

- The architecture of a software system has a significant influence on non-functional system properties, such as reliability, efficiency, and security.

- Architectural design involves understanding the issues that are critical for your product and creating system descriptions that show components and their relationships.

- The principal role of architectural descriptions is to provide a basis for the development team to discuss the system organization. Informal architectural diagrams are effective in architectural description because they are fast and easy to draw and share.

- System decomposition involves analyzing architectural components and representing them as a set of finer-grain components.

- To minimize complexity, you should separate concerns, avoid functional duplication, and focus on component interfaces.

- Web-based systems often have a common layered structure, including user interface layers, application-specific layers, and a database layer.

- The distribution architecture in a system defines the organization of the servers in that system and the allocation of components to these servers.

- Multi-tier client–server and service-oriented architectures are the most commonly used architectures for web-based systems.

- Making decisions about technologies such as database and cloud technologies is an important part of the architectural design process.

RECOMMENDED READING

"Software Architecture and Design" This excellent series of articles provides sound, practical advice on general principles of software architecture and design. It includes a discussion of layered architectures in Chapter 3, under architectural patterns and styles. (Microsoft, 2010)

https://docs.microsoft.com/en-us/previous-versions/msp-n-p/ee658093(v%3dpandp.10)

"Five Things Every Developer Should Know about Software Architecture" This is a good explanation of why designing a software architecture is consistent with agile software development. (S. Brown, 2018)

https://www.infoq.com/articles/architecture-five-things

"Software Architecture Patterns" This is a good general introduction to layered architectures, although I don't agree that layered architectures are as difficult to change as the author suggests. (M. Richards, 2015, login required)

https://www.oreilly.com/ideas/software-architecture-patterns/page/2/layered-architecture

"What is the 3-Tier Architecture?" This is a very comprehensive discussion of the benefits of using a three-tier architecture. The author argues that is isn't necessary to use more than three tiers in any system. (T. Marston, 2012)

http://www.tonymarston.net/php-mysql/3-tier-architecture.html

"Five Reasons Developers Don't Use UML and Six Reasons to Use It" This article sets out arguments for using the UML when designing software architectures. (B. Pollack, 2010)

https://saturnnetwork.wordpress.com/2010/10/22/
five-reasons-developers-dont-use-uml-and-six-reasons-to-use-it/

"Mobile vs. Desktop: 10 key differences" This blog post summarizes the issues to be considered when designing mobile and desktop products. (S. Hart, 2014)

https://www.paradoxlabs.com/blog/mobile-vs-desktop-10-key-differences/

"To SQL or NoSQL? That's the Database Question" This is a good, short introduction to the pros and cons of relational and NoSQL databases. (L. Vaas, 2016)

https://arstechnica.com/information-technology/2016/03/
to-sql-or-nosql-thats-the-database-question/

I recommend articles on cloud-computing and service-oriented architecture in Chapters 5 and 6.

PRESENTATIONS, VIDEOS, AND LINKS

https://iansommerville.com/engineering-software-products/software-architecture

EXERCISES

4.1 Extend the IEEE definition of software architecture to include a definition of the activities involved in architectural design.

4.2 An architecture designed to support security may be based on either a centralized model, where all sensitive information is stored in one secure place, or a distributed model, where information is spread around and stored in many different places. Suggest one advantage and one disadvantage of each approach.

4.3 Why is it important to try to minimize complexity in a software system?

4.4 You are developing a product to sell to finance companies. Giving reasons for your answer, consider the issues that affect architectural decision making (Figure 4.4) and suggest which two factors are likely to be most important.

4.5 Briefly explain how structuring a software architecture as a stack of functional layers helps to minimize the overall complexity in a software product.

4.6 Imagine your manager has asked you whether or not your company should move away from informal architectural descriptions to more formal descriptions based on the UML. Write a short report giving advice to your manager. If you don't know what the UML is, then you should do a bit of reading to understand it. The article by Pollack in Recommended Reading can be a starting point for you.

4.7 Using a diagram, show how the generic architecture for a web-based application can be implemented using a multi-tier client–server architecture.

4.8 Under what circumstances would you push as much local processing as possible onto the client in a client–server architecture?

4.9 Explain why it would not be appropriate to use a multi-tier client–server architecture for the iLearn system.

4.10 Do some background reading and describe three fundamental differences between relational and NoSQL databases. Suggest three types of software product that might benefit from using NoSQL databases, explaining why the NoSQL approach is appropriate.

5
Cloud-Based Software

The convergence of powerful, multicore computer hardware and high-speed networking has led to the development of "the cloud." Put simply, the cloud is a very large number of remote servers that are offered for rent by companies that own these servers. You can rent as many servers as you need, run your software on these servers, and make them available to your customers. Your customers can access these servers from their own computers or other networked devices such as a tablet or a TV. You may rent a server and install your own software, or you may pay for access to software products that are available on the cloud.

The remote servers are "virtual servers," which means they are implemented in software rather than hardware. Many virtual servers can run simultaneously on each cloud hardware node, using virtualization support that is built in to the hardware. Running multiple servers has very little effect on server performance. The hardware is so powerful that it can easily run several virtual servers at the same time.

Cloud companies such as Amazon and Google provide cloud management software that makes it easy to acquire and release servers on demand. You can automatically upgrade the servers that you are running, and the cloud management software provides resilience in the event of a server failure. You can rent a server for a contracted amount of time or rent and pay for servers on demand. Therefore, if you need resources for only a short time, you simply pay for the time that you need.

The cloud servers that you rent can be started up and shut down as demand changes. This means that software that runs on the cloud can be scalable, elastic, and resilient (Figure 5.1). I think that scalability, elasticity, and resilience are the fundamental differences between cloud-based systems and those hosted on dedicated servers.

Figure 5.1 Scalability, elasticity, and resilience

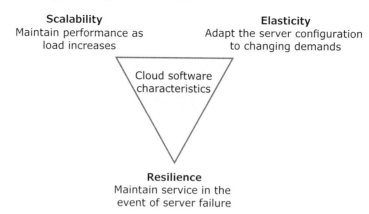

Scalability reflects the ability of your software to cope with increasing numbers of users. As the load on your software increases, the software automatically adapts to maintain the system performance and response time. Systems can be scaled by adding new servers or by migrating to a more powerful server. If a more powerful server is used, this is called scaling up. If new servers of the same type are added, this is called scaling out. If your software is scaled out, copies of your software are created and executed on the additional servers.

Elasticity is related to scalability but allows for scaling down as well as scaling up. That is, you can monitor the demand on your application and add or remove servers dynamically as the number of users changes. This means that you pay for only the servers you need, when you need them.

Resilience means that you can design your software architecture to tolerate server failures. You can make several copies of your software available concurrently. If one of these fails, the others continue to provide a service. You can cope with the failure of a cloud data center by locating redundant servers in different places.

If you are setting up a new software product company or development project, it isn't cost effective to buy server hardware to support software development. Rather, you should use cloud-based servers that are accessed from your development machines. The benefits of adopting this approach rather than buying your own servers are shown in Table 5.1.

I recommend that using the cloud for both development and product delivery, as a cloud service, should be the default choice for new software product development. The only exceptions might be if you are delivering products for a specialized hardware platform, or your customers have security requirements that forbid the use of external systems.

Table 5.1 Benefits of using the cloud for software development

Factor	Benefit
Cost	You avoid the initial capital costs of hardware procurement.
Startup time	You don't have to wait for hardware to be delivered before you can start work. Using the cloud, you can have servers up and running in a few minutes.
Server choice	If you find that the servers you are renting are not powerful enough, you can upgrade to more powerful systems. You can add servers for short-term requirements, such as load testing.
Distributed development	If you have a distributed development team, working from different locations, all team members have the same development environment and can seamlessly share all information.

All major software vendors now offer their software as cloud services. Customers access the remote service through a browser or mobile app rather than installing it on their own computers. Well-known examples of software delivered as a service include mail systems such as Gmail and productivity products such as Office 365.

This chapter introduces some fundamental ideas about cloud-based software that you have to consider when making architectural decisions. I explain the idea of containers as a lightweight mechanism to deploy software. I explain how software can be delivered as a service, and I introduce general issues in cloud-based software architecture design. Chapter 6 focuses on a service-oriented architectural pattern that is particularly relevant to cloud-based systems—namely, microservices architecture.

5.1 Virtualization and containers

All cloud servers are virtual servers. A virtual server runs on an underlying physical computer and is made up of an operating system plus a set of software packages that provide the server functionality required. The general idea is that a virtual server is a stand-alone system that can run on any hardware in the cloud.

This "run anywhere" characteristic is possible because the virtual server has no external dependencies. An external dependency means you need some

Figure 5.2 Implementing a virtual server as a virtual machine

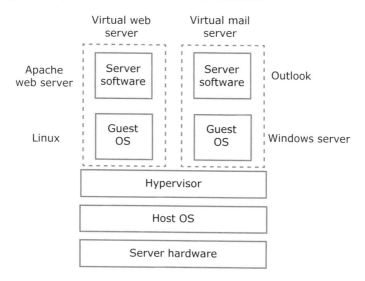

software, such as a database management system, that you are not developing yourself. For example, if you are developing in Python, you need a Python compiler, a Python interpreter, various Python libraries, and so on.

When you run software on different computers, you often encounter problems because some of the external software that you rely on is unavailable or is different in some way from the version that you're using. If you use a virtual server, you avoid these problems. You load all of the software that you need, so you are not relying on software being made available by someone else.

Virtual machines (VMs), running on physical server hardware, can be used to implement virtual servers (Figure 5.2). The details are complex, but you can think of the hypervisor as providing a hardware emulation that simulates the operation of the underlying hardware. Several of these hardware emulators share the physical hardware and run in parallel. You can run an operating system and then install server software on each hardware emulator.

The advantage of using a virtual machine to implement virtual servers is that you have exactly the same hardware platform as a physical server. You can therefore run different operating systems on virtual machines that are hosted on the same computer. For example, Figure 5.2 shows that Linux and Windows can run concurrently on separate VMs. You may want to do this so that you can run software that is available for only one particular operating system.

Figure 5.3 Using containers to provide isolated services

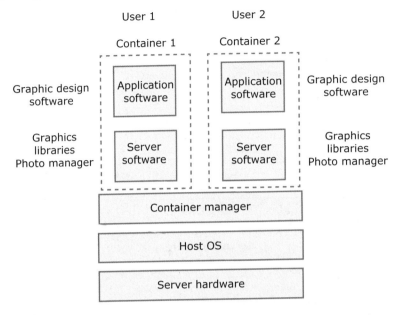

The problem with implementing virtual servers on top of VMs is that creating a VM involves loading and starting up a large and complex operating system (OS). The time needed to install the OS and set up the other software on the VM is typically between 2 and 5 minutes on public cloud providers such as AWS. This means that you cannot instantly react to changing demands by starting up and shutting down VMs.

In many cases, you don't really need the generality of a virtual machine. If you are running a cloud-based system with many instances of applications or services, these all use the same operating system. To cater to this situation, a simpler, lightweight, virtualization technology called "containers" may be used.

Using containers dramatically speeds up the process of deploying virtual servers on the cloud. Containers are usually megabytes in size, whereas VMs are gigabytes. Containers can be started up and shut down in a few seconds rather than the few minutes required for a VM. Many companies that provide cloud-based software have now switched from VMs to containers because containers are faster to load and less demanding of machine resources.

Containers are an operating system virtualization technology that allows independent servers to share a single operating system. They are particularly useful for providing isolated application services where each user sees their own version of an application. I show this in Figure 5.3, where a graphics design system product uses basic graphics libraries and a photo management system. A container with the graphics support software and the application is created for each user of the software.

To create and use a container, you use client software to create the container and to load software into that container. You then deploy the container that you have created onto a Linux server. Using fundamental OS features, the container management system ensures that the process executing in the container is completely isolated from all other processes.

Containers are a lightweight mechanism for running applications in the cloud and are particularly effective for running small applications such as stand-alone services. At the time of writing this book in 2018, containers are not the best mechanism for running large, shared databases. If your application depends on a large, shared database that provides continuous service, running this database on a VM is still the best option. VMs and containers can coexist on the same physical system, so applications running in containers can access the database efficiently.

Containers were first introduced in the mid-2000s with developments in the Linux operating system. Several companies, such as Google and Amazon, developed and used their own version of containers to manage large server clusters. However, containers really became a mainstream technology around 2015. An open-source project called Docker provided a standard means of container management that is fast and easy to use. Docker is now the most widely used container technology, so I discuss the Docker model of containers here.

Docker is a container management system that allows users to define the software to be included in a container as a Docker image. It also includes a run-time system that can create and manage containers using these Docker images. Figure 5.4 shows the different elements of the Docker container system and their interactions. I explain the function of each of the elements in the Docker container system in Table 5.2.

Docker images are directories that can be archived, shared, and run on different Docker hosts. Everything that's needed to run a software system—binaries, libraries, system tools, and so on—is included in the directory. Therefore, the image can act as a stand-alone filesystem for the virtual server. Because of the way Docker has implemented its filesystem, the image includes only the files that are different from standard operating system files. It does not include all the other operating system files that are unchanged. Consequently, images are usually compact and therefore fast to load.

Figure 5.4 The Docker container system

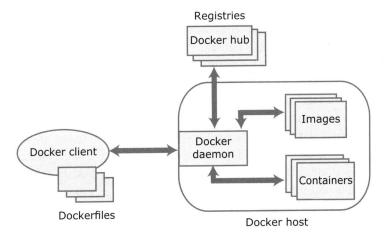

Table 5.2 The elements of the Docker container system

Element	Function
Docker daemon	This is a process that runs on a host server and is used to set up, start, stop, and monitor containers, as well as building and managing local images.
Docker client	This software is used by developers and system managers to define and control containers.
Dockerfiles	Dockerfiles define runnable applications (images) as a series of setup commands that specify the software to be included in a container. Each container must be defined by an associated Dockerfile.
Image	A Dockerfile is interpreted to create a Docker image, which is a set of directories with the specified software and data installed in the right places. Images are set up to be runnable Docker applications.
Docker hub	This is a registry of images that has been created. These may be reused to set up containers or as a starting point for defining new images.
Containers	Containers are executing images. An image is loaded into a container and the application defined by the image starts execution. Containers may be moved from server to server without modification and replicated across many servers. You can make changes to a Docker container (e.g., by modifying files) but you then must commit these changes to create a new image and restart the container.

The filesystem used in Docker images is called a union filesystem. I don't go into details of this here, but it is a bit like an incremental backup, where you simply add the changed files to your backup. Backup software allows you to merge them with previous backups to restore your whole filesystem. In a union filesystem, you start with a base filesystem with updates that are specific to an image layered on top of this base. Each update is added as a new layer. The file system software integrates the layers so that you have a complete, isolated filesystem.

A Docker image is a base layer, usually taken from the Docker registry, with your own software and data added as a layer on top. This layered model means that updating Docker applications is fast and efficient. Each update to the filesystem is a layer on top of the existing system. To change an application, all you have to do is ship the changes that you have made to its image, often just a small number of files. You don't have to include any files that are unchanged.

When a container is created, the image is loaded and the files in that image are set as read-only. A read-write layer is added by the Docker daemon to manage local container information, and various initialization parameters are set up by the container management system. A process is then initialized to run the software defined in the image.

Docker includes a mechanism, called a bridge network, that enables containers to communicate with each other. This means you can create systems made up of communicating components, each of which runs in its own container. Consequently, you can quickly deploy a large number of communicating containers to implement a complex distributed system. You use a management system such as Kubernates to manage the set of deployed containers.

You don't need to understand the Docker communication mechanisms to understand the principles of containers, so I don't say any more about this. I include links to information on container communications in the Recommended Reading section.

From a cloud software engineering perspective, containers offer four important benefits:

1. They solve the problem of software dependencies. You don't have to worry about the libraries and other software on the application server being different from those on your development server. Instead of shipping your product as stand-alone software, you can ship a container that includes all of the support software that your product needs.

2. They provide a mechanism for software portability across different clouds. Docker containers can run on any system or cloud provider where the Docker daemon is available.

Figure 5.5 Everything as a service

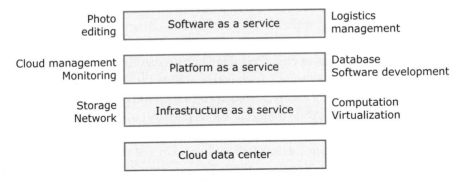

3. They provide an efficient mechanism for implementing software services and so support the development of service-oriented architectures, which I cover in Chapter 6.

4. They simplify the adoption of DevOps. This is an approach to software support where the same team is responsible for both developing and supporting operational software. I cover DevOps in Chapter 10.

5.2 Everything as a service

Very few of us employ a personal, full-time hairdresser. Instead, when we need a haircut, we "rent" a hairdresser for a while and pay that person to cut our hair. The hairdresser is providing a hairdressing service, and we pay for the time we are using that service. The same approach can be applied to software products. Rather than buy a software product, we can rent it when we need it.

This idea of a service that is rented rather than owned is fundamental to cloud computing. Instead of owning hardware, you can rent the hardware that you need from a cloud provider. If you have a software product, you can use that rented hardware to deliver the product to your customers. In cloud computing, this has been developed into the idea of "everything as a service."

For software product developers, there are currently three levels where everything as a service is most relevant. I show these levels in Figure 5.5, which also includes some examples of possible services at each level.

1. *Infrastructure as a service (IaaS)* This is a basic service level that all major cloud providers offer. They provide different kinds of infrastructure service, such as a compute service, a network service, and a storage service. These infrastructure services may be used to implement virtual cloud-based servers. The key benefits of using IaaS are that you don't incur the capital costs of buying hardware and you can easily migrate your software from one server to a more powerful server. You are responsible for installing the software on the server, although many preconfigured packages are available to help with this. Using the cloud provider's control panel, you can easily add more servers if you need to as the load on your system increases.

2. *Platform as a service (PaaS)* This is an intermediate level where you use libraries and frameworks provided by the cloud provider to implement your software. These provide access to a range of functions, including SQL and NoSQL databases. Using PaaS makes it easy to develop auto-scaling software. You can implement your product so that as the load increases, additional compute and storage resources are added automatically.

3. *Software as a service (SaaS)* Your software product runs on the cloud and is accessed by users through a web browser or mobile app. We all know and use this type of cloud service—mail services such as Gmail, storage services such as Dropbox, social media services such as Twitter, and so on. I discuss SaaS in more detail later in this chapter.

If you are running a small or medium-sized product development company, it is not cost effective to buy server hardware. If you need development and testing servers, you can implement these using infrastructure services. You can set up a cloud account with a credit card and be up and running within a few minutes. You don't have to raise capital to buy hardware, and it is easy to respond to changing demand by upscaling and downscaling your system on the cloud. You can implement your product on the cloud using PaaS and deliver your product as a software service.

There are now many companies offering public cloud services to businesses including large, well-known providers such as Amazon, Google, and Microsoft. They all use different interfaces and control panels, so I do not explain the details of acquiring and setting up servers on the cloud. All cloud providers have introductory tutorials that explain how to do this. I include links to these tutorials in the Recommended Reading section.

Figure 5.6 Management responsibilities for SaaS, IaaS, and PaaS

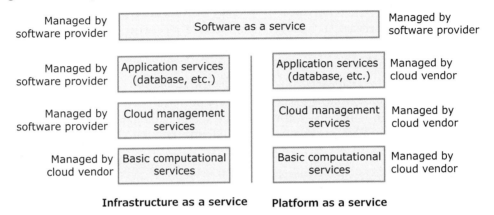

An important difference between IaaS and PaaS is the allocation of system management responsibilities. Figure 5.6 shows who has management responsibilities for SaaS, IaaS, and PaaS.

If you are using IaaS, you have the responsibility for installing and managing the database, the system security, and the application. If you use PaaS, you can devolve responsibility of managing the database and security to the cloud provider. In SaaS, assuming that a software vendor is running the system on a cloud, the software vendor manages the application. Everything else is the cloud provider's responsibility.

When clouds were introduced (around 2010), there was a clear distinction between IaaS and PaaS. Amazon presented Amazon Web Services (AWS) as IaaS. Google, on the other hand, presented their cloud platform as a PaaS environment where you could use Google's cloud primitives to create auto-scaling environments and other features. In practice now, there is very little real difference between these levels, with all cloud providers supporting some form of PaaS.

You may also come across the idea of function as a service (FaaS), which is supported by Amazon's Lambda service. In this relatively recent development it is possible to implement a cloud service and start this up and shut it down each time it is used. All you need to do is upload the software implementing the service to the cloud provider and they create the service automatically. When it is accessed, a server running this service is automatically started.

FaaS offers two main benefits:

1. You don't have to manage a server to run your service. The cloud provider takes full responsibility for this.

2. You pay for only the time that the function is executing rather than rent the underlying server on which the function runs. This leads to a significant savings for services, such as recovery services, that have to be available on demand and do not run continuously.

Function as a service is a developing area that I think will become increasingly widely used. At the time of writing in 2018, however, it is not sufficiently mature to cover in an introductory textbook.

5.3 Software as a service

When software products were introduced, they had to be installed on the customer's own computers. Sometimes the buyer of the software had to configure the software to their own operating environment and deal with software updates. Updated software was not always compatible with other software in the company, so it was common for software users to run older versions of the product to avoid these compatibility problems. This meant the software product company sometimes had to maintain several different versions of their product at the same time.

Many software products are still delivered in this way but, increasingly, software products are being delivered as a service. If you deliver your software product as a service, you run the software on your servers, which you may rent from a cloud provider. Customers don't have to install software, and they access the remote system through a web browser or dedicated mobile app (Figure 5.7). The payment model for SaaS is usually a subscription. Users pay a monthly fee to use the software rather than buy it outright.

Many software providers deliver their software as a cloud service, but also allow users to download a version of the software so that they can work without a network connection. For example, Adobe offers the Lightroom photo management software as both a cloud service and a download that runs on the user's own computer. This gets around the problem of reduced performance due to slow network connections.

For the majority of web-based software products, I think it makes sense for product developers to deliver these as a service. Table 5.3 shows the benefits of this approach for product providers.

Customers benefit from SaaS by avoiding large up-front payments for software and always having access to the latest version. However, some disadvantages in this delivery model dissuade many people from using software that is delivered in this way. These advantages and disadvantages are shown in Figure 5.8.

Figure 5.7 Software as a service

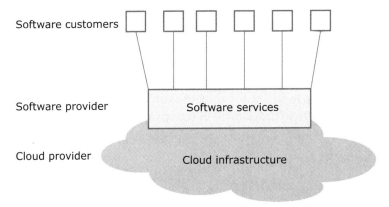

Table 5.3 Benefits of SaaS for software product providers

Benefit	Explanation
Cash flow	Customers either pay a regular subscription or pay as they use the software. This means you have a regular cash flow, with payments throughout the year. You don't have a situation where you have a large cash injection when products are purchased but very little income between product releases.
Update management	You are in control of updates to your product, and all customers receive the update at the same time. You avoid the issue of several versions being simultaneously used and maintained. This reduces your costs and makes it easier to maintain a consistent software code base.
Continuous deployment	You can deploy new versions of your software as soon as changes have been made and tested. This means you can fix bugs quickly so that your software reliability can continuously improve.
Payment flexibility	You can have several different payment options so that you can attract a wider range of customers. Small companies or individuals need not be discouraged by having to pay large upfront software costs.
Try before you buy	You can make early free or low-cost versions of the software available quickly with the aim of getting customer feedback on bugs and how the product could be approved.
Data collection	You can easily collect data on how the product is used and so identify areas for improvement. You may also be able to collect customer data that allow you to market other products to these customers.

Figure 5.8 Advantages and disadvantages of SaaS for customers

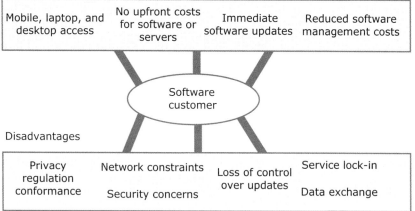

One of the most significant business benefits of using SaaS is that customers do not incur the capital costs of buying servers or the software itself. Customer cash flow is improved with software being a monthly operational cost rather than a significant capital expenditure. To maintain access to a service-based software product, however, customers have to continue to pay, even if they rarely use the software. This contrasts with software that you can buy for a one-off payment. Once you have bought this software, you can keep it as long as you wish without further payments.

The universal use of mobile devices means that customers want to access software from these devices as well as from desktop and laptop computers. Delivering SaaS means that customers can access the software from any platform at any time. People can use the software from multiple devices without having to install the software in advance. However, this may mean that software developers have to develop mobile apps for a range of platforms in order to maintain their customer base.

A further benefit of SaaS for customers **is** that they don't have to employ staff to install and update the system. This transfers the problems of ensuring a reliable and consistent service to the SaaS provider rather than local system administrators. However, this may lead to a loss of local expertise. A lack of expertise may make it more difficult for customers to revert to self-hosted software if they need to do so.

A characteristic of SaaS is that updates can be delivered quickly. New features are immediately available to all customers. As I explain in Chapter 10, many companies now practice continuous deployment where new versions

Table 5.4 Data storage and management issues for SaaS

Issue	Explanation
Regulation	Some countries, such as EU countries, have strict laws on the storage of personal information. These may be incompatible with the laws and regulations of the country where the SaaS provider is based. If an SaaS provider cannot guarantee that their storage locations conform to the laws of the customer's country, businesses may be reluctant to use their product.
Data transfer	If software use involves a lot of data transfer, the software response time may be limited by the network speed. This is a problem for individuals and smaller companies who can't afford to pay for very high speed network connections.
Data security	Companies dealing with sensitive information may be unwilling to hand over the control of their data to an external software provider. As we have seen from a number of high-profile cases, even large cloud providers have had security breaches. You can't assume that they always provide better security than the customer's own servers.
Data exchange	If you need to exchange data between a cloud service and other services or local software applications, this can be difficult unless the cloud service provides an API that is accessible for external use.

of the software are delivered every day. Customers have no control over when software upgrades are installed, however. If incompatibilities with the customer's way of working are introduced in an update, they have to make immediate changes to continue using the software.

Other disadvantages of SaaS are related to storage and data management issues (Table 5.4). These are important to some customers, especially large multinational companies. They are the fundamental reasons some companies remain reluctant to use cloud-based software and prefer to run software on their own servers.

If you are developing a system that does not deal with personal and financial information, SaaS is usually the best way to deliver your software product. Where national or international data protection regulations apply, however, the choice is more difficult. You must use a cloud provider that stores data in permitted locations. If this is impractical, you may have to provide customer-installed software, where the data are stored on the customer's own servers.

In some ways, developing software as a service is no different from developing software with a browser interface that runs on organizational servers. In those situations, however, you can make assumptions about the available network speed and bandwidth, the electric power available, and the users of

Figure 5.9 Design issues for SaaS

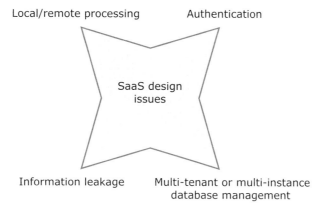

the system. For SaaS, your customers are from different organizations. They access the system on unknown devices, so you need to design your software to take this into account. Factors that you have to consider are shown in Figure 5.9.

A software product may be designed so that some features are executed locally in the user's browser or mobile app and some on a remote server. Local execution reduces network traffic and so increases user response speed. This is useful when users have a slow network connection. However, local processing increases the electric power needed to run the system. This is not a problem if there is a connection to grid or mains power, but it is an issue when battery-powered mobile devices are used to access the application. The best way to distribute local and remote processing depends on the type of application and the expected usage of the system. Consequently, it is difficult to give general advice on this topic apart from "experiment and be prepared to change."

On all shared systems, users have to authenticate themselves to show that they are accredited to use the system. You can set up your own authentication system, but this means users have to remember another set of authentication credentials. People don't like this, so for individual users, many systems allow authentication using the user's Google, Facebook, or LinkedIn credentials. However, this is not usually acceptable for businesses that prefer their users to authenticate using their business credentials. You may need to set up a federated authentication system that delegates authentication to the business where the user works. I explain federated authentication in Chapter 7.

Information leakage is a particular risk for cloud-based software. If you have multiple users from multiple organizations, a security risk is that information leaks from one organization to another. This can happen in a number of different ways, so you need to be very careful in designing your security system to avoid it.

Multi-tenancy means that the system maintains the information from different organizations in a single repository rather than maintaining separate copies of the system and database. This can lead to more efficient operation. However, the developer has to design software so that each organization sees a virtual system that includes its own configuration and data. In a multi-instance system, each customer has their own instance of the software and its database.

5.4 Multi-tenant and multi-instance systems

Many cloud-based systems are multi-tenant systems, in which all customers are served by a single instance of the system and a multi-tenant database. Business users interact with what appears to be a dedicated system for their company. The database is partitioned so that customer companies have their own space and can store and access their own data.

An alternative SaaS implementation is to provide a separate copy of the system and database for each user. These are called multi-instance systems. I discuss these in Section 5.4.2.

5.4.1 Multi-tenant systems

In a multi-tenant database, a single database schema, defined by the SaaS provider, is shared by all of the system's users. Items in the database are tagged with a tenant identifier, representing a company that has stored data in the system. The database access software uses this tenant identifier to provide "logical isolation," which means that users seem to be working with their own database. Figure 5.10 illustrates this situation using a simplified stock management database table. The tenant identifier (column 1) is used to identify the rows in the database that are exclusive to that tenant.

The advantages and disadvantages of using a multi-tenant database are shown in Table 5.5.

Mid-size and large businesses that are buying software as a service rarely want to use generic multi-tenant software. They want a version of the software that is adapted to their own requirements and that presents their staff with a customized version of the software. Table 5.6 summarizes some business requirements for the customization of SaaS.

Figure 5.10 An example of a multi-tenant database

Stock management					
Tenant	Key	Item	Stock	Supplier	Ordered
T516	100	Widg 1	27	S13	2017/2/12
T632	100	Obj 1	5	S13	2017/1/11
T973	100	Thing 1	241	S13	2017/2/7
T516	110	Widg 2	14	S13	2017/2/2
T516	120	Widg 3	17	S13	2017/1/24
T973	100	Thing 2	132	S26	2017/2/12

In a multi-tenant system, where all users share a single copy of the system, providing these features means that the software's user interface and access control system have to be configurable and it must be possible to create "virtual databases" for each business customer.

Table 5.5 Advantages and disadvantages of multi-tenant databases

Advantages	Disadvantages
Resource utilization The SaaS provider has control of all the resources used by the software and can optimize the software to make effective use of these resources.	**Inflexibility** Customers must all use the same database schema with limited scope for adapting this schema to individual needs. I explain possible database adaptations later in this section.
Security Multi-tenant databases have to be designed for security because the data for all customers are held in the same database. They are, therefore, likely to have fewer security vulnerabilities than standard database products. Security management is also simplified as there is only a single copy of the database software to be patched if a security vulnerability is discovered.	**Security** As data for all customers are maintained in the same database, there is a theoretical possibility that data will leak from one customer to another. In fact, there are very few instances of this happening. More seriously, perhaps, if there is a database security breach, then it affects all customers.
Update management It is easier to update a single instance of software rather than multiple instances. Updates are delivered to all customers at the same time so all use the latest version of the software.	**Complexity** Multi-tenant systems are usually more complex than multi-instance systems because of the need to manage many users. There is, therefore, an increased likelihood of bugs in the database software.

Table 5.6 Possible customizations for SaaS

Customization	Business need
Authentication	Businesses may want users to authenticate using their business credentials rather than the account credentials set up by the software provider. I explain in Chapter 7 how federated authentication makes this possible.
Branding	Businesses may want a user interface that is branded to reflect their own organization.
Business rules	Businesses may want to be able to define their own business rules and workflows that apply to their own data.
Data schemas	Businesses may want to be able to extend the standard data model used in the system database to meet their own business needs.
Access control	Businesses may want to be able to define their own access control model that sets out the data that specific users or user groups can access and the allowed operations on that data.

User interface configurability is relatively easy to implement by using user profiles for each customer (Figure 5.11). This user profile includes information about how the system should look to users and security profiles that define the access permissions of both the organization and individual users. The figure shows profiles for all companies, but co2 and co5 do not have any logged-in users.

Figure 5.11 User profiles for SaaS access

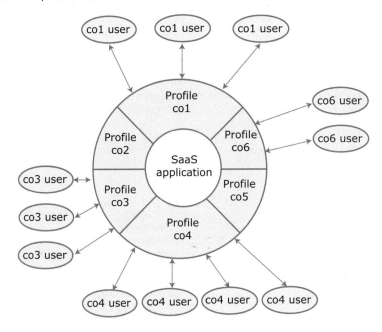

Figure 5.12 Database extensibility using additional fields

Stock management								
Tenant	Key	Item	Stock	Supplier	Ordered	Ext 1	Ext 2	Ext 3
T516	100	Widg 1	27	S13	2017/2/12			
T632	100	Obj 1	5	S13	2017/1/11			
T973	100	Thing 1	241	S13	2017/2/7			
T516	110	Widg 2	14	S13	2017/2/2			
T516	120	Widg 3	17	S13	2017/1/24			
T973	100	Thing 2	132	S26	2017/2/12			

When a SaaS product detects that the user is from a particular organization, it looks for the user profile for that organization. The software uses profile information to create a personalized version of the interface to be presented to users. To detect a user, you can ask them to either select their organization or provide their business email address. As well as a business profile, there may also be an individual profile for each user that defines what features and system data they are allowed to access.

The user interface is designed using generic elements, such as the company name and logo. At run time, web pages are generated by replacing these generic elements with the company name and logo taken from the profile associated with each user. Menus may also be adapted, with some features disabled if they are not needed by the user's business.

Individual users are usually happy to accept a shared fixed schema in a multi-tenant database and adapt their work to fit that schema. However, corporate users may wish to extend or adapt the schema to meet their specific business needs. There are two ways to do this if you are using a relational database system:

1. Add a number of extra fields to each table and allow customers to use these fields as they wish.

2. Add a field to each table that identifies a separate "extension table," and allow customers to create these extension tables to reflect their needs.

I illustrate these situations in Figures 5.12 and 5.13.

It is relatively easy to extend the database by providing additional fields. You add some extra columns to each database table and define a customer

Figure 5.13 Database extensibility using tables

Main database table

Tab1

Tenant	ID	Item	Stock	Supplier	Ordered	Ext 1
			Stock management			
T516	100	Widg 1	27	S13	2017/2/12	E123
T632	100	Obj 1	5	S13	2017/1/11	E200
T973	100	Thing 1	241	S13	2017/2/7	E346
T516	110	Widg 2	14	S13	2017/2/2	E124
T516	120	Widg 3	17	S13	2017/1/24	E125
T973	100	Thing 2	132	S26	2017/2/12	E347

Tab2

Field names

Tenant	Name	Type
T516	'Location'	String
T516	'Weight'	Integer
T516	'Fragile'	Bool
T632	'Delivered'	Date
T632	'Place'	String
T973	'Delivered'	Date

Extension table showing the
field names for each company
that needs database extensions

Field values   Tab3

Record	Tenant	Value
E123	T516	'A17/S6'
E123	T516	'4'
E123	T516	'False'
E200	T632	'2017/1/15'
E200	T632	'Dublin'
E346	T973	'2017/2/10'
...		

Value table showing the value of
extension fields for each record

profile that maps the column names that the customer wants to these extra
columns. However, this approach has two major problems:

1. It is difficult to know how many extra columns you should include. If you
    have too few, customers will find that there aren't enough for what they
    need to do. However, if you cater to customers who need a lot of extra
    columns, you will find that most customers don't use them, so you will
    have a lot of wasted space in your database.

2. Different customers are likely to need different types of columns. For example, some customers may wish to have columns whose items are string types; others may wish to have columns that are integers. You can get around this by maintaining everything as strings. However, this means that either you or your customer has to provide conversion software to create items of the correct type.

An alternative approach to database extensibility is to add any number of additional fields and to define the names, types, and values of these fields. The names and types of these values are held in a separate table, accessed using the tenant identifier. Unfortunately, using tables in this way adds complexity to the database management software. Extra tables must be managed and information from them integrated into the database.

Figure 5.13 illustrates a situation where the extension column in the database includes an identifier for the added field values. The names and types of these fields are held in a separate table. They are linked to the values using a tenant identifier. Table Tab1 is the main database table that maintains information about the stock of different items. In this example, there are three tenants: T516, T632, and T973.

Tab1 has a single extension field (Ext1) that links to a separate table, Tab3. Each linked row in T1 has one or more rows in Tab3, where the number of rows represents the number of extension fields. For example, row 1 in Tab1 has three extension fields. The values of these fields are provided in Table Tab3 and the field names in Table Tab2. Therefore, the extension fields for T516/Item 100 are 'Location', 'Weight', and 'Fragile'. Their values are 'A17/S6', '4', and 'False'. The extension fields for T634/Item 100 are 'Delivered' and 'Place', and their values are '2017/1/15' and 'Dublin'.

Corporate users may also want to define their own validation rules and access permissions for their own database. You can implement this using a customer profile that stores this information but, again, it adds complexity to your software.

The major concern of corporate customers with multi-tenant databases is security. As information from all customers is stored in the same database, a software bug or an attack could lead to the data of some or all customers being exposed to others. This means that you have to implement stringent security precautions in any multi-tenant system. I don't cover security issues in detail, but I briefly mention two important issues: multilevel access control and encryption.

Multilevel access control means that access to data must be controlled at both the organizational level and the individual level. You need to have organizational level access control to ensure that any database operations act on only that organization's data. So, the first stage is to execute the operation on the database, selecting the items that are tagged with the organization's identifier. Individual users accessing the data should also have their own access permissions. Therefore, you must make a further selection from the database to present only those data items that an identified user is allowed to access.

Encryption of data in a multi-tenant database reassures corporate users that their data cannot be viewed by people from other companies if some kind of system failure occurs. Encryption, as I discuss in Chapter 7, is the process of applying a function to data to obscure its value. The encrypted data are stored and decrypted only when accessed with the appropriate key. However, encryption and decryption are computationally intensive operations and so slow down database operation. Consequently, multi-tenant databases that use encryption usually encrypt only sensitive data.

5.4.2 Multi-instance systems

Multi-instance systems are SaaS systems where each customer has its own system that is adapted to its needs, including its own database and security controls. Multi-instance, cloud-based systems are conceptually simpler than multi-tenant systems and avoid security concerns such as data leakage from one organization to another.

There are two types of multi-instance system:

1. *VM-based multi-instance systems* In these systems, the software instance and database for each customer run in its own virtual machine. This may appear to be an expensive option, but it makes sense when your product is aimed at corporate customers who require 24/7 access to their software and data. All users from the same customer may access the shared system database.

2. *Container-based multi-instance systems* In these systems, each user has an isolated version of the software and database running in a set of containers. Generally, the software uses a microservices architecture, with each service running in a container and managing its own database. This approach is suited to products in which users mostly work independently, with relatively little data sharing. Therefore, it is most suited for products that serve individuals rather than business customers or for business products that are not data intensive.

Table 5.7 Advantages and disadvantages of multi-instance databases

Advantages	Disadvantages
Flexibility Each instance of the software can be tailored and adapted to a customer's needs. Customers may use completely different database schemas and it is straightforward to transfer data from a customer database to the product database.	**Cost** It is more expensive to use multi-instance systems because of the costs of renting many VMs in the cloud and the costs of managing multiple systems. Because of the slow startup time, VMs may have to be rented and kept running continuously, even if there is very little demand for the service.
Security Each customer has its own database so there is no possibility of data leakage from one customer to another.	**Update management** Many instances have to be updated so updates are more complex, especially if instances have been tailored to specific customer needs.
Scalability Instances of the system can be scaled according to the needs of individual customers. For example, some customers may require more powerful servers than others.	
Resilience If a software failure occurs, this will probably affect only a single customer. Other customers can continue working as normal.	

It is possible to run containers on a virtual machine, so it is also possible to create hybrid systems where a business could have its own VM-based system and then run containers on top of this for individual users. As container technology develops, I suspect this type of system will become increasingly common.

The advantages and disadvantages of using multi-instance databases are shown in Table 5.7.

Early vendors of SaaS, such as Salesforce.com, developed their systems as multi-tenant systems because this was the most cost-effective way to provide a responsive system for users. The shared database could run on powerful servers, with all data being available as soon as a user logged on to the system. The alternative at that time was multi-instance VM-based systems, and these were significantly more expensive.

However, container-based multi-instance systems are not necessarily significantly more expensive to run than multi-tenant systems. There is no need

Figure 5.14 Architectural decisions for cloud software engineering

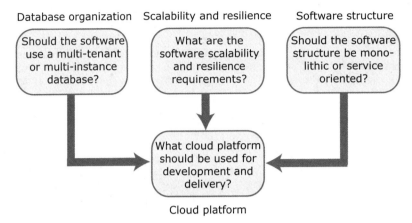

Cloud platform

to have VMs constantly available, as containers can be started quickly in response to user demand. As I discuss in Chapter 6 though, container-based databases are not suitable for transaction-based applications in which the database must be consistent at all times.

5.5 Cloud software architecture

As part of the architectural design process for your software you should decide on the most important software attributes, the delivery platform, and the technology used. If you decide to use the cloud as your delivery platform, you have to make a number of cloud-specific architectural decisions. I show these as questions in Figure 5.14.

Choosing the most appropriate cloud platform for development and delivery of your application is important. As I show in Figure 5.14, the answers to questions on database organization, scalability and resilience, and software structure are factors in that decision.

5.5.1 Database organization

There are three possible ways of providing a customer database in a cloud-based system:

1. As a multi-tenant system, shared by all customers for your product. This may be hosted in the cloud using large, powerful servers.

Table 5.8 Questions to ask when choosing a database organization

Factor	Key questions
Target customers	Do customers require different database schemas and database personalization? Do customers have security concerns about database sharing? If so, use a multi-instance database.
Transaction requirements	Is it critical that your products support ACID transactions where the data are guaranteed to be consistent at all times? If so, use a multi-tenant database or a VM-based multi-instance database.
Database size and connectivity	How large is the typical database used by customers? How many relationships are there between database items? A multi-tenant model is usually best for very large databases, as you can focus effort on optimizing performance.
Database interoperability	Will customers wish to transfer information from existing databases? What are the differences in schemas between these and a possible multi-tenant database? What software support will they expect to do the data transfer? If customers have many different schemas, a multi-instance database should be used.
System structure	Are you using a service-oriented architecture for your system? Can customer databases be split into a set of individual service databases? If so, use containerized, multi-instance databases.

2. As a multi-instance system, with each customer database running on its own virtual machine.

3. As a multi-instance system, with each database running in its own container. The customer database may be distributed over several containers.

Deciding which approach to choose is a critical architectural decision. In Table 5.8 I show some of the questions you have to ask when making this decision.

As I have discussed, different types of customers have different expectations about software products. If you are targeting consumers or small businesses, they do not expect to have branding and personalization, use of a local authentication system, or varying individual permissions. This means you can use a multi-tenant database with a single schema.

Large companies are more likely to want a database that has been adapted to their needs. This is possible, to some extent, with a multi-tenant system, as

I discussed in Section 5.4. However, it is easier to provide a tailored product if you use a multi-instance database.

If your product is in an area such as finance, where the database has to be consistent at all times, you need a transaction-based system. This means you should use either a multi-tenant database or a database per customer running on a virtual machine. All users from each customer share the VM-based database.

If your customers need a single large relational database that has many linked tables, then a multi-tenant approach is usually the best design choice. However, if your database can be limited in size and does not have many connected tables, it may be possible to split the database into smaller independent databases. Each of these databases can then be implemented as a separate instance running in its own container.

If you are targeting business customers, they may want to transfer information between their local databases and your cloud-based database while they are using your product. As these customers will not all be using the same database technology and schemas, it is much easier to use a separate database for each customer. You can then replicate their data organization in the customer instance. In a multi-tenant system, the time required to adapt the data to the multi-tenant schema slows down the system's response.

If you are building your system as a service-oriented system, your services should each have its own independent database. You should use a multi-instance database in this situation. You need to design your database as a separate distributed system. This, of course, adds complexity and may be a factor in deciding whether to use a service-oriented or an object-oriented approach to design.

5.5.2 Scalability and resilience

The scalability of a system reflects its ability to adapt automatically to changes in the load on that system. The resilience of a system reflects its ability to continue to deliver critical services in the event of system failure or malicious system use.

You achieve scalability in a system by making it possible to add new virtual servers (scaling out) or increase the power of a system server (scaling up) in response to increasing load. In cloud-based systems, scaling out rather than scaling up is the normal approach used. This means your software has to be organized so that individual software components can be replicated and run in parallel. Load-balancing hardware or software is used to direct requests to

Figure 5.15 Using a standby system to provide resilience

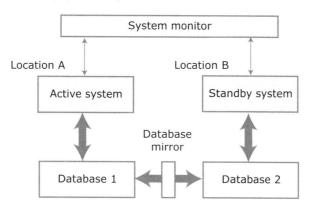

different instances of these components. If you develop your software using the cloud provider's support for PaaS, then this can automatically scale your software as demand increases.

To achieve resilience, you need to be able to restart your software quickly after a hardware or software failure. Figure 5.15 shows how this can be achieved.

Several variants to the system organization shown in Figure 5.15 all use the same fundamental approach:

1. Replicas of the software and data are maintained in different locations.

2. Database updates are mirrored so that the standby database is a working copy of the operational database.

3. A system monitor continually checks the system status. It can switch to the standby system automatically if the operational system fails.

To protect against hardware failure or failure of the cloud management software, you need to deploy your main system and backup system in different physical locations. You should use virtual servers that are not hosted on the same physical computer. Ideally, these servers should be located in different data centers. If a physical server fails or if there is a wider data center failure, then operation can be switched automatically to the software copies elsewhere.

If software copies are run in parallel, switching may be completely transparent with no effects on users. Figure 5.15 shows a "hot standby" system, where data in different locations are synced so that there is only a minimal delay in bringing up the new system. A cheaper alternative is to use a "cool standby" approach. In a cool standby system, the data are restored from a backup and the transactions are replayed to update the backup to the system state immediately before failure. If you use a cool standby approach, your system will be unavailable until the backup restore is complete.

System monitoring can range from regular checking that your system is up and delivering service to more comprehensive monitoring of the load and the response times of your software. Data from the monitor may be used to decide if you need to scale your system up or down. System monitors can also provide early warnings of problems with your software or server. They may be able to detect external attacks and report these to the cloud provider.

5.5.3 Software structure

An object-oriented approach to software engineering has been the dominant mode of development since the mid-1990s. This approach is suitable for the development of client–server systems built around a shared database. The system itself is, logically, a monolithic system with distribution across multiple servers running large software components. The traditional multi-tier client–server architecture that I discussed in Chapter 4 is based on this distributed system model. All the business logic and processing are implemented in a single system.

The alternative to a monolithic approach to software organization is a service-oriented approach, where the system is decomposed into fine-grain, stateless services. Because it is stateless, each service is independent and can be replicated, distributed, and migrated from one server to another. The service-oriented approach is particularly suitable for cloud-based software with services deployed in containers.

I recommend that you normally use a monolithic approach to build your prototype and perhaps the first release of your software product. Development frameworks usually include support for implementing systems based on a model-view-controller model. Consequently, monolithic MVC systems can be built fairly quickly. When you are experimenting with a system, it is usually easier to do so using a single program as you don't have to identify services, manage a large number of distributed services, support multiple databases, and so on.

Software products are often delivered on mobile devices as well as browser-based systems. Different parts may have to be updated at different times, and you may need to respond quickly to infrastructure change, such as a mobile OS upgrade. Sometimes you have to scale parts of a system to cope with increasing load even though other parts are unaffected. In those circumstances, I recommend that you use a service-oriented architecture based on microservices.

Figure 5.16 Technical issues in cloud platform choice

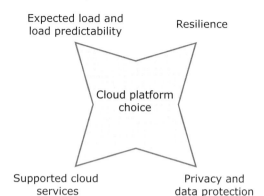

5.5.4 Cloud platform

Many different cloud platforms are now available. These may be general-purpose clouds such as Amazon Web Services or lesser-known platforms oriented around a specific application, such as the SAP Cloud Platform. There are also smaller national providers that provide more limited services but may be more willing to adapt their services to the needs of different customers. There is no "best" platform; you should choose a cloud provider based on your background and experience, the type of product you are developing, and the expectations of your customers.

You need to consider both technical issues and business issues when choosing a cloud platform for your product. Figure 5.16 shows the main technical issues in cloud platform choice.

In addition to their basic IaaS services, cloud vendors usually provide other services such as database services, "big data" services, and so on. Using these services can reduce your development costs and time to market, so you should choose a provider whose services best support your application area. You may also need to consider software compatibility. For example, if you have developed business products for a .NET environment, they can usually be transferred fairly easily to the Microsoft Azure cloud.

Some systems have a predictable usage pattern, and there is no need to design for unexpected spikes in usage. If it is likely that your system will experience large spikes in demand, however, you should choose a provider that offers PaaS libraries that make it easier to write elastic software. As I have discussed, resilience relies on replication, so you need to use a provider that has data centers in different locations and that supports replication across these locations.

Figure 5.17 Business issues in cloud platform choice

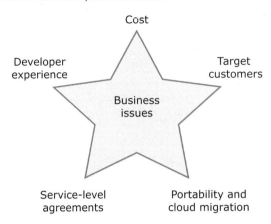

Privacy and data protection are technical and business issues. Some countries and areas, such as the European Union, have strict requirements on data protection and on where data are stored. From a technical perspective, if you have customers in different countries, you need to use a cloud provider that has international data centers and that can provide guarantees on storage locations.

The business issues you have to consider when choosing a cloud provider are shown in Figure 5.17.

Cost is obviously a critical factor in choosing a cloud platform, particularly for small product companies. The costs of cloud services from different providers vary quite significantly, particularly for software with varying usage patterns. However, it is difficult to work out the real costs and the trade-off between direct and indirect costs such as cloud management. Although it may be tempting to choose the provider that appears to offer the lowest costs, you must always ask yourself why that provider is cheaper and what compromises have been made to provide a lower-price service.

If your development team have experience with a particular cloud platform, it makes sense to use that platform if possible. Your team will not have to spend time learning about a new system and so the overall product development time will be reduced.

If you are offering business products, you need to think carefully about the expectations of your customers. There may be commercial advantages in allowing your software to interoperate with other software used by your customers. Many businesses run their software on platforms such as Salesforce and Microsoft Azure, so you should consider these as a deployment platform for your product. Some companies prefer to deal with trusted providers, such as IBM, so prefer software that will run on that provider's cloud. Of course, if you are targeting a specific market, such as users of SAP software, you should choose the cloud platform used by that software.

Service-level agreements (SLAs) define the performance and availability of a service that's delivered to customers. Your customers will expect a certain level of service, and to deliver this, you need a comparable service level from your cloud provider. Cloud SLAs set out the service that a cloud provider guarantees to provide and the penalties if it fails to do so. If you have specific requirements and you are a large customer, you should choose a provider that will negotiate SLAs. Large providers such as Amazon and Google simply offer most customers an SLA on a "take it or leave it" basis with no room for negotiation.

Portability and cloud migration are both technical and business issues. In choosing a provider, you need to think about the possibility that you may wish to move your software to another provider in future. You may be unhappy with the service provided, or you may need services that are not available from your current provider. Containers have simplified the problems of cloud migration, as they are stand-alone entities supported by all cloud providers. You can easily restart your software in a container from a different provider.

If you use cloud provider platform services in your software implementation, however, these have to be reimplemented on a different system. Not all services from Amazon (say) are available on Google, and vice versa. Therefore, this software has to be rewritten if it is migrated.

KEY POINTS

- The cloud is made up of a large number of virtual servers that you can rent for your own use. You and your customers access these servers remotely over the Internet and pay for the amount of server time used.

- Virtualization is a technology that allows multiple server instances to be run on the same physical computer. This means you can create isolated instances of your software for deployment on the cloud.

- Virtual machines are physical server replicas on which you run your own operating system, technology stack, and applications.

- Containers are a lightweight virtualization technology that allow rapid replication and deployment of virtual servers. All containers run the same operating system. Docker is currently the most widely used container technology.

- A fundamental feature of the cloud is that "everything" can be delivered as a service and accessed over the Internet. A service is rented rather than owned and is shared with other users.

▪ Infrastructure as a service (IaaS) means that computing, storage, and other services are available in the cloud. There is no need to run your own physical servers.

▪ Platform as a service (PaaS) means using services provided by a cloud platform vendor to make it possible to auto-scale your software in response to demand.

▪ Software as a service (SaaS) means that application software is delivered as a service to users. This has important benefits for users, such as lower capital costs, and for software vendors, such as simpler deployment of new software releases.

▪ Multi-tenant systems are SaaS systems where all users share the same database, which may be adapted at run time to their individual needs. Multi-instance systems are SaaS applications where each user has their own separate database.

▪ The key architectural issues for cloud-based software are the cloud platform to be used, whether to use a multi-tenant or multi-instance database, scalability and resilience requirements, and whether to use objects or services as the basic components in the system.

RECOMMENDED READING

"SaaS vs. PaaS vs. IaaS—An Ultimate Guide on When to Use What" This succinct introduction to everything as a service discusses not only what the terms mean but also when it is appropriate to use these services. (S. Patel, 2015)

https://www.linkedin.com/pulse/saas-vs-paas-iaas-ultimate-guide-when-use-what-sonia-patel

Cloud vendor tutorials

These are links to the tutorials provided by the major public cloud vendors (Amazon, Google, and Microsoft) that explain how to set up and get started with their services.
https://aws.amazon.com/getting-started/
https://cloud.google.com/docs/tutorials#getting_started
https://docs.microsoft.com/en-us/azure/

"A Beginner-Friendly Introduction to Containers, VMs and Docker"

This easy-to-read article explains both virtual machine and container technology as well as Docker, which is the most widely used container system. (P. Kasireddy, 2016)
https://medium.freecodecamp.com/a-beginner-friendly-introduction-to-containers-vms-and-docker-79a9e3e119b

"The Docker Ecosystem: Networking and Communications"

Most articles on container communications dive into technicalities quickly without presenting a broad picture of the issues. This article is an exception, and I recommend reading it before any of the more detailed technical tutorials. (J. Ellingwood, 2015)

https://www.digitalocean.com/community/tutorials/the-docker-ecosystem-networking-and-communication

"Multi tenancy vs. Multi instance in CCaaS/UCaaS Clouds"

Most articles on this topic argue for one solution or another, but this is a balanced article that looks at the advantages and disadvantages of each approach. (A. Gangwani, 2014) http://www.contactcenterarchitects.com/wp-content/uploads/2014/12/Who-Leads-Whom-CCaaS_UCaaS_Whitepaper3.76-by-Ankush-Gangwani.pdf

PRESENTATIONS, VIDEOS, AND LINKS

https://iansommerville.com/engineering-software-products/cloud-based-software

EXERCISES

5.1. Why should companies that are developing software products use cloud servers to support their development process?

5.2. Explain the fundamental difference between virtualization using a VM and virtualization using a container.

5.3. Explain why it is simple and fast to deploy a replica of a container on a new server.

5.4. Explain what is meant by IaaS and PaaS. Explain why the distinction between these categories of services is becoming increasingly blurred and why they may be merged in the near future.

5.5. What are the benefits to software product vendors of delivering software as a service? In what situations might you decide not to deliver software in this way?

5.6. Using an example, explain why EU data protection rules can cause difficulties for companies that offer software as a service.

5.7. What is the fundamental difference between a multi-tenant SaaS system and a multi-instance SaaS system?

5.8. What are the key issues that have to be considered when deciding whether to implement a multi-tenant or a multi-instance database when software is delivered as a service?

5.9. Why isn't cost the most important factor to consider when choosing a cloud platform for development and software delivery?

5.10. What do you need to do to deliver a resilient cloud-based system that offers your software as a service?

6

Microservices Architecture

One of the most important decisions a software architect has to make is how to decompose a system into components. Component decomposition is critical because the components can then be developed in parallel by different people or teams. They can be reused and replaced if their underlying technology changes, and they can be distributed across multiple computers.

To take advantage of the benefits of cloud-based software—scalability, reliability, and elasticity—you need to use components that can be easily replicated, run in parallel, and moved between virtual servers. This is difficult with components, such as objects, that maintain local state because you need to find a way of maintaining state consistency across components. Therefore, it is best to use stateless software services that maintain persistent information in a local database.

A software service is a software component that can be accessed from remote computers over the Internet. Given an input, a service produces a corresponding output, without side effects. The service is accessed through its published interface and all details of the service implementation are hidden. The manager of a service is called the service provider, and the user of a service is called a service requestor.

Services do not maintain any internal state. State information is either stored in a database or maintained by the service requestor. When a service request is made, the state information may be included as part of the request and the updated state information is returned as part of the service result. As there is no local state, services can be dynamically reallocated from one virtual server to another. They can be replicated to reflect increases in the number of service requests made, making it simpler to create applications that can scale depending on load.

Software services are not a new idea and the notion of "service-oriented architecture" was developed in the late 1990s. This introduced the principle that services should be independent and stand alone, they should have defined and publicly accessible interfaces, and services in the same system can be implemented using different technologies.

To operate effectively, services must use a standard protocol for communication and a standard format for interface description. After various experiments in the 1990s with service-oriented computing, the idea of Web Services emerged in the early 2000s. These were based on XML-based protocols and standards, such as SOAP for service interaction and WSDL for interface description. They were supplemented by a range of additional XML-based standards covering service orchestration (how services are combined to create new functionality), reliable messaging, quality of service, and so on.

Web Services standards and protocols involve services exchanging large and complex XML texts. It takes a significant amount of time to analyze the XML messages and extract the encoded data, which slows down systems built using these web services. Even small, single-function web services have a significant message management overhead.

Most software services are simple, however; they don't need the generality that's inherent in the design of web service protocols. Consequently, modern service-oriented systems use simpler, "lighter weight" service-interaction protocols that have lower overheads and consequently faster execution. These have simple interfaces and usually use a more efficient format for encoding message data.

As service-oriented ideas were being developed, companies such as Amazon were rethinking the concept of a service. Web services were generally thought of as implementations of traditional software components that could be distributed over a network. So, there might be business services, user interface (UI) services, logging services, and so on. These services usually shared a database and provided an API that was used by the system's user interface module. In practice, it was not easy to scale or move individual services without affecting other parts of the system.

Amazon's approach was to rethink what a service should be. They concluded that a service should be related to a single business function. Instead of relying on a shared database and other services in the system, services should be completely independent, with their own database. They should also manage their own user interface. Replacing or replicating a service should therefore be possible without having to change any other services in the system.

This type of service has become known as a "microservice." Microservices are small-scale, stateless services that have a single responsibility. Software products that use microservices are said to have a microservices architecture.

If you need to create cloud-based software products that are adaptable, scalable, and resilient, then I recommend that you use a microservices architecture.

A microservices architecture is based on services that are fine-grain components with a single responsibility. For example, a coarse-grain authentication component or service might manage user names, check passwords, handle forgotten passwords, and send texts for two-factor authentication. In a microservice-based system, you may have individual microservices for each of these, such as get-login-name, check-password, and so on.

Before going on to discuss microservices in more detail, I'll introduce microservices using a short example. Consider a system that uses an authentication module that provides the following features:

- user registration, where users provide information about their identity, security information, mobile (cell) phone number, and email address;

- authentication using user ID (UID)/password;

- two-factor authentication using code sent to mobile phone;

- user information management—for example, ability to change password or mobile phone number;

- password reset.

In principle, each of these features can be implemented as a separate service that uses a central shared database to hold authentication information. A user interface service can then manage all aspects of user communication.

In a microservices architecture, however, these features are too large to be microservices. To identify the microservices that might be used in the authentication system, you need to break down the coarse-grain features into more detailed functions. Figure 6.1 shows what these functions might be for user registration and UID/password authentication.

At this stage, you might think you have identified the microservices that you need. Each of the functions shown in Figure 6.1 could be implemented as a single microservice. However, remember that each microservice has to manage its own data. If you have very specific services, data often have to be replicated across several services. There are various ways of keeping data consistent, but they all potentially slow down the system. I explain how replicate data can be reconciled later in the chapter.

Alternatively, you can look at the data used for authentication and identify a microservice for each logical data item that has to be managed. This minimizes the amount of replicate data management that is required. Therefore,

Figure 6.1 Functional breakdown of authentication features

User registration

| Set up new login ID |
| Set up new password |
| Set up password recovery information |
| Set up two-factor authentication |
| Confirm registration |

Authenticate using UID/password

| Get login ID |
| Get password |
| Check credentials |
| Confirm authentication |

you might have a UID management service, a password management service, and so on. The operations supported by these services allow information to be created, read, and modified.

As I discuss later, these operations map onto the operations available for RESTful services. Figure 6.2 shows the microservices that could be used to implement user authentication. Other services, of course, would be required for registration. The convention that I use in figures in this chapter is that round-edged rectangles represent microservices and ellipses represent service data.

Figure 6.2 Authentication microservices

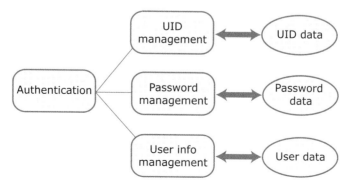

Table 6.1   Characteristics of microservices

Characteristic	Explanation
Self-contained	Microservices do not have external dependencies. They manage their own data and implement their own user interface.
Lightweight	Microservices communicate using lightweight protocols, so that service communication overheads are low.
Implementation independent	Microservices may be implemented using different programming languages and may use different technologies (e.g., different types of database) in their implementation.
Independently deployable	Each microservice runs in its own process and is independently deployable, using automated systems.
Business-oriented	Microservices should implement business capabilities and needs, rather than simply provide a technical service.

6.1 Microservices

Microservices are small-scale services that may be combined to create applications. They should be independent, so that the service interface is not affected by changes to other services. It should be possible to modify the service and re-deploy it without changing or stopping other services in the system. Table 6.1 summarizes these essential characteristics of microservices.

Microservices communicate by exchanging messages. A message that is sent between services includes some administrative information, a service request, and the data required to deliver the requested service. For example, an authentication service may send a message to a login service that includes the name input by the user. Services return a response to service request messages. This response includes data representing the reply to the service request. The reply from the login service might be a token associated with a valid user name or might be an error saying that there is no registered user.

Your aim in designing a microservice should be to create a service that has high cohesion and low coupling. Cohesion and coupling are ideas that were developed in the 1970s to reflect the interdependence of components in a software system. Briefly:

■ Coupling is a measure of the number of relationships that one component has with other components in the system. Low coupling means that components do not have many relationships with other components.

- Cohesion is a measure of the number of relationships that parts of a component have with each other. High cohesion means that all of the component parts that are needed to deliver the component's functionality are included in the component.

Low coupling is important in microservices because it leads to independent services. So long as you maintain its interface, you can update a service without having to change other services in the system. High cohesion is important because it means that the service does not have to call lots of other services during execution. Calling other services involves communications overhead, which can slow down a system.

The aim of developing highly cohesive services has led to a fundamental principle that underlies microservice design: the "single responsibility principle." Each element in a system should do one thing only and it should do it well. However, the problem with this is that "one thing only" is difficult to define in a way that is applicable to all services.

If you take the single responsibility principle literally, you would implement separate services for creating and changing a password and for checking that a password is correct. However, these simple services would all have to use a shared password database. This is undesirable because it increases the coupling between these services. Responsibility, therefore, should not always mean a single, functional activity. In this case, I would interpret a single responsibility as the responsibility to maintain stored passwords, and I would design a single microservice to do this.

The term "microservices" implies that services are small-scale components, so developers often ask "How big should a microservice be?" Unfortunately, there is no easy way to answer this question. I don't think it is sensible to use a measure such as lines of code, especially as services can be written in different programming languages. Rather, I think the "rule of twos" is perhaps the most useful when you are thinking about the size of microservices:

- It should be possible for a microservice to be developed, tested, and deployed by a service development team in two weeks or less.

- The team size should be such that the whole team can be fed by no more than two large pizzas (Amazon's guideline). This places an upper limit on the team size of eight to ten people (depending on how hungry they are).

You may think that, because microservices have to do only one thing, there really isn't a lot of code involved. Aren't they just like a function or a

Figure 6.3 Password management functionality

User functions	Supporting functions
Create password	Check password validity
Change password	Delete password
Check password	Back up password database
Recover password	Recover password database
	Check database integrity
	Repair password database

class in a program? Why might a development team of eight to ten people be needed? In essence, this many people may be needed because the team is not just responsible for implementing the service functionality. They must also develop all the code that is necessary to ensure that a microservice is completely independent, such as UI code, security code, and so on.

Furthermore, members of the service team are usually responsible for testing services, maintaining the team's software development environment, and supporting the service after it has been deployed. Testing is not simply the unit testing of the service functionality but also the testing of its interactions with other services in the overall system. The testing process is usually automated, and it requires a lot of time and effort to program comprehensive service tests.

Although microservices should focus on a single responsibility, this does not mean they are like functions that do only one thing. Responsibility is a broader concept than functionality, and the service development team has to implement all the individual functions that implement the service's responsibility. To illustrate this, Figure 6.3 shows the range of functionality that might be included in a password management microservice.

In addition to this functionality, the independence of microservices means that each service has to include support code that may be shared in a monolithic system. Figure 6.4 shows support code that is needed in all microservices. For many services, you need to implement more support code than the code that delivers the service functionality.

Message management code in a microservice is responsible for processing incoming and outgoing messages. Incoming messages have to be checked for validity, and the data extracted from the message format are used. Outgoing messages have to be packed into the correct format for service communication.

Figure 6.4 Microservice support code

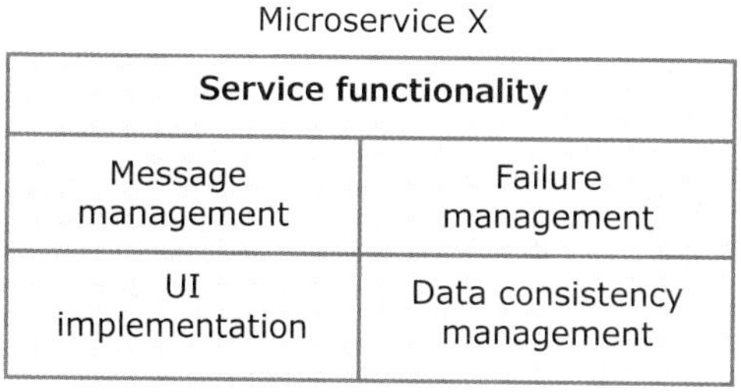

Microservice X

Service functionality	
Message management	Failure management
UI implementation	Data consistency management

Failure management code in a microservice has two concerns. First, it has to cope with circumstances where the microservice cannot properly complete a requested operation. Second, if external interactions are required, such as a call to another service, it has to handle the situation where that interaction does not succeed because the external service returns an error or does not reply.

Data consistency management is needed when the data used in a microservice are also used by other services. In those cases, there needs to be a way of communicating data updates between services and ensuring that the changes made in one service are reflected in all services that use the data. I explain consistency management and failure management later in this chapter.

For complete independence, each microservice should maintain its own user interface. Microservice support teams must agree on conventions for this interface and, within these conventions, each microservice may offer a user interface that is tailored to the microservice's responsibility.

6.2 Microservices architecture

A microservices architecture is not like a layered application architecture that defines the common set of components used in all applications of a particular kind. Rather, a microservices architecture is an *architectural style*— a tried and tested way of implementing a logical software architecture. For web-based applications, this architectural style is used to implement logical client-server architectures, where the server is implemented as a set of interacting microservices.

The microservices architectural style aims to address two fundamental problems with the multi-tier software architecture for distributed systems, which I introduced in Chapter 4:

Table 6.2 A photo-printing system for mobile devices

Imagine that you are developing a photo-printing service for mobile devices. Users can upload photos to your server from their phone or specify photos from their Instagram account that they would like to be printed. Prints can be made at different sizes and on different media.

Users can choose print size and print medium. For example, they may decide to print a picture onto a mug or a T-shirt. The prints or other media are prepared and then posted to their home. They pay for prints either using a payment service such as Android or Apple Pay or by registering a credit card with the printing service provider.

1. When a monolithic architecture is used, the whole system has to be rebuilt, retested, and re-deployed when any change is made. This can be a slow process, as changes to one part of the system can adversely affect other components. Frequent application updates are therefore impossible.

2. As the demand on the system increases, the whole system has to be scaled, even if the demand is localized to a small number of system components that implement the most popular system functions. Larger servers must be used, and this significantly increases the costs of renting cloud servers to run the software. Depending on how virtualization is managed, starting up a larger server can take several minutes, with the system service degraded until the new server is up and running.

Microservices are self-contained and run in separate processes. In cloud-based systems, each microservice may be deployed in its own container. This means a microservice can be stopped and restarted without affecting other parts of the system. If the demand on a service increases, service replicas can be quickly created and deployed. These do not require a more powerful server, so scaling out is typically much cheaper than scaling up.

Let's start with an example to see what a system that uses a microservices architecture might look like. Table 6.2 is a brief description of a photo-printing system.

In a monolithic client–server system, the photo-printing functionality would be implemented in the business logic tier, with all information held in a common database. By contrast, a microservices architecture uses separate services for each area of functionality. Figure 6.5 is a diagram of a possible high-level system architecture for a photo-printing system. Some of the services shown might be decomposed into more specialized microservices, but I do not show this here.

The API gateway shown in Figure 6.5 is an important component that insulates the user app from the system's microservices. The gateway is a single

Figure 6.5 A microservices architecture for a photo-printing system

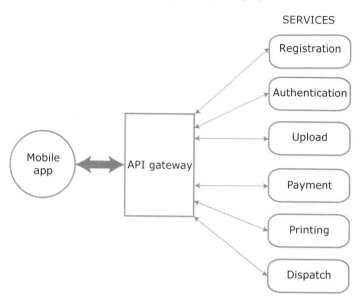

point of contact and translates service requests from the app into calls to the microservices used in the system. This means that the app does not need to know what service communication protocol is being used. Using a gateway also means it is possible to change the service decomposition by splitting or combining services without affecting the client app.

6.2.1   Architectural design decisions

In a microservice-based system, the development teams for each service are autonomous. They make their own decisions about how best to provide the service. This means the system architect should not make technology decisions for individual services; these are left to the service implementation team. For practical reasons, however, teams should not use too many different technologies. There are costs, such as the purchase and maintenance of a development environment, in supporting each technology used. It also takes time and effort for developers to learn about new technologies when they move from one team to another.

Although individual microservices are independent, they have to coordinate and communicate to provide the overall system service. Therefore, to design a microservices architecture, you have to consider the key design issues shown in Figure 6.6.

Figure 6.6 Key design questions for microservices architecture

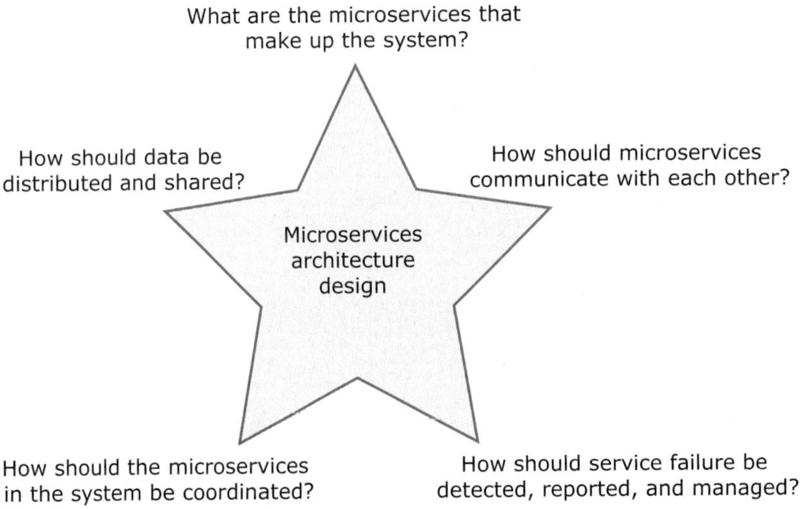

One of the most important jobs for a system architect is to decide how the overall system should be decomposed into a set of microservices. As I explained in the introduction, this is not just a matter of making each system function as a microservice. Too many microservices in a system mean that there will be many service communications and the time needed for process communications slows down the system. Too few microservices means that each service must have more functionality. The services will be larger, with more dependencies, so changing them is likely to be more difficult.

Unfortunately, there is no simple method you can follow to decompose a system into microservices. However, some general design guidelines may be helpful:

1. *Balance fine-grain functionality and system performance* In single-function services, changes are typically limited to few services. If each of your services offers only a single, very specific service, however, it is inevitable that you will need to have more service communications to implement user functionality. This slows down a system because each service has to bundle and unbundle messages sent from other services.

2. *Follow the "common closure principle"* This means that elements of a system that are likely to be changed at the same time should be located within the same service. Most new and changed requirements should therefore affect only a single service.

3. *Associate services with business capabilities* A business capability is a discrete area of business functionality that is the responsibility of an individual or a group. For example, the provider of a photo-printing system will have a group responsible for sending photos to users (dispatch capability), a set of printing machines (print capability), someone responsible for finance (payment service), and so on. You should identify the services that are required to support each business capability.

4. *Design services so that they have access to only the data that they need* In situations with an overlap between the data used by different services, you need to have a mechanism that ensures that data changes in one service are propagated to other services that use the same data.

One possible starting point for microservice identification is to look at the data that services have to manage. It usually makes sense to develop microservices around logically coherent data, such as passwords, user identifiers, and so on. This avoids the problem of having to coordinate the actions of different services to ensure that shared data are consistent.

Experienced microservice developers argue that the best way to identify the microservices in a system is to start with a monolithic architecture based on the traditional multi-tier client–server model that I described in Chapter 4. Once you have experience of a system and some data about how it is used, it is much easier to identify the functionality that should be encapsulated in microservices. You should then refactor your monolithic software into a microservices architecture.

6.2.2   Service communications

Services communicate by exchanging messages. These messages include information about the originator of the message as well as the data that are the input to or output from the request. The messages that are exchanged are structured to follow a message protocol. This is a definition of what must be included in each message and how each component of the message can be identified.

When you are designing a microservices architecture, you have to establish a standard for communications that all microservices should follow. Key decisions that you have to make are:

■ Should service interaction be synchronous or asynchronous?

■ Should services communicate directly or via message broker middleware?

■ What protocol should be used for messages exchanged between services?

Figure 6.7 Synchronous and asynchronous microservice interaction

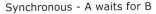
Synchronous - A waits for B

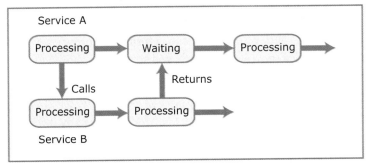

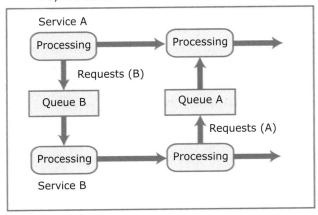
Asynchronous - A and B execute concurrently

Figure 6.7 illustrates the difference between synchronous and asynchronous interaction.

In a synchronous interaction, service A issues a request to service B. Service A then suspends processing while service B is processing the request. It waits until service B has returned the required information before continuing execution.

In an asynchronous interaction, service A issues the request that is queued for processing by service B. Service A then continues processing without waiting for service B to finish its computations. Sometime later, service B completes the earlier request from service A and queues the result to be retrieved by service A. Service A therefore has to check its queue periodically to see if a result is available.

Synchronous interaction is less complex than asynchronous interaction. Consequently, synchronous programs are easier to write and understand. There will

Figure 6.8 Direct and indirect service communication

Direct communication - A and B send messages to each other

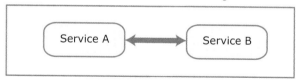

Indirect communication - A and B communicate through a message broker

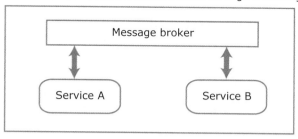

probably be fewer difficult-to-find bugs. On the other hand, asynchronous interaction is often more efficient than synchronous interaction, as services are not idle while waiting for a response. Services that interact asynchronously are loosely coupled, so making changes to these services should be easier. If service developers don't have much experience in concurrent programming, however, it usually takes longer to develop a reliable asynchronous system.

I recommend starting with the simplest approach, which is synchronous interaction. However, you should be prepared to rewrite some services to interact asynchronously if you find that the performance of the synchronous system is not good enough.

Direct service communication requires that interacting services know each other's addresses. The services interact by sending requests directly to these addresses. Indirect communication involves naming the service that is required and sending that request to a message broker (sometimes called a message bus). The message broker is then responsible for finding the service that can fulfill the service request. Figure 6.8 shows these communication alternatives.

Direct service communication is usually faster, but it means that the requesting service must know the URI (uniform resource identifier) of the requested service. If that URI changes, then the service request will fail.

Indirect communication requires additional software (a message broker) but services are requested by name rather than a URI. The message broker finds the address of the requested service and directs the request to it. This is particularly useful where services exist in several versions. The requesting service does not need to know the specific version being used. By default, the message broker can direct requests to the most recent version.

Message brokers, such as the API gateway shown in Figure 6.5, route a service request to the correct service. They may also handle message translation from one format to another. A service that accesses another service through a message broker does not need to know details of where that service is located or its message format. RabbitMQ is an example of a widely used message broker.

Message brokers can support synchronous and asynchronous interactions. A requesting service simply sends a service request to the message broker and either waits for a response or continues processing. When the service request is complete, the message broker takes care of ensuring that the response is in the right format and informs the original service that it is available.

If you use a message broker, it is easier to modify and replace services without affecting the clients using these services. However, this flexibility means that the overall system becomes more complex. Direct service communication is simple and easy to understand. It is usually faster to develop products using direct service communication.

A message protocol is an agreement between services that sets out how messages between these services should be structured. Protocols can be strictly defined, as in the Advanced Message Queuing Protocol (AMQP) that is supported by RabbitMQ and other message brokers. The protocol definition sets out what data must be included in a message and how they must be organized. The message broker rejects messages that do not follow the definition.

However, the most widely used approach to direct service communication does not have a formal definition. RESTful services follow the REST architectural style with the message data represented using JSON. The operations offered by these services can be represented using the verbs supported by the HTTP Internet Protocol: GET, PUT, POST, and DELETE. The service is represented as a resource that has its own URI.

Because of the ubiquity of RESTful services, I focus on how you can use this approach rather than a more complex approach based on message brokers and AMQP. In Section 6.3, I explain the fundamentals of RESTful services and show how they can be organized.

6.2.3 Data distribution and sharing

A general rule of microservice development is that each microservice should manage its own data. In an ideal world, the data managed by each service would be completely independent. There would be no need to propagate data changes made in one service to other services.

In the real world, however, complete data independence is impossible. There will always be overlaps between the data used in different services. Consequently, as an architect, you need to think carefully about sharing data and managing data consistency. You need to think about the microservices as an interacting system rather than as individual units. This means:

1. You should isolate data within each system service with as little data sharing as possible.

2. If data sharing is unavoidable, you should design microservices so that most sharing is read-only, with a minimal number of services responsible for data updates.

3. If services are replicated in your system, you must include a mechanism that can keep the database copies used by replica services consistent.

Multi-tier client–server systems use a shared database architecture where all system data are maintained in a shared database. Access to those data is managed by a database management system (DBMS). The DBMS can ensure that the data are always consistent and that concurrent data updates do not interfere with each other.

Failure of services in the system and concurrent updates to shared data have the potential to cause database inconsistency. Without controls, if services A and B are updating the same data, the value of that data depends on the timing of the updates. However, by using ACID transactions, the DBMS serializes the updates and avoids inconsistency.

An ACID transaction bundles a set of data updates into a single unit so that either all updates are completed or none of them are. The database is always consistent because, in the event of some kind of failure, there are no partial updates to the data. You need this for some kinds of system. For example, if you move money from account A to account B within the same bank, it would be unacceptable for account A to be debited without crediting the same amount to account B.

When you use a microservices architecture, this kind of transaction is difficult to implement efficiently unless you can confine the data involved in the transaction to a single microservice. However, this almost certainly means that you have to break the rule of a microservice having a single responsibility. Consequently, if you are implementing a system, such as a banking system, where absolute data consistency at all times is a critical requirement, you should normally use a shared database architecture.

In any distributed system, there is a trade-off between data consistency and performance. The stricter the requirements for data consistency, the more computing you have to do to ensure that the data are consistent. Furthermore, you may need to implement locks on data to ensure that updates do not interfere with each other. This means services could be slow because the data that they need are locked. The service using the data must finish its operation and release the lock on the data.

Systems that use microservices have to be designed to tolerate some degree of data inconsistency. The databases used by different services or service replicas need not be completely consistent all of the time. Of course, you need a means to ensure that the common data are eventually made consistent. This may execute when the load on the system is relatively light so that overall system performance is unaffected.

Two types of inconsistency have to be managed:

1. *Dependent data inconsistency* The actions or failures of one service can cause the data managed by another service to become inconsistent.

2. *Replica inconsistency* Several replicas of the same service may be executing concurrently. These all have their own database copy and each updates its own copy of the service data. You need a way of making these databases "eventually consistent" so that all replicas are working on the same data.

To illustrate these inconsistency issues, consider a simple example of a user placing an online order for a book. This triggers a number of services, including:

■ a stock management service that reduces the number of books in stock by 1 and increases the number of books that are "pending sale" by 1;

■ an order service that places the order in a queue of orders to be fulfilled.

These services are dependent because a failure of the ordering service means that the stock level for the book ordered is incorrect. To manage this situation, you need to be able to detect service failure. When a failure is detected, you need to initiate actions to correct the stock level for the book.

One way of managing this inconsistency is to use a "compensating transaction," which is a transaction that reverses the previous operation. In this case, when the failure of the ordering service is detected, a compensating transaction may be created. This is processed by the stock management service, which increments the stock level for the book that was not actually ordered, so it is still available.

However, compensating transactions do not guarantee that problems will not arise. For example, in the time gap between the failure of the order service

Figure 6.9 Using a pending transaction log

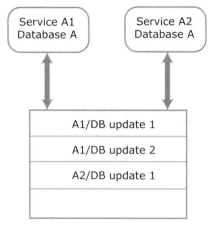

Pending transactions log

and the issue of the compensating transaction, another order could be placed. If the failed order had reduced the number in stock to zero, then the new order would not succeed.

To illustrate the problem of replica inconsistency, consider a situation where two identical instances of a stock management service (A and B) are in use. Each has its own stock database. Imagine the following scenario:

▪ Service A updates the number of books in stock for book X.

▪ Service B updates the number of books in stock for book Y.

The stock databases used in each service are now inconsistent. Service A does not have the correct stock level for book Y, and service B does not have the correct stock level for book X. There needs to be a way for each instance of the service to update its own database so that all of the database replicas become consistent. To do this, you use an "eventual consistency" approach.

Eventual consistency means the system guarantees that the databases will eventually become consistent. You can implement eventual consistency by maintaining a transaction log, as shown in Figure 6.9. When a database change is made, it is recorded on a "pending updates" log. Other service instances look at this log, update their own database, and indicate that they have made the change. After all services have updated their own database, the transaction is removed from the log.

When a service starts to process a service request, the service replica handling the request checks the log to see if the data required in that request have been updated. If so, it updates its own data from the log and then initiates its own operation. Otherwise, the database can be updated from the log whenever the load on the service is relatively light.

In practice, you sometimes need a more complex approach than a simple transaction log to deal with the timing issues that can arise with concurrent database updates. I don't cover these more complex aspects of eventual consistency here.

6.2.4 Service coordination

Most user sessions involve a series of interactions in which operations have to be carried out in a specific order. This is called a workflow. As an example, the workflow for UID/password authentication in which there is a limited number of allowed authentication attempts is shown in Figure 6.10. For simplicity, I've ignored the situation where users have forgotten their password or UID. Operations are shown in round-edged rectangles, relevant state values are in boxes, and choices are indicated by a diamond symbol.

In this example workflow, the user is allowed three login attempts before the system indicates that the login has failed. The user must input both a user name and then a password even if the user name is invalid. You should implement authentication like this so that a malicious user does not know whether an incorrect login name or an incorrect password caused the failure.

One way to implement this workflow is to define the workflow explicitly (either in a workflow language or in code) and to have a separate service that executes the workflow by calling the component services in turn. This is called "orchestration," reflecting the notion that an orchestra conductor instructs the musicians when to play their parts. In an orchestrated system, there is an overall controller. The workflow shown in Figure 6.10 would be managed by an authentication controller component.

An alternative approach that is often recommended for microservices is called "choreography." This term is derived from dance rather than music, where there is no "conductor" for the dancers. Rather, the dance proceeds as dancers observe one another. Their decision to move on to the next part of the dance depends on what the other dancers are doing.

In a microservices architecture, choreography depends on each service emitting an event to indicate that it has completed its processing. Other services watch for events and react accordingly when events are observed. There is no explicit service controller. To implement service choreography,

Figure 6.10 Authentication workflow

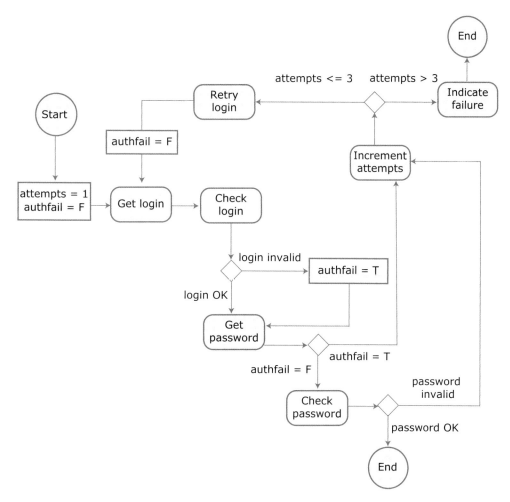

you need additional software such as a message broker that supports a publish and subscribe mechanism. Publish and subscribe means that services "publish" events to other services and "subscribe" to those events that they can process.

Figure 6.11 shows this difference between choreography and orchestration.

A problem with service choreography is that there is no simple correspondence between the workflow and the actual processing that takes place. This makes choreographed workflows harder to debug. If a failure occurs during workflow processing, it is not immediately obvious what service has failed. Furthermore, recovering from a service failure is sometimes difficult to implement in a choreographed system.

Figure 6.11 Orchestration and choreography

Service orchestration   Service choreography

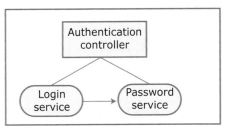
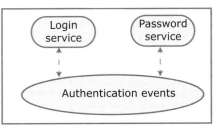

In an orchestrated approach, if a service fails, the controller knows which service has failed and where the failure has occurred in the overall process. In a choreographed approach, you need to set up a service monitoring system that can detect service failures and unavailability and react to correct these. In the example shown in Figure 6.10, you may need a reporting service that examines the authentication events and reports failures to the user if you implement this using service choreography.

In his book *Building Microservices*, Sam Newman[1] recommends that service choreography usually be preferred to service orchestration. He argues that using service choreography leads to a less tightly coupled system that is, therefore, easier to change than an orchestrated system.

I disagree with this recommendation because of the debugging and failure management issues I have explained. Service coordination using orchestration is simpler to implement than service choreography. I advise that you start with the simplest approach (orchestration). You should rewrite your software using service choreography only if you find that the inflexibility of orchestrated services is slowing down your software, or if you have problems making software changes.

6.2.5   Failure management

The reality of any large-scale system is that things go wrong. Even when certain types of failure have a low probability, if there are thousands of service instances in a cloud-based system, failures will inevitably occur. Consequently, services have to be designed to cope with failure.

---

[1]Sam Newman, Building Microservices (Sebastopol, CA: O'Reilly Media, 2015).

Table 6.3 Failure types in a microservices system

Failure type	Explanation
Internal service failure	These are conditions that are detected by the service and can be reported to the service requestor in an error message. An example of this type of failure is a service that takes a URL as an input and discovers that this is an invalid link.
External service failure	These failures have an external cause that affects the availability of a service. Failure may cause the service to become unresponsive and actions have to be taken to restart the service.
Service performance failure	The performance of the service degrades to an unacceptable level. This may be due to a heavy load or an internal problem with the service. External service monitoring can be used to detect performance failures and unresponsive services.

The three kinds of failure you have to deal with in a microservices system are shown in Table 6.3.

The simplest way to report microservice failures is to use HTTP status codes, which indicate whether or not a request has succeeded. Service responses should include a status that reflects the success or otherwise of the service request. Status code 200 means the request has been successful, and codes from 300 to 500 indicate some kind of service failure. Requests that have been successfully processed by a service should always return the 200 status code.

Imagine a situation where a service is given a URL by a calling service but, for some reason, this URL is unreachable. An HTTP GET request made to the unreachable URL returns a status code of 404. The requested service then has to inform the service requester that the operation has not completed successfully. It then returns the 404 code to the calling service to indicate that the service request had failed because of an unreachable resource.

System architects have to ensure that there is an agreed standard on what the HTTP status codes actually mean so that all services return the same status code for the same type of failure. HTTP status codes were designed for web interaction, but your services will have other types of failure that should be reported using status codes.

For example, if a service accepts an input structure representing an order and this is malformed in some way, you might use status code 422, which is defined to mean "Unprocessable entity." If all your services understand that this code means that a service has received a malformed input, then they can cooperate to provide the client with helpful failure information.

One way to discover whether a service that you are requesting is unavailable or running slowly is to put a timeout on the request. A timeout is a counter that is associated with the service requests and starts running when the request is made. Once the counter reaches some predefined value, such as 10 seconds, the calling service assumes that the service request has failed and acts accordingly.

Martin Fowler[2] explains that the problem with the timeout approach is that every service call to a "failed service" is delayed by the timeout value, so the whole system slows down. Instead of using timeouts explicitly when a service call is made, he suggests using a circuit breaker. Like an electrical circuit breaker, this immediately denies access to a failed service without the delays associated with timeouts.

Figure 6.12 illustrates the idea of a circuit breaker. In this example, service S1 makes a request to service S2. Instead of calling a service directly, the service call is routed through a circuit breaker.

The circuit breaker includes a service timeout mechanism that starts when service S1 sends a request to service S2. If service S2 responds quickly, then the response is returned to the calling service. If service S2 does not respond after several retries, however, the circuit breaker assumes that service S2 has failed, and it blows. This means that when a future call is made to the service that is timing out, the circuit breaker immediately responds with a failure status code. The requesting service does not need to wait for the requested service to time out before detecting a problem.

If you use a circuit breaker, you can include code within the circuit breaker that tests whether the failed service has recovered. Periodically, the circuit breaker sends a request to the failed service. If the called service responds quickly, the circuit breaker "resets" the circuit so that future external service calls are routed to the now-available service. To keep the diagram simple, however, I do not show this in Figure 6.12.

A circuit breaker is an example of a service monitoring system. In a production microservices system, it is important to monitor the performance of services in detail. As well as overall service response time, you may monitor the response time of each service operation. This helps you identify possible bottlenecks in the system. You should also monitor the failures that services detect, as this may give you pointers to ways that the service can be improved. Generally, service monitors produce detailed logs, and a "monitoring dashboard" is used to analyze and present these logs to the system managers.

---

[2]https://martinfowler.com/bliki/CircuitBreaker.html

Figure 6.12 Using a circuit breaker to cope with service failure

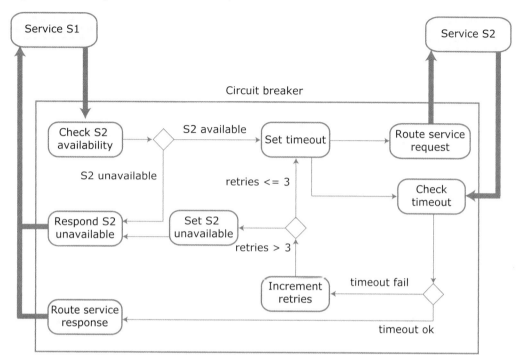

6.3 RESTful services

Microservices may communicate synchronously or asynchronously, using different protocols for message organization and communication. I don't have space to go into all of the possible protocols here, so I focus on one of the most commonly used approaches for service interaction—namely, the RESTful "protocol."

Strictly speaking, there is no such thing as a RESTful protocol, as this approach has not been standardized. Rather, it is a set of conventions for service communication based on the HTTP Internet Protocol and the hierarchical representation of resources. RESTful services follow the REST (REpresentational State Transfer) architectural style and communicate using the HTTP protocol.

The REST architectural style is based on the idea of transferring representations of digital resources from a server to a client. This is the fundamental approach used in the web, where the resource is a page to be displayed in the user's browser. An HTML representation is generated by the server in

Table 6.4 RESTful service principles

Principle	Explanation
Use HTTP verbs	The basic methods defined in the HTTP protocol (GET, PUT, POST, DELETE) must be used to access the operations made available by the service.
Stateless services	Services must never maintain internal state. As I have already explained, microservices are stateless, so fit with this principle.
URI addressable	All resources must have a URI, with a hierarchical structure, that is used to access subresources.
Use XML or JSON	Resources should normally be represented in JSON or XML or both. Other representations, such as audio and video representations, may be used if appropriate.

response to an HTTP GET request and is transferred to the client for display by a browser or a special-purpose app.

The same resource may be represented in different ways. For example, if you think of this book as a resource, it has at least four electronic representations:

1. A representation in a format known as Markdown. This text format is used by the Ulysses editor, which I used to write the book.

2. A representation in Microsoft Word, which is the representation I used to deliver the book to the publisher for typesetting and editing.

3. A representation in Adobe InDesign, which is the typeset representation of the book for printing.

4. A PDF representation, which is the delivery representation for some electronic versions of the book.

The server managing the resource is responsible for delivering that resource in the representation requested by the client. For RESTful microservices, JSON is the most commonly used representation for digital resources. XML may be used as an alternative. XML is a markup language, like HTML, where each element has opening and closing tags. These are structured notations based on plain text that can be used to represent structured data such as database records. I show examples of each of these representations later in this section, in Table 6.7.

The RESTful architectural style assumes client–server interaction and is defined by a number of RESTful principles as shown in Table 6.4.

Table 6.5 RESTful service operations

Action	Implementation
Create	Implemented using HTTP POST, which creates the resource with the given URI. If the resource has already been created, an error is returned.
Read	Implemented using HTTP GET, which reads the resource and returns its value. GET operations should never update a resource so that successive GET operations with no intervening PUT operations always return the same value.
Update	Implemented using HTTP PUT, which modifies an existing resource. PUT should not be used for resource creation.
Delete	Implemented using HTTP DELETE, which makes the resource inaccessible using the specified URI. The resource may or may not be physically deleted.

Resources that are accessed via their unique URI[3] and RESTful services operate on these resources. You can think of a resource as any chunk of data, such as credit card details, an individual's medical record, a magazine or newspaper, a library catalog, and so on. Therefore, the following URI might be used to reference this book in a publisher's catalog:

http://bookpublisher.com/catalog/computer-science/software-engineering/sommerville/Engineering-Software-Products

Four fundamental operations act on resources. Table 6.5 shows these operations and explains how they are mapped to the standard HTTP verbs.

To illustrate how this works, imagine a system that maintains information about incidents, such as traffic delays, roadworks, and accidents on a national road network. This system can be accessed via a browser using this URL:

https://trafficinfo.net/incidents/

Users can query the system to discover incidents on the roads they are planning to travel.

With a RESTful web service, you need to design the resource structure so that incidents are organized hierarchically. For example, incidents may be recorded according to the road identifier (e.g., A90), the location (e.g., Stonehaven), the carriageway direction (e.g., north), and an incident number (e.g., 1). Therefore, each incident can be accessed using its URI:

https://trafficinfo.net/incidents/A90/stonehaven/north/1

---

[3]A URI (uniform resource identifier) is a means of identifying resources. For practical purposes, you can think of it as the same as a URL. There are subtle differences, which are explained here: https://danielmiessler.com/study/url-uri/#gs.uK=UmgM

Table 6.6 Incident description

Incident ID: A90N17061714391

Date: 17 June 2017

Time reported: 1439

Severity: Significant

Description: Broken-down bus on north carriageway. One lane closed. Expect delays of up to 30 minutes.

Accessing this URI returns a description of the incident, including the time reported, its status such as minor, significant, or serious, and a narrative explanation as shown in Table 6.6.

Four operations are supported by this information service:

1. *Retrieve* returns information about a reported incident or incidents; accessed using the GET verb.

2. *Add* adds information about a new incident; accessed using the POST verb.

3. *Update* updates the information about a reported incident; accessed using the PUT verb.

4. *Delete* deletes an incident. The DELETE verb is used when an incident has been cleared.

RESTful microservices accept HTTP requests based on the RESTful style, process these requests, and create HTTP responses to them (Figure 6.13).

Figure 6.13 HTTP request and response processing

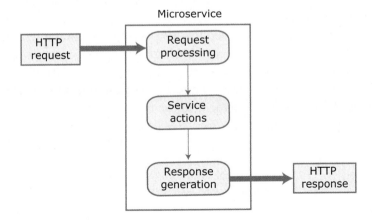

Figure 6.14 HTTP request and response message organization

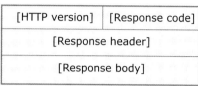

Figure 6.14 shows how requests for a RESTful service and the responses from that service are structured and organized as HTTP messages.

The request and response header component of a message includes metadata about the message body as well as other information about the server, the length of the message, and so on. Most of these details are unimportant and some elements are usually created automatically by your web development environment. For microservices, the critical elements are:

1. *Accept* specifies the content-types that can be processed by the requesting service and that are therefore acceptable in the service response. Commonly used types are text/plain and text/json. These specify that the response can be either plain text or JSON.

2. *Content-Type* specifies the content-type of the request or response body. For example, text/json specifies that the request body includes structured JSON text.

3. *Content-Length* specifies the length of the text in the response body. If this is zero, it means there is no text in the request/response body.

Table 6.7 XML and JSON incident descriptions

XML	JSON

<id>
A90N17061714391
</id>
<date>
20170617
</date>
<time>
1437
</time>
. . .
<description>
Broken-down bus on north carriageway. One lane closed. Expect delays of up to 30 minutes.
</description>
	{
	id: "A90N17061714391",
	"date": "20170617",
	"time": "1437",
	"road_id": "A90",
	"place": "Stonehaven",
	"direction": "north",
	"severity": "significant",
	"description": "Broken-down bus on north carriageway. One lane closed. Expect delays of up to 30 minutes."
	}

Figure 6.15 A GET request and the associated response

REQUEST

| GET | incidents/A90/stonehaven/ | HTTP/1.1 |

Host: trafficinfo.net
...
Accept: text/json, text/xml, text/plain
Content-Length: 0

RESPONSE

| HTTP/1.1 | 200 |

...
Content-Length: 461
Content-Type: text/json

```
{
    "number": "A90N17061714391",
    "date": "20170617",
    "time": "1437",
    "road_id": "A90",
    "place": "Stonehaven",
    "direction": "north",
    "severity": "significant",
    "description": "Broken-down bus on north
    carriageway. One lane closed. Expect
delays of up to 30 minutes."
}
{
    "number": "A90S17061713001",
    "date": "20170617",
    "time": "1300",
    "road_id": "A90",
    "place": "Stonehaven",
    "direction": "south",
    "severity": "minor",
    "description": "Grass cutting on verge.
Minor delays"
}
```

The body of the request or response includes the service parameters and is usually represented in JSON or XML. Table 6.7 shows how a message body might be structured in XML and JSON.

XML is a flexible notation, but quite a lot of overhead is involved in parsing and constructing XML messages. As I explained in Chapter 4, JSON is a simpler structured notation that is more widely used than XML because it is easier to read and process.

Figure 6.15 shows the structure of a GET request for information about incidents at Stonehaven and the message generated by the server in response to that request. If there are no incidents, the service returns status code 204, which indicates that the request has been successfully processed but there is no associated content.

The diagram is largely self-explanatory but these are the key points:

1. The GET request has no message body and a corresponding Content-Length of zero. GET requests only need a message body if you have to specify that some kind of selector is to be applied to the information that is to be returned.

2. The URI specified in the GET request does not include the name of the host server. The name is specified separately. It is mandatory to provide a host name in the request header.

3. The response includes a 200 response code, which means that the request has been successfully processed.

As the HTML transfer protocol used by most RESTful services is a request/response protocol, RESTful services are normally synchronous services.

6.4 Service deployment

After a system has been developed and delivered, it has to be deployed on servers, monitored for problems, and updated as new versions become available. Traditionally, the tasks of managing an operational system were seen as separate from development. The system admin team had different skills from the system developers.

When a system is composed of tens or even hundreds of microservices, deployment of the system is more complex than for monolithic systems. The service development teams decide which programming language, database, libraries, and other support software should be used to implement their service. Consequently, there is no "standard" deployment configuration for all services. Furthermore, services may change very quickly and there is the potential for a "deployment bottleneck" if a separate system admin team is faced with the problem of updating several services at the same time.

Consequently, when a microservices architecture is used, it is now normal practice for the development team to be responsible for deployment and service management as well as software development. This approach is known as DevOps—a combination of "development" and "operations." I discuss general issues of DevOps and the benefits of this approach in Chapter 10.

Figure 6.16 A continuous deployment pipeline

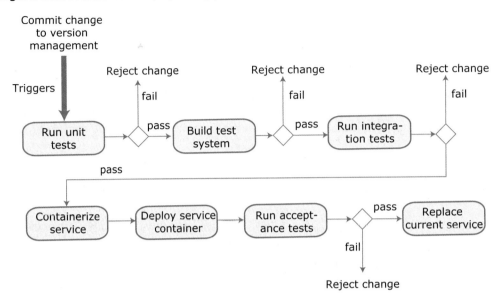

A general principle of microservice-based development is that the service development team has full responsibility for their service, including the responsibility of deciding when to deploy new versions of that service. Good practice in this area is now to adopt a policy of continuous deployment. Continuous deployment means that as soon as a change to a service has been made and validated, the modified service is re-deployed.

This contrasts with the approach used for software products that are installed on a user's own computer. In this situation, the software is deployed in a series of releases. New versions of the software are released periodically, typically three or four times per year. Changes to the system to introduce new features and to fix non-critical bugs are bundled into each new release. Critical bug fixes may be distributed as patches between releases.

Continuous deployment depends on automation so that as soon as a change is committed, a series of automated activities is triggered to test the software. If the software "passes" these tests, it then enters another automation pipeline that packages and deploys the software. Figure 6.16 is a simplified diagram of the continuous deployment process.

The deployment of a new service version starts with the programmer committing the code changes to a code management system such as Git (covered in Chapter 10). This automatically triggers a set of automated tests that run using the modified service. If all service tests run successfully, a new version of the system that incorporates the changed service is created. Another set of automated system tests are then executed. If these run successfully, the service is ready for deployment.

Deployment involves adding the new service to a container and installing the container on a server. Automated "whole system" tests are then executed. If these system tests run successfully, the new version of the service is put into production.

Containers (covered in Chapter 5) are usually the best way to package a cloud service for deployment. Recall that a container is a virtualized environment that includes all the software that a service needs. Containers are a deployment unit that can execute on different servers so that the service development team does not have to take server configuration issues into account. As service dependencies can be predefined and a service container created, deploying a microservice simply involves loading the executable code into the container and then deploying that container on a server or servers.

A large-scale system of microservices may involve managing tens or possibly hundreds of containers that are deployed in the cloud. Managing a large set of communicating containers is a significant problem, so container management systems such as Kubernetes automate container deployment and management. Kubernetes provides Docker container scheduling on a cluster of servers, service discovery, load balancing, and server resource management. Container management is too specialized for this book, so I don't go into any more detail here. However, I provide a link to information about Kubernetes in the Recommended Reading section of this chapter.

A general risk of deploying new software services is that unanticipated problems will be caused by the interactions between the new version of the service and existing services. Testing can never completely eliminate this risk. Consequently, in a microservices architecture, you need to monitor the deployed services to detect problems. If a service fails, you should roll back to an older version of the service.

If you use an API gateway, as shown in Figure 6.5, you could do this by accessing services through a "current version" link. When you introduce a new version of a service, you maintain the old version but change the current version link to point at the new service. If the monitoring system detects problems, it then switches the link back to the older service. I illustrate this in Figure 6.17.

In Figure 6.17, a service request for a cameras service, which might be included in a road incidents information system, is routed to version 002 of that service. The response is returned through the service monitor. If the monitor detects a problem with version 002, it switches the "current version link" back to version 001 of the cameras service.

Figure 6.17 Versioned services

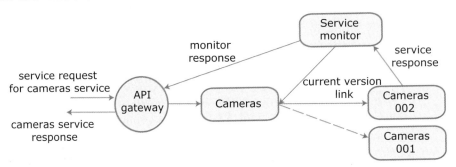

Many service changes are transparent to other services. They do not change the service's API, so dependent services should be unaffected by the change. However, service API's must sometimes change. Services that use the changed service have to be modified, but they must be able to access the service using the older API until those changes have been made.

You can do this by ensuring that the identifier for each service includes the service version number. For example, if you use RESTful services, you can include this version number as part of the resource's URI:

https://trafficinfo.net/incidents/cameras/001/A90/stonehaven/north/1

In this example, the version number is 001. When you introduce a new version of the service, you update the version number. It makes sense to use a numbering convention so that you can identify whether a new version has introduced an API change. For example, you can indicate API changes by changing the first digit of the version number so that version 001 becomes version 101:

https://trafficinfo.net/incidents/cameras/101/A90/stonehaven/north/1

User services can be informed of the API change and can, in time, be changed to use the new service version with the updated API.

KEY POINTS

▪ A microservice is an independent and self-contained software component that runs in its own process and communicates with other microservices using lightweight protocols.

▪ Microservices in a system can be implemented using different programming languages and database technologies.

- Microservices have a single responsibility and should be designed so that they can be easily changed without having to change other microservices in the system.

- Microservices architecture is an architectural style in which the system is constructed from communicating microservices. It is well suited to cloud-based systems where each microservice can run in its own container.

- The two most important responsibilities of architects of a microservices system are to decide how to structure the system into microservices and to decide how microservices should communicate and be coordinated.

- Communication and coordination decisions involve microservice communication protocols, data sharing, whether services should be centrally coordinated, and failure management.

- The RESTful architectural style is widely used in microservice-based systems. Services are designed so that the HTTP verbs—GET, POST, PUT, and DELETE—map onto the service operations.

- The RESTful style is based on digital resources that, in a microservices architecture, may be represented using XML or, more commonly, JSON.

- Continuous deployment is a process in which new versions of a service are put into production as soon as a service change has been made. It is a completely automated process that relies on automated testing to check that the new version is of production quality.

- If continuous deployment is used, you may need to maintain multiple versions of deployed services so that you can switch to an older version if problems are discovered in a newly deployed service.

RECOMMENDED READING

Building Microservices This book is an excellent and readable overview of microservices and the issues to be considered when constructing microservices architectures. (S. Newman, O'Reilly, 2015)

"Microservices" This is probably the most readable introduction to microservices that I have found. I highly recommend it. (J. Lewis and M. Fowler, 2014)

https://martinfowler.com/articles/microservices.html

"RESTful Web Services: A Tutorial" Many tutorials on RESTful web services are available and naturally they are very similar. This tutorial is a comprehensive and clear introduction to the RESTful approach to web service implementation. (M. Vaqqas, 2014)

http://www.drdobbs.com/web-development/restful-web-services-a-tutorial/240169069

"Is REST Best in a Microservices Architecture?" This article questions whether the RESTful approach is the best one to use in a microservices architecture. It suggests that in many circumstances a better approach is to use asynchronous messaging through a message broker. (C. Williams, 2015)

https://capgemini.github.io/architecture/is-rest-best-microservices/

"Kubernetes Primer" This is a good introduction to the Kubernetes container management system. (CoreOS, 2017)

https://coreos.com/resources/index.html#ufh-i-339012759-kubernetes-primer

"Continuous Delivery" Continuous delivery is often used as another name for continuous deployment. This blog includes a series of articles on this topic that expand on the material in this chapter. (J. Humble, 2015)

https://continuousdelivery.com/

PRESENTATIONS, VIDEOS, AND LINKS

https://iansommerville.com/engineering-software-products/microservices-architecture

EXERCISES

6.1 What are the advantages of using services as the fundamental component in a distributed software system?

6.2 Based on the functional breakdown of the authentication features shown in Figure 6.1, create a corresponding breakdown for two-factor authentication and password recovery.

6.3 Explain why microservices should have low coupling and high cohesion.

6.4 What are the principal problems with multi-tier software architectures? How does a microservices architecture help with these problems?

6.5 Explain the differences between synchronous and asynchronous microservices interactions.

6.6 Explain why each microservice should maintain its own data. Explain how data in service replicas can be kept consistent?

6.7 What is a timeout and how is it used in service failure management? Explain why a circuit breaker is a more efficient mechanism than timeouts for handling external service failures.

6.8 Explain what is meant by a "resource." How do RESTful services address resources and operate on them?

6.9 Consider the Upload service for photographs to be printed as shown in Figure 6.5. Suggest how this might be implemented and then design a RESTful interface for this service, explaining the function of each of the HTTP verbs. For each operation, identify its input and output.

6.10 Why should you use continuous deployment in a microservices architecture? Briefly explain each of the stages in the continuous deployment pipeline.

7

Security and Privacy

Software security should always be a high priority for product developers and users. If you don't prioritize security, you and your customers will inevitably suffer losses from malicious attacks. The aim of the attacks may be to steal data or hijack a computer for some criminal purpose. Some attacks try to extort money from a user by encrypting data and demanding a fee for the decryption key, or by threatening a denial of service attack on their servers.

In the worst case, these attacks could put product providers out of business. If providers are delivering a product as a service and it is unavailable or if customer data are compromised, customers are liable to cancel their subscriptions. Even if they can recover from the attacks, this will take a lot of time and effort that would have been better spent working on their software.

Figure 7.1 shows the three main types of threat that computer systems face. Some attacks may combine these threats. For example, a ransomware attack is a threat to the integrity of a system, as it damages data by encrypting them. This makes normal service impossible. Therefore, it is also a threat to the availability of a system.

Security is a system-wide problem. Application software is dependent on an execution platform that includes an operating system, a web server, a language run-time system, and a database. We also depend on frameworks and code generation tools to reuse software that others have developed. Figure 7.2 is a diagram of a system stack that shows the infrastructure systems that your software product may use.

Attacks may target any level in this stack, from the routers that control the network to the reusable components and libraries used by your product. However, attackers usually focus on software infrastructure—the operating system, web browsers, messaging systems, and databases. Everyone uses these, so they are the most effective targets for external attacks.

Figure 7.1 Types of security threat

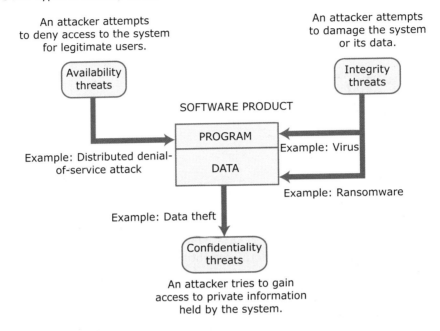

Figure 7.2 System infrastructure stack

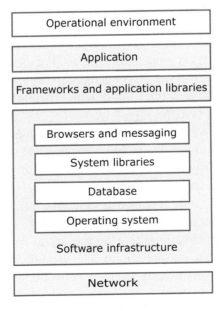

Table 7.1 Security management

Procedure	Explanation
Authentication and authorization	You should have authentication and authorization standards and procedures that ensure that all users have strong authentication and that they have properly set up access permissions. This minimizes the risk of unauthorized users accessing system resources.
System infrastructure management	Infrastructure software should be properly configured, and security updates that patch vulnerabilities should be applied as soon as they become available.
Attack monitoring	The system should be regularly checked for possible unauthorized access. If attacks are detected, it may be possible to put resistance strategies in place that minimize the effects of the attack.
Backup	Backup policies should be implemented to ensure that you keep undamaged copies of program and data files. These can then be restored after an attack.

Maintaining the security of your software infrastructure is a system management rather than a software development issue. You need management procedures and policies to minimize the risk of a successful attack that could ultimately compromise your application system (Table 7.1). Software, such as browsers and operating systems, needs to be updated to ensure that security flaws are fixed. They must be correctly configured so that there are no loopholes that attackers can use to gain access.

Operational security focuses on helping users to maintain security. Attacks on users are very common. Generally, the aim of the attacker is to trick users into disclosing their credentials or accessing a website that includes malware such as a key-logging system. To maintain operational security, you need procedures and practices that advise users how to use your system securely and regular reminders to users of these procedures.

If you offer your product as a cloud-based service, you should include features that help users manage operational security and deal with security problems that may arise. For example:

1. Auto-logout addresses the common problem of users forgetting to log out from a computer used in a shared space. This feature reduces the chances of an unauthorized person gaining access to the system.

2. User command logging makes it possible to discover actions taken by users that have deliberately or accidentally damaged some system resources. This feature helps to diagnose problems and recover from them and also deters malicious legitimate users, as they know that their behavior will be logged.

3. Multifactor authentication reduces the chances of an intruder gaining access to the system using stolen credentials.

Security is a huge topic and my aim here is to introduce some important aspects that are relevant to product developers. This chapter gives you a basic understanding of the issues, but I don't cover detailed security implementation.

7.1 Attacks and defenses

Many types of attack may affect a software system. They depend on the type of system, the way it has been implemented, the potential vulnerabilities in the system, and the environment where the system is used. I focus here on some of the most common types of attack on web-based software.

The targets of the attacks on a computer system may be the system provider or the users of the system. Distributed denial-of-service attacks (see Section 7.1.4) on servers aim to disable access to a system so that users are locked out and the system provider loses revenue. Ransomware attacks disable individual systems in some way and demand a ransom from users to unlock their computers. Data theft attacks may target personal data that can be sold or credit card numbers that can be used illegally.

A fundamental requirement for most attacks is for attackers to be able to authenticate themselves to your system. This usually involves stealing the credentials of a legitimate user. The most common way of doing this is to use social engineering techniques where users click on an apparently legitimate link in an email. This may take them to a lookalike site where they enter their credentials, which are then available to the attacker. Alternatively, the link may take them to a website that installs malware, such as a key logger, that records the user's keystrokes and sends them to the attackers.

7.1.1   Injection attacks

Injection attacks are a type of attack where a malicious user uses a valid input field to input malicious code or database commands. These malicious instructions are then executed, causing some damage to the system. Code can be injected that leaks system data to the attackers. Common types of injection attack include buffer overflow attacks and SQL poisoning attacks.

Buffer overflow attacks are possible when systems are programmed in C or C++. These languages do not automatically check that an assignment to an array element is within the array bounds. You can declare a buffer as an array of a specific size, but the run-time system does not check whether an input exceeds the length of that buffer.

An attacker who understands how the system memory is organized can carefully craft an input string that includes executable instructions. This overwrites the memory and, if a function return address is also overwritten, control can then be transferred to the malicious code.

Modern software products are not usually developed in C or C++, so this type of attack is unlikely to be a major problem for web-based and mobile software products. Most programming languages check for buffer overflows at run time and reject long, malicious inputs. Operating systems and libraries are often written in C or C++, however. If inputs are passed directly from your system to an underlying system function, buffer overflow is a possibility.

SQL poisoning attacks are attacks on software products that use an SQL database. They take advantage of a situation where a user input is part of an SQL command. For example, the following SQL command is intended to retrieve a database record for a single account holder:

```
SELECT * FROM AccountHolders WHERE accountnumber = '34200645'
```

This statement should return those records in the table called Accountholders where the accountnumber field matches '34200645'. The single quotes identify a string to be matched against the named field.

Normally, the account number is input on a form. Let's assume you use a function called getAccountNumber to retrieve this. You can then create this SQL command:

```
accNum = getAccountNumber ()
SQLstat = "SELECT * FROM AccountHolders WHERE accountnumber = '"
+ accNum + "';"
database.execute (SQLstat)
```

This creates a valid SQL statement by catenating the SELECT part with the input variable accNum and adding a semicolon to end the SQL statement. Single quotes must still be included, as the value of accNum is substituted. This generated SQL statement can then be run against the database.

Now imagine that a malicious user inputs the account number as "10010010' OR '1' = '1". When this is inserted into the SQL query, it becomes

```
SELECT * from AccountHolders WHERE accountnumber = '10010010' OR '1' = '1';
```

The final condition is obviously always true, so the query is equivalent to

```
SELECT * from AccountHolders
```

Therefore, details of all account holders are returned and displayed to the malicious user.

SQL poisoning attacks are possible only when the system does not check the validity of the inputs. In this case, if we know that account numbers are eight digits, then the input function getAccountNumber should include an input check for characters other than digits. This would then reject the injected SQL code.

Validating all user inputs is the key to combating injection attacks. I explain how input validation can be implemented in Chapter 8.

7.1.2 Cross-site scripting attacks

Cross-site scripting attacks are another form of injection attack. An attacker adds malicious Javascript code to a web page that is returned from a server to a client, and this script is executed when the page is displayed in the user's browser. The malicious script may steal customer information or direct customers to another website that may try to capture personal data or display advertisements. Cookies may be stolen, which makes a session hijacking attack possible.

The various kinds of cross-site scripting attacks are described in the XSS scripting tutorial that I include in the Recommended Reading section. They all take the same general form, shown in Figure 7.3, which shows an attack to steal a session cookie.

There are three actors in the scenario shown in Figure 7.3: an attacker, a legitimate website that provides user services, and a victim of the attack, who accesses the legitimate website.

Figure 7.3 Cross-site scripting attack

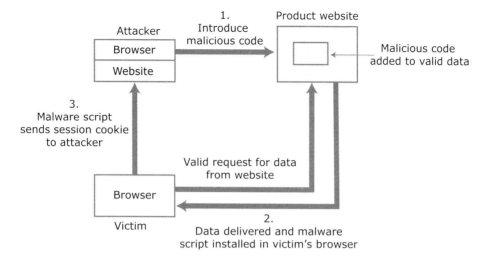

In the simplest type of cross-site scripting attack, the attacker replaces some legitimate information on the website with a malicious script. When the victim accesses that information, a web page is generated that includes the malicious script as well as the legitimate information requested by the victim. This is sent to the victim's browser, where the malicious code is executed. In this example, the malware steals the session cookie. This gives the attacker access to user information on the product website.

As with other types of injection attack, cross-site scripting attacks may be avoided by input validation. Attackers often add the malicious script to the database using a legitimate form. If this is checked for invalid inputs, then the malicious script can be rejected. Another line of defense is to check input from the database before adding it to a generated page. Finally, it is possible to use the HTML "encode" command, which states that information added to a web page is not executable but should be treated as data by the client's browser.

7.1.3   Session hijacking attacks

When a user authenticates with a web application, a session is created. A session is a time period during which the user's authentication is valid. The user doesn't have to re-authenticate for subsequent system interactions. The session is closed when the user logs out from a system. Alternatively, the session may be closed when the system "times out" because there have been no user inputs for a period of time.

Table 7.2 Actions to reduce the likelihood of session hijacking

Action	Explanation
Traffic encryption	Always encrypt the network traffic between clients and your server. This means setting up sessions using https rather than http. If traffic is encrypted, it is harder to monitor to find session cookies.
Multifactor authentication	Always use multifactor authentication and require confirmation of new actions that may be damaging. For example, before a new payee request is accepted, you could ask the user to confirm their identity by inputting a code sent to their phone. You could also ask for password characters to be input before every potentially damaging action, such as transferring funds.
Short timeouts	Use relatively short timeouts on sessions. If there has been no activity in a session for a few minutes, the session should be ended and future requests directed to an authentication page. This reduces the likelihood that an attacker can access an account if a legitimate user forgets to log off when they have finished work.

The authentication process involves placing a token on the user's computer or mobile device. This is called a session cookie. It is sent from the server to the client at the beginning of a session. The session cookie is used by the server to keep track of user actions. Each time the user makes an http request, the session cookie is sent to the server so that it can link this to previous actions.

Session hijacking is a type of attack where an attacker acquires a valid session cookie and uses it to impersonate a legitimate user. There are several ways an attacker can find out the session cookie value, including cross-site scripting attacks and traffic monitoring. In a cross-site scripting attack, the installed malware sends session cookies to the attackers. Traffic monitoring involves attackers capturing the traffic between the client and the server. The session cookie can then be identified by analyzing the data exchanged. Traffic monitoring is relatively easy if unsecured Wi-Fi networks are used and unencrypted data are exchanged.

Session hijacking may be active or passive. In active session hijacking, the attacker takes over a user session and carries out user actions on a server. So, if a user is logged on to a bank, the attacker can set up a new payee account and transfer money to this account. Passive session hijacking occurs when the attacker simply monitors the traffic between the client and the server, looking for valuable information such as passwords and credit card numbers.

Table 7.2 shows various actions you can take to reduce the likelihood of a session hijacking attack.

7.1.4 Denial-of-service attacks

Denial-of-service attacks are attacks on a software system that are intended to make that system unavailable for normal use. They might be used by malicious attackers who disagree with the policies or actions of the product vendor. Alternatively, attackers might threaten a product provider with a denial of service attack and demand payment not to carry out the threat. They set the level of "ransom" lower than the amount they expect the product provider to lose if their system is out of service.

Distributed denial-of-service (DDOS) attacks are the most common type of denial-of-service attacks. These involve distributed computers that have usually been hijacked as part of a botnet, sending hundreds of thousands of requests for service to a web application. There are so many of these that legitimate users are denied access.

Combating a DDOS attack is a system-level activity. Most cloud providers have specialist software available that can detect and drop incoming packets and thus help restore your services to normal operation.

Other types of denial-of-service attacks target application users. For example, user lockout attacks take advantage of a common authentication policy that locks out a user after a number of failed authentication attempts. Users often use their email address as their login name, so if an attacker has access to a database of email addresses, he or she can try to log in using these addresses. The aim is to lock users out rather than gain access and so deny the service to these users.

There have been so many security breaches that it is relatively easy to get lists of email addresses, and these are often used as user identifiers. If you don't lock accounts after failed validation, then you run the risk of attackers being able to log in to your system. If you do, you may be denying access to legitimate users.

You can take two actions to reduce the damage that such an attack may cause:

1. *Temporary lockouts* If you lock out a user for a short time after failed authentication, the user can regain access to your system after a few minutes. This makes it much more complex for attackers to continue their attack, as they have to continually repeat previous login attempts.

2. *IP address tracking* You may log the IP addresses normally used by users to access your system. If there are failed login attempts from a different IP address, then you can lock out further attempts from that address but allow logins from the user's usual IP addresses.

Sometimes attackers are simply vandals whose aim is to crash an application with no monetary motive. They try to do this by inputting very long strings into forms in the hope that these will not be detected. These attacks are relatively simple to circumvent by using input validation and by handling all exceptions that arise when unexpected input is detected.

7.1.5   Brute force attacks

Brute force attacks are attacks on a web application where the attacker has some information, such as a valid login name, but does not have the password for the site. The attacker creates different passwords and tries to log in with each of these. If the login fails, the attacker then repeatedly tries again with a different password.

Attackers may use a string generator that generates every possible combination of letters and numbers and use these as passwords. You may think this would take a long time, but all strings of six characters or fewer can be generated in a few seconds. You can check this using one of the password checkers on the web.[1] The time required to generate passwords depends on the length of the password, so long passwords are more secure.

To speed up the process of password discovery, attackers take advantage of the fact that many users choose easy-to-remember passwords. They start by trying passwords from the published lists of the most common passwords. They then usually try a dictionary attack, using all the words in a dictionary. People find it difficult to remember random character strings, so they choose real words that have some significance for them.

Because brute force attacks involve successive retries, many sites block users after a small number of attempts. The problem with this, as I explained in Section 7.1.4, is that this action blocks out legitimate users. An attacker who has a list of user logins and blocks access to all of them can cause widespread disruption.

Brute force attacks rely on users setting weak passwords, so you can circumvent them by insisting that users set long passwords that are not in a dictionary and are not common words. Two-factor authentication, explained in the next section, is also an effective way of deterring these attacks.

---

[1]For example: https://howsecureismypassword.net/

Figure 7.4 Authentication approaches

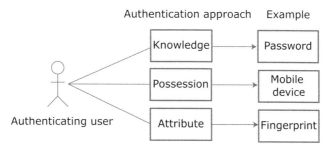

7.2 Authentication

Authentication is the process of ensuring that a user of your system is who they claim to be. You need authentication in all software products that maintain user information so that only the providers of that information can access and change it. You also use authentication to learn about your users so that you can personalize their experience of using your product.

Authentication in software products is based on one or more of three approaches—namely, user knowledge, user possession, and user attributes (Figure 7.4).

Knowledge-based authentication relies on users providing secret, personal information when registering to use the system. Each time a user logs on, the system asks for some or all of this information. If the information provided matches the registered information, the authentication is successful. Passwords are the most widely used method of knowledge-based authentication. An alternative, which is often used with passwords, is personal questions that the authenticating user must answer, such as "name of first school" or "favorite film."

Possession-based authentication relies on the user having a physical device that can be linked to the authenticating system. This device can generate or display information that is known to the authenticating system. The user then inputs this information to confirm that they possess the authenticating device.

The most commonly used version of this type of authentication relies on the user providing their mobile phone number when registering for an account. The authenticating system sends a code to the user's phone number. The user has to input this code to complete the authentication.

An alternative approach, which is used by some banks, is based on a special-purpose device that can generate one-time codes. The device calculates

Table 7.3 Weaknesses of password-based authentication

Weakness	Explanation
Insecure passwords	Users choose passwords that are easy to remember. However, it is also easy for attackers to guess or generate these passwords, using either a dictionary or a brute force attack.
Phishing attacks	Users click on an email link that points to a fake site that tries to collect their login and password details.
Password reuse	Users use the same password for several sites. If there is a security breach at one of these sites, attackers then have passwords that they can try on other sites.
Forgotten passwords	Users regularly forget their passwords, so you need to set up a password recovery mechanism to allow these to be reset. This can be a vulnerability if users' credentials have been stolen and attackers use that mechanism to reset their passwords.

a code based on some aspect of the user input. The user inputs this code and it is compared with the code generated by the authenticating system, using the same algorithm as that encoded in the device.

Attribute-based authentication is based on a unique biometric attribute of the user, such as a fingerprint, which is registered with the system. Some mobile phones can authenticate in this way; others use face recognition for authentication. In principle, this is a very secure approach to authentication, but there are still reliability issues with the hardware and recognition software. For example, fingerprint readers often don't work if the user has hot, damp hands.

Each of these approaches to authentication has advantages and disadvantages. Therefore, to strengthen authentication, many systems now use multi-factor authentication, which combines approaches. Service providers, such as Google, offer two-stage authentication; after inputting a password, the user has to input a code sent to the mobile phone. Using a phone provides another level of security, as the phone has to be unlocked using a code, fingerprint, or in some other way.

If your product is delivered as a cloud service, the most practical authentication approach is knowledge-based authentication based on a password, possibly backed up with other techniques. Everyone is familiar with this authentication method. Unfortunately, password-based authentication has well-known weaknesses, as listed in Table 7.3.

You can reduce the risks of password-based authentication by forcing users to set strong passwords. However, this increases the chances that they will forget their password. You may also ask that individual letters rather than the whole password are input, which means the whole password is not revealed to key-logging malware. You may augment password-based authentication with knowledge-based authentication and require users to answer questions as well as input a password.

The level of authentication that you need depends on your product. If you do not store confidential user information but use authentication to recognize your users, then knowledge-based authentication may be all you need. If you hold confidential user details, however, such as financial information, you should not use knowledge-based authentication on its own. People are now used to two-stage authentication, so you should use phone-based authentication as well as passwords and possibly personal questions.

Implementing a secure and reliable authentication system is expensive and time-consuming. Although toolkits and libraries, such as OAuth, are available for most of the major programming languages, there is still a lot of programming effort involved. Unlike some other aspects of a product, you can't release partial implementations of an authentication system with the aim of extending them in later releases.

For this reason, it is best to think of authentication as a service, even if you are not using a service-oriented approach to build your product. An authentication service can be outsourced using a federated identity system. If you build your own system, you can use a "safer" programming language, such as Java, with more extensive checking and static analysis tools to develop your authentication service. This increases the chances of finding vulnerabilities and programming errors. Your authentication service can also be used for other products that you may develop.

7.2.1 Federated identity

You have almost certainly used websites that offer the opportunity to "Login with Google" or "Login with Facebook." These sites rely on what is called a "federated identity" approach, where an external service is used for authentication.

The advantage of federated identity for users is that they have a single set of credentials that are stored by a trusted identity service. Instead of logging into a service directly, you provide your credentials to a known service that confirms your identity to the authenticating service. You don't have to keep track of different user IDs and passwords. Because your credentials are stored in fewer places, the chances of a security breach where these are revealed is reduced.

Figure 7.5 Federated identity

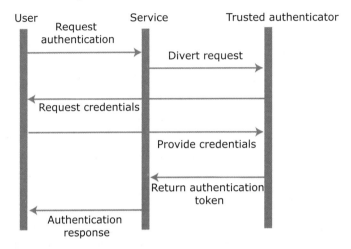

Figure 7.5 is a simplified description of the sequence of actions in a federated identity system.

Consider a product that offers a "Login with Google" option. A user who clicks on this is diverted to the Google identity service. This service validates the user's identity using their Google account credentials. It then returns a token to the diverting site to confirm that the user is a registered Google user. If the user is already logged into a Google service, such as Gmail, then the identity is already registered and there is no need for the user to input any further information.

There are two advantages of using federated identities for authentication:

1. You don't have to maintain your own database of passwords and other secret information. System attackers often try to gain access to this database, so if you maintain your own, you have to take stringent security precautions to protect it. Implementing and maintaining an authentication system are expensive processes for small product companies. Large companies, such as Google and Facebook, have the resources and the expertise to do this.

2. The identity provider may give additional information about users that can be used to personalize your service or to target advertising at users. Of course, when you set up a federated identity system with a major provider, then you have to ask users whether they are willing to share their information with you. There is no guarantee they will agree to this.

Identity verification using Google or Facebook as a trusted service is acceptable for consumer products that are aimed at individual customers. For business products, you can still use federated identity, with authentication based on the business's own identity management system.

If you use a product such as Office 365, you can see how this works. You identify yourself initially to Office 365 using your business email address. The identity management system discovers the business domain from your address and looks up the business's own identity management server. You are diverted to this server, where you input your business credentials, and a token is then sent to the Office 365 system that validates your identity.

Some people dislike federated identity services because of privacy concerns. User information has to be shared with the third-party identity service as a condition of using the service. If Google is the identity service, it therefore knows what software you are using. It can update the data that it holds about you with this information to improve its targeting of personalized advertisements.

There are various ways to implement federated authentication, but most of the major companies that offer federated authentication services use the OAuth protocol. This standard authentication protocol has been designed to support distributed authentication and the return of authentication tokens to the calling system.

However, OAuth tokens do not include information about the authenticated user. They only indicate that access should be granted. This means it is not possible to use OAuth authentication tokens to make decisions on user privileges—for example, what resources of the system they should have access to. To get around this problem, an authentication protocol called OpenID Connect has been developed that provides user information from the authenticating system. Most of the major authentication services now use this, except Facebook, which has developed its own protocol on top of OAuth.

7.2.2 Mobile device authentication

The ubiquity of mobile devices (tablets and phones) means that companies that offer a cloud-based product usually offer users a mobile app to access their service. You can, of course, use exactly the same approach to authentication on a mobile device as you do on a browser. This will probably annoy your users, however, and dissuade them from using your app. Mobile keyboards are fiddly and prone to errors; if you insist on strong passwords, as you should, there's a good chance that users will mistype them.

Figure 7.6 Mobile device authentication

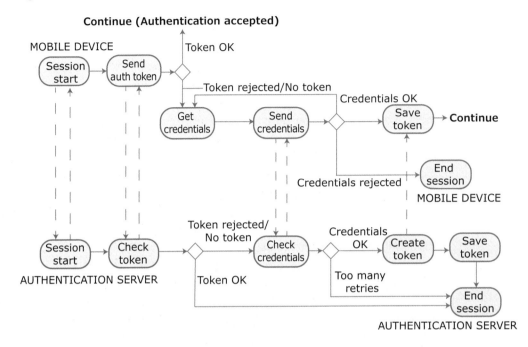

As an alternative to using a login/password pair, a commonly used approach to mobile authentication is to install an authentication token on the mobile device. When the app starts, the token is sent to the service provider to identify the user of the device. This approach to authentication is shown in Figure 7.6.

Users register through the app vendor's website and create an account where they define their authentication credentials. When they install the app, users authenticate themselves using these authentication credentials. These credentials are sent over a secure connection to the authentication server. This server then issues an authentication token that is installed on the user's mobile device. Subsequently, when the app starts, it sends this token to the authentication server to confirm the user's identity. For added security, the authentication token may expire after some period of time so that users have to periodically re-authenticate themselves to the system.

A potential weakness in this approach is that if a device is stolen or lost, then someone who is not the device owner can get access to your product. You can guard against this by checking that the device owner has set up a device passcode or biometric identification that should protect the device from unauthorized access. Otherwise, you require the user to re-authenticate with your app every time it starts up.

Figure 7.7 Elements of an access control policy

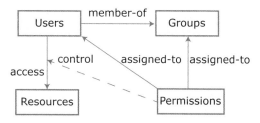

Issuing individual users digital certificates and using certificate-based authentication is a variant of token-based authentication where the token is a digital certificate (see the Recommended Reading section). This is a more secure approach than simple authentication tokens because certificates are issued by trusted providers and their validity can be checked. The same certificate can be used to provide single sign-on across a range of applications. There is a significant overhead in managing certificates, however. You have to either do this yourself or outsource the management to a security service.

You must always encrypt authentication information when it is being sent from the client device to the authentication server. You do this using an https rather than an http connection between the client and the server. I explain secure transmission in Section 7.4.

7.3 Authorization

Authentication involves a user proving their identity to a software system. Authorization is a complementary process in which that identity is used to control access to software system resources. For example, if you use a shared folder on Dropbox, the folder's owner may authorize you to read the contents of that folder but not to add new files or overwrite files in the folder.

When a business wants to define the type of access that users get to resources, this is based on an access control policy. This policy is a set of rules that define what information (data and programs) is controlled, who has access to that information, and the type of access that is allowed (Figure 7.7).

For example, an access control policy may specify that nurses and doctors have access to all medical records stored on the system. Doctors may modify information on a record, but nurses may only add new information. Patients may read their own records and may issue a request for correction if they find what they believe is an error.

If you are developing a product for individual use, you probably don't need to include access control features. Your access control policy is simply that the individual user is allowed to create, read, and modify all of their own information. If you have a multiuser business system or share information in individual accounts, however, then access control is essential.

Explicit access control policies are important for both legal and technical reasons. Data protection rules limit access to personal data, and this must be reflected in the defined access control policy. If this policy is incomplete or does not conform to the data protection rules, then there may be subsequent legal action in the event of a data breach. Technically, an access control policy can be a starting point for setting up the access control scheme for a system. For example, if the access control policy defines the access rights of students, then when new students are registered, they all get these rights by default.

Access control lists (ACLs) are used in most file and database systems to implement access control policies. ACLs are tables that link users with resources and specify what those users are permitted to do. For example, for this book I would like to be able to set up an ACL to a book file that allows reviewers to read that file and annotate it with comments. However, they are not allowed to edit the text or to delete the file.

If ACLs are based on individual permissions, then these lists can become very large. However, you can dramatically cut their size by allocating users to groups and then assigning permissions to the group (Figure 7.8). If you use a hierarchy of groups, then you can add permissions or exclusions to subgroups and individuals.

Figure 7.8 shows examples of ACLs in a university associated with resources A, B, and C. Resource A is a public document that anyone can read. However, it can only be created and edited by staff in the institution and can only be deleted by system administrators. Resource B is an executable program. Anyone can execute it, but only system administrators can create and delete it. Resource C is a student information system. Administrative staff can create, read, and edit records in the system. Teaching staff can read and edit records of students in their department. Students can only read their own record. To ensure that student information is retained, no one has permission to delete student data.

Unless you have a very specialized product, it is not worth developing your own access control system for authorization. Rather, you should use the ACL mechanisms in the underlying file or database system. However, you may decide to implement your own control panel for the ACL system that reflects the data and file types used in your product. This makes it easier to set up and revoke access permissions and reduces the chances of authorization errors.

Figure 7.8 Access control lists

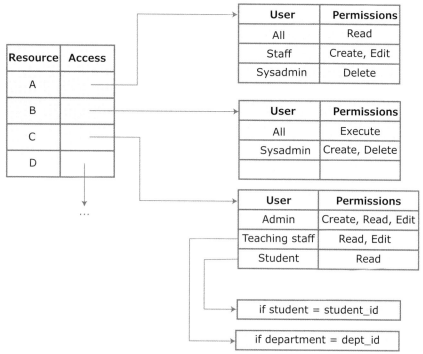

7.4 Encryption

Encryption is the process of making a document unreadable by applying an algorithmic transformation to it. The encryption algorithm uses a secret key as the basis of this transformation. You can decode the encrypted text by applying the reverse transformation. If you choose the right encryption algorithm and secret key, then it is virtually impossible for anyone else to make the text readable without the key.

This encryption and decryption process is shown in Figure 7.9.

Figure 7.9 Encryption and decryption

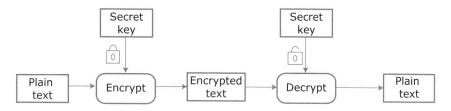

Table 7.4 Technology and encryption

During World War II, the German military used an encryption system based on an electromechanical coding machine called Enigma. They believed it to be practically uncrackable because of the number of combinations that would have to be tested to break the code.

However, Alan Turing, a pioneering British computer scientist, designed two early computers, one electro-mechanical (Bombe) and one electronic (Colossus), specifically to crack the Enigma encryption. These computers could carry out thousands of operations per second, and it became possible to decode a large percentage of encrypted German messages. This was said to have saved thousands of Allied lives and to have hastened the defeat of Nazi Germany by the Allies.

Modern encryption techniques enable you to encrypt data so that they are practically uncrackable using currently available technology. However, history has demonstrated that apparently strong encryption may be crackable when new technology becomes available (Table 7.4). Quantum computers are particularly suited to very fast decryption of text that is encrypted using current encryption algorithms. If commercial quantum systems become available, we will have to use a completely different approach to encryption on the Internet.

Encryption is a complex topic; most engineers, including me, are not experts in the design and implementation of encryption systems. Consequently, I don't give advice on what encryption schemes to use, how to manage encryption keys, and so on. What I aim to do here is give an overview of encryption and make you aware of what you have to think about when making decisions about it.

7.4.1 Symmetric and asymmetric encryption

Symmetric encryption, illustrated in Figure 7.10, has been used for hundreds of years. In a symmetric encryption scheme, the same encryption key is used for both encoding and decoding the information that is to be kept secret. If Alice and Bob wish to exchange a secret message, both must have a copy of the encryption key. Alice encrypts the message with this key. When Bob receives the message, he decodes it using the same key to read its contents.

The fundamental problem with a symmetric encryption scheme is securely sharing the encryption key. If Alice simply sends the key to Bob, an attacker may intercept the message and gain access to the key. The attacker can then decode all future secret communications.

Figure 7.10 Symmetric encryption

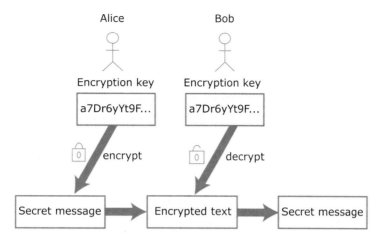

An alternative approach, called asymmetric encryption (Figure 7.11), does not require secret keys to be shared. An asymmetric encryption scheme uses different keys for encrypting and decrypting messages. Each user has a public and a private key. Messages may be encrypted using either key but can only be decrypted using the other key.

As the name suggests, public keys may be published and shared by the key owner. Anyone can access and use a published public key. However, a message can only be decrypted by the user's private key, so is readable by only the intended recipient. For example, in Figure 7.11, Alice encrypts a

Figure 7.11 Asymmetric encryption

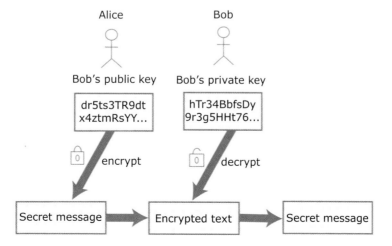

Figure 7.12 Encryption for authentication

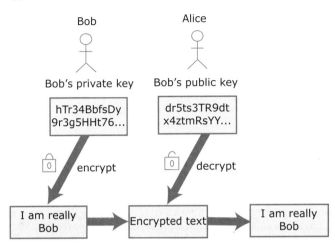

secret message using Bob's public key. Bob decrypts the message using his private key, which only he knows. The message cannot be decrypted with Bob's public key.

Asymmetric encryption can also be used to authenticate the sender of a message by encrypting it with a private key and decrypting it with the corresponding public key. Let's assume Alice wants to send a message to Bob and she has a copy of his public key. However, she is not sure whether or not the public key that she has for Bob is correct, and she is concerned that the message may be sent to the wrong person. Figure 7.12 shows how private/public key encryption can be used to verify Bob's identity. Bob uses his private key to encrypt a message and sends it to Alice. If Alice can decrypt the message using Bob's public key, then Alice has the correct key.

As there isn't a secure key exchange problem, an obvious question is "Why not always use asymmetric rather than symmetric encryption?" The reason is that, for the same level of security (measured by the time required to crack the code), asymmetric encryption takes about 1000 times longer than symmetric encryption. This is proportional to the length of the text being encoded so, in practice, asymmetric encryption is used only for encoding relatively short messages.

Symmetric and asymmetric encryption can be used together. This is the basis of the world's most extensively used encryption scheme for exchanging secure messages on the web. I use this as an example of how to combine symmetric and asymmetric encryption.

Table 7.5 Elements of digital certificates

Certificate element	Explanation
Subject information	Information about the company or individual whose website is being visited. Applicants apply for a digital certificate from a certificate authority who checks that the applicant is a valid organization.
Certificate authority information	Information about the certificate authority (CA) who has issued the certificate.
Certificate information	Information about the certificate itself, including a unique serial number and a validity period, defined by start and end dates.
Digital signature	The combination of all of the above data uniquely identifies the digital certificate. The signature data are encrypted with the CA's private key to confirm that the data are correct. The algorithm used to generate the digital signature is also specified.
Public key information	The public key of the CA is included along with the key size and the encryption algorithm used. The public key may be used to decrypt the digital signature.

7.4.2 TLS and digital certificates

The https protocol is a standard protocol for securely exchanging texts on the web. Basically, it is the standard http protocol plus an encryption layer called TLS (Transport Layer Security). TLS has replaced the earlier SSL (Secure Socket Layer) protocol, which was found to be insecure. This encryption layer has two uses:

- to verify the identity of the web server;

- to encrypt communications so that they cannot be read by an attacker who intercepts the messages between the client and the server.

TLS encryption depends on a digital certificate that is sent from the web server to the client. Digital certificates are issued by a certificate authority (CA), which is a trusted identity verification service. Organizations that buy a digital certificate have to provide information to the CA about their identity, and this identity information is encoded in the digital certificate. Therefore, if a certificate is issued by a recognized CA, the identity of the server can be trusted. Web browsers and apps that use https include a list of trusted certificate providers.

Table 7.5 shows the information that is included in a digital certificate.

Figure 7.13 Using symmetric and asymmetric encryption in TLS

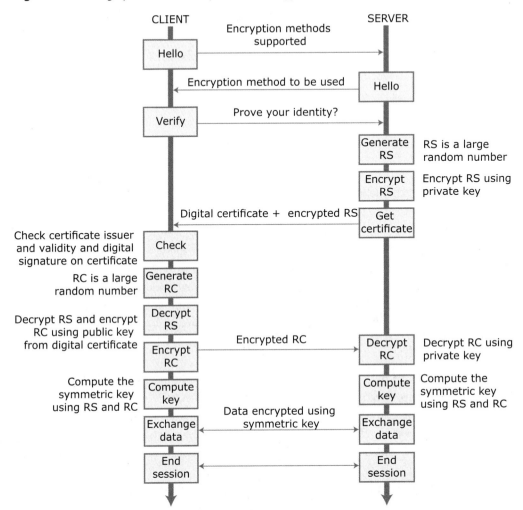

The CA encrypts the information in the certificate using their private key to create a unique signature. This signature is included in the certificate along with the public key of the CA. To check that the certificate is valid, you can decrypt the signature using the CA's public key. The decrypted information should match the other information in the certificate. If not, the certificate has been forged and should be rejected.

When a client and server wish to exchange encrypted information, they communicate to set up a TLS connection. They then exchange messages, as shown in Figure 7.13, to establish the encryption key that both the client and the server will use.

The digital certificate that the server sends to the client includes the server's public key. The server also generates a long random number, encrypts it using its private key, and sends this to the client. The client can then decrypt this using the server's public key and, in turn, generates its own long random number. It encrypts this number using the server's public key and sends it to the server, which decrypts the message using its private key. Both client and server then have two long random numbers.

The agreed encryption method includes a way of generating an encryption key from these numbers. The client and server independently compute the key that will be used to encrypt subsequent messages using a symmetric approach. All client—server traffic is then encrypted and decrypted using that computed key. There is no need to exchange the key itself.

7.4.3   Data encryption

As a product provider, you inevitably store information about your users and, for cloud-based products, user data. User information may include personal information such as addresses, phone numbers, email addresses, and credit card numbers. User data may include documents that the users have created or business databases.

For example, say your product is a cloud-based system for labs that allows them to store and process information on tests of new pharmaceuticals. The database includes information about experiments, the participants in these experiments, and the test results. Theft of these data may compromise the privacy of the participants in the test, and disclosure of the test results may affect the financial position of the testing company.

Encryption can be used to reduce the damage that may occur from data theft. If information is encrypted, it is impossible, or very expensive, for thieves to access and use the unencrypted data. Therefore, you should encrypt user data whenever it is practicable to do so. The practicality of encryption depends on the encryption context:

1. *Data in transit* The data are being moved from one computer to another. Data in transit should always be encrypted. When transferring the data over the Internet, you should always use the https rather than the http protocol to ensure encryption.

2. *Data at rest* The data are being stored. If data are not being used, then the files where the data are stored should be encrypted so that theft of these files will not lead to disclosure of confidential information.

Figure 7.14 Encryption levels

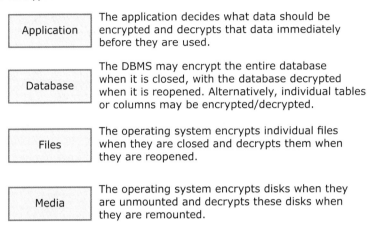

Application	The application decides what data should be encrypted and decrypts that data immediately before they are used.
Database	The DBMS may encrypt the entire database when it is closed, with the database decrypted when it is reopened. Alternatively, individual tables or columns may be encrypted/decrypted.
Files	The operating system encrypts individual files when they are closed and decrypts them when they are reopened.
Media	The operating system encrypts disks when they are unmounted and decrypts these disks when they are remounted.

3. *Data in use* The data are being actively processed. There are problems in using encryption with data that are in use. Encrypting and decrypting the data slow down the system response time. Furthermore, implementing a general search mechanism with encrypted data is impossible because of the difficulties in matching search terms with encrypted data.

Encryption of data is possible at four different levels in the system (Figure 7.14). Generally, more protection is afforded at the higher levels in this stack, as the data are decrypted for a shorter period of time.

Media-level encryption is where an entire disk is encrypted. This provides some limited protection and can be used to protect the data on laptops and portable media if they are lost or stolen. This level is not really relevant to product developers.

File-level encryption involves encrypting entire files and is relevant if you maintain some information in files rather than store everything in a DBMS. Generally, this means you have to provide your own encryption system for your system files. You should not trust the encryption used by cloud providers, such as Dropbox, as they hold the keys and so can access your data.

Most database management systems provide some support for encryption:

1. *Database file encryption* The files in which the database holds its data are encrypted. When the DBMS requests data from a file, it is decrypted as it is transferred to the system's memory and encrypted when it is written back to the file.

2. *"Column-level" encryption* Specific columns in a relational database system are encrypted. For example, if your database holds personal information, you should encrypt the column that holds the user's credit card number. The column need only be decrypted when the number is retrieved—for example, sent in a transaction to the credit card company.

Application-level encryption allows you, as a product developer, to decide what and when data should be encrypted. You implement an encryption scheme within your product to encrypt and decrypt confidential data. Each user of your product chooses a personal encryption key. The data are encrypted in the application that generates or modifies the data rather than relying on database encryption. Consequently, all stored data are always encrypted. You should not store the encryption keys used.

Unfortunately, application-level encryption has several drawbacks:

1. As I said, most software engineers are not encryption experts. Implementing a trustworthy encryption system is complex and expensive, and there is a real possibility that you will make mistakes. This means your system may not be as secure as you intended.

2. Encryption and decryption can significantly affect the performance of your application. The time needed for encryption and decryption slows down the system. Users may either reject your software or not use the encryption feature.

3. In addition to encryption, you need to provide key management functionality, which I cover in the next section. Normally, this involves writing extra code to integrate your application with a key management system.

If you decide to implement encryption in your application, crypto libraries are available for most programming languages. For symmetric encryption, the AES and Blowfish algorithms are very secure, but you should always develop or bring in specialist expertise to help you choose the encryption approach that is most appropriate for your product.

7.4.4 Key management

A general problem in any encryption system is key management. This is the process of ensuring that encryption keys are securely generated, stored, and accessed by authorized users. Businesses may have to manage tens of thousands

Figure 7.15 Using a KMS for encryption management

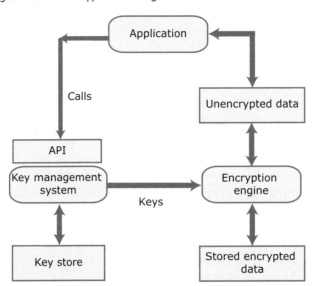

of encryption keys. Because of the huge number of encryption keys and digital certificates that have to be managed, it is impractical to do key management manually. You need to use some kind of automated key management system (KMS).

Key management is important because if you get it wrong, unauthorized users may be able to access your keys and so decrypt supposedly private data. Even worse, if you lose encryption keys, then your encrypted data may be permanently inaccessible.

A KMS is a specialized database designed to securely store and manage encryption keys, digital certificates, and other confidential information. It may provide functionality such as key generation—for example, a public key/private key pair, access control that governs which people and applications can access keys, and key transfer that securely transfers the keys from the KMS to other network nodes.

Figure 7.15 shows the elements of an encryption system with access coordinated using a KMS.

Businesses may be required by accounting and other regulations to keep copies of all of their data for several years. For example, in the United Kingdom, tax and company data have to be maintained for at least six years, with a longer retention period for some types of data. Data protection regulations may require that these data be stored securely, so the data should be encrypted.

To reduce the risks of a security breach, however, encryption keys should be changed regularly. This means that archival data may be encrypted with a different key from the current data in your system. Therefore, a KMS must maintain multiple timestamped versions of keys so that system backups and archives can be decrypted if required.

Some elements of KMS functionality may be provided as a standard OS facility, such as Apple's MacOS Keychain, but this is really only suitable for personal or perhaps small business use. More complex KMS products and services are available for large businesses. Amazon, Microsoft, and Google provide KMSs that are specifically designed for cloud-based products.

7.5 Privacy

Privacy is a social concept that relates to the collection, dissemination, and appropriate use of personal information held by a third party, such as a company or a hospital. The importance of privacy has changed over time, and individuals have their own views on what degree of privacy is important. Culture and age also affect peoples' views on what privacy means. For example:

- Some people may be willing to reveal information about their friends and colleagues by uploading their contacts list to a software system; others do not wish to do so.

- Younger people were early adopters of the first social networks, and many of them seem to be less inhibited about sharing personal information on these platforms than older people.

- In some countries, the level of income earned by an individual is seen as a private matter; in others, all tax returns are openly published.

To maintain privacy, you need to have a secure system. However, security and privacy are not the same thing. Facebook is a secure system with few breaches of its security. There have been several privacy breaches, however, because the features of the system prevent or make it difficult for users to control who sees their personal information. In a medical information system, if an external attacker gains access to the medical records, this is a security failure. If the information in the system is used to send unwanted marketing information about care homes, this is a privacy failure.

Figure 7.16 Data protection laws

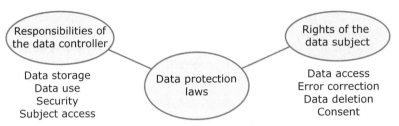

People have different opinions on privacy, so it is impossible to establish objective "privacy standards" based on a definition of "sensitive personal information." Few people would argue against maintaining the privacy of health information. But what about location information—should this be private or not? Knowing an individual's location can enhance the user experience in many products. This information can be misused, however, so some people don't want to disclose their locations or won't allow other companies to use their location information.

In many countries, the right to individual privacy is protected by data protection laws. These laws limit the collection, dissemination, and use of personal data to the purposes for which they were collected. For example, a travel insurance company may collect health information to assess their level of risk. This is legal and permissible. However, it would not be legal for those companies to use this information to target online advertising of health products, unless their users had given specific permission for this.

Figure 7.16 shows the areas that may be covered by data protection laws. These laws differ from country to country, and some country's laws do not cover all areas. The European Union's data protection regulations (GDPR) are among the most stringent in the world, and I base my discussion here on these regulations. The legislation does not only apply to European companies. The GDPR applies to all companies that hold data about EU citizens, irrespective of where these companies are based. Therefore, U.S., Indian, and Chinese companies that allow EU citizens to create accounts must follow the GDPR.

Data protection laws typically refer to data subjects and data controllers. The data subject is the individual whose data are being managed, and the data controller is the manager of the data. The term "data owner" is ambiguous, so it is not usually used. Data subjects have the right to access the stored data and to correct mistakes. They must give their consent for the use of their data and may ask for relevant data to be deleted. The data controller is responsible

Table 7.6 Data protection principles

Data protection principle	Explanation
Awareness and control	Users of your product must be made aware of what data are collected when they are using your product, and must have control over the personal information that you collect from them.
Purpose	You must tell users why data are being collected and you must not use those data for other purposes.
Consent	You must always have the consent of a user before you disclose their data to other people.
Data lifetime	You must not keep data for longer than you need to. If a user deletes an account, you must delete the personal data associated with that account.
Secure storage	You must maintain data securely so that it cannot be tampered with or disclosed to unauthorized people.
Discovery and error correction	You must allow users to find out what personal data you store. You must provide a way for users to correct errors in their personal data.
Location	You must not store data in countries where weaker data protection laws apply unless there is an explicit agreement that the stronger data protection rules will be upheld.

for storing data securely in a location covered by data protection legislation. The controller must provide subject access to the data and should use it only for the purpose for which it was collected.

Data protection laws are based on a set of privacy principles that reflect good privacy practice (Table 7.6).

There are three business reasons why you should pay attention to information privacy:

1. If you are offering a product directly to consumers and you fail to conform to privacy regulations, then you may be subject to legal action by product buyers or by a data regulator. If your conformance is weaker than the protection offered by data protection regulations in some countries, you cannot sell your product in these countries.

2. If your product is a business product, business customers require privacy safeguards so that they are not put at risk of privacy violations and legal action by users.

3. If personal information is leaked or misused, even if this is not seen as a violation of privacy regulations, your reputation may be seriously damaged. Customers may stop using your product because of this.

The information that your software needs to collect depends on the functionality of your product and on the business model you use. You should not collect personal information that you do not need. Say you are developing a service-oriented learning environment. You need to collect information about the learners using the system, the services they use, the learning modules they access, and their performance in assessments. You do not need information on the ethnic background of users, their family circumstances, or what other software they use.

To maintain the privacy of user data, you should establish a privacy policy that defines how personal and sensitive information about users is collected, stored, and managed. The general data protection principles, shown in Table 7.6, should serve as a framework for the development of a privacy policy for your product.

Software products use data in different ways, so your privacy policy has to define the personal data that you will collect and how you will use those data. Product users should be able to review your privacy policy and change their preferences regarding the information that you store. For example, users should be able to state whether or not they want to receive marketing emails from you. Your privacy policy is a legal document and it should be auditable to check that it is consistent with the data protection laws in countries where your software is sold.

Unfortunately, too many software companies bury their privacy policy in a long "terms and conditions" document that, in practice, nobody reads. They therefore get away with collecting user data that are not needed for their product and using these data in ways that users would not expect. This is not illegal, but it is unethical. The GDPR now requires software companies to provide a summary of their privacy policy, written in plain language rather than legal jargon.

Some software business models are based on providing free access to the software and using the users' data in some way to generate revenue. The data may be used to target advertising at users or to provide services that are paid for by other companies. If you use this model, you should make clear that you collect data for this purpose and that your service depends on monetizing user data in some way. You should always allow users to opt out of the use of their data by other companies.

Privacy becomes particularly challenging when your product includes sharing features that allow users to see what other users are doing and how they use your product. Facebook is the prime example of this. There have been many controversies over Facebook privacy and the ways in which the company uses user data and provides privacy controls for users. Facebook provides extensive privacy controls, but these are not all located in the same place and they are sometimes difficult to find. Consequently, many Facebook users inadvertently reveal personal information that they might prefer to keep private.

If your product includes social network functionality so that users can share information, you should ensure that users understand how to control the information they share. Ideally, you should offer a "privacy dashboard," where all privacy controls are in one place and are clear to users. If the functionality of your system depends on mining user information, you should make clear to users that setting privacy controls may limit the functionality that your system offers.

KEY POINTS

- Security is a technical concept that relates to a software system's ability to protect itself from malicious attacks that may threaten its availability, the integrity of the system and its data, and the theft of confidential information.

- Common types of attack on software products are injection attacks, cross-site scripting attacks, session hijacking attacks, denial-of-service attacks, and brute force attacks.

- Authentication may be based on something a user knows, something a user has, or some physical attribute of the user.

- Federated authentication involves devolving responsibility for authentication to a third party, such as Facebook or Google, or to a business's authentication service.

- Authorization involves controlling access to system resources based on the user's authenticated identity. Access control lists are the most commonly used mechanism to implement authorization.

- Symmetric encryption involves encrypting and decrypting information using the same secret key. Asymmetric encryption uses a key pair—a private key and a public key. Information encrypted using the public key can only be decrypted using the private key.

- A major issue in symmetric encryption is key exchange. The TLS protocol, which is used to secure web traffic, gets around this problem by using asymmetric encryption for transferring the information required to generate a shared key.

▪ If your product stores sensitive user data, you should encrypt that data when they are not in use.

▪ A key management system (KMS) stores encryption keys. Using a KMS is essential because a business may have to manage thousands or even millions of keys and may have to decrypt historical data that were encrypted using an obsolete encryption key.

▪ Privacy is a social concept that relates to how people feel about the release of their personal information to others. Different countries and cultures have different ideas about what information should and should not be private.

▪ Data protection laws have been passed in many countries to protect individual privacy. They require companies that manage user data to store them securely, to ensure that they are not used or sold without the permission of users, and to allow users to view and correct personal data held by the system.

RECOMMENDED READING

Security in Computing, 5th edition

There are lots of general books on computer security that cover many of the same topics. All give a reasonable overview of security fundamentals such as authentication, authorization, and encryption. This is the book that I used when writing this chapter. (C. P. Pfleeger and S. L. Pfleeger. Prentice Hall, 2015)

Schneier on Security

Bruce Schneier is a well-known security expert who writes in a very readable way. His blog covers a wide range of general security topics. (B. Schneier, various dates)
https://www.schneier.com/

"The Basics of Web Application Security"

This is an excellent introduction from Martin Fowler's team on possible security threats to web applications and safeguards you can use to counter these threats. (C. Cairns and D. Somerfield, 2017)
https://martinfowler.com/articles/web-security-basics.html

"Excess XSS: A comprehensive tutorial on cross-site scripting"

This is a comprehensive tutorial on cross-site scripting attacks and how they can be prevented.
(J. Kallin and I. Lobo Valbuena, 2016)
https://excess-xss.com/

"Certificates and Authentication"

This easy-to-read introduction explains how certificates can be used in the authentication process. (Redhat, undated)
https://access.redhat.com/documentation/en-US/Red_Hat_Certificate_System/8.0/html/
Deployment_Guide/Introduction_to_Public_Key_Cryptography-Certificates_and_Authentication.html

"5 Common Encryption Algorithms and the Unbreakables of the Future"

Encryption is a complex topic and you need to choose an encryption algorithm carefully. This article introduces five commonly used encryption algorithms, but you need to investigate them in much more detail before making a choice. (StorageCraft, 2017)
https://www.storagecraft.com/blog/5-common-encryption-algorithms/

"What Is GDPR? The summary guide to GDPR compliance in the UK"

GDPR (General Data Protection Regulation) is a major change to data protection legislation in Europe that came into force in 2018. This WIRED article is a good summary of general data protection issues as well as a discussion of how GDPR has strengthened data protection. (M. Burgess, 2018)
http://www.wired.co.uk/article/what-is-gdpr-uk-eu-legislation-compliance-summary-fines-2018

PRESENTATIONS, VIDEOS, AND LINKS

https://iansommerville.com/engineering-software-products/security-and-privacy

EXERCISES

7.1. Briefly describe the three main types of threat that have to be considered when planning how to secure a software product against cyberattacks.

7.2. Explain in your own words what you understand by an SQL injection attack. Explain how you can use data validation to avoid such attacks.

7.3. What do you think are the advantages and disadvantages of using a special-purpose device rather than a mobile phone in two-factor authentication? (*Hint:* Think about the problems of using a mobile phone as an authentication device.)

7.4. Suggest, giving reasons, appropriate forms of authentication for the following products:

 a. An e-learning product for teachers and students, funded by advertising, that allows users to recommend videos and other learning material on a range of topics.

 b. A personal finance app for mobile devices that can automatically transfer funds between different accounts based on rules set up by the user.

 c. A human resources product for businesses that helps manage the process of recruiting new staff.

7.5. What is the difference between symmetric and asymmetric encryption? Why do we need both encryption methods?

7.6. Explain why it is normally preferable to use a database's built-in encryption support rather than implement your own application-level encryption.

7.7. Explain how encryption keys are securely exchanged in the TLS protocol.

7.8. What are the problems in maintaining confidential information that, by law, has to be kept for a number of years? How can a key management system help with these problems?

7.9. Why is it difficult to establish a set of privacy standards that can be applied internationally in software products?

7.10. A Chinese e-commerce company decides to expand its business into the European Union. It proposes to use a local cloud vendor for application server provision but to transfer user information to servers in China for analysis. Explain why this information transfer might be illegal, according to data protection legislation. (*Hint:* Look at the issues related to keeping data anonymous.)

8

Reliable Programming

To create a successful software product you must do more than provide a set of useful features that meets customer needs. Customers have to be confident that your product will not crash or lose information, and users have to be able to learn to use the software quickly and without mistakes. In short, you need to create a "high-quality" product that people want to use.

Saying that a program is high quality is a shorthand way of referring to a set of desirable program attributes that make programs usable and practically useful. I introduced the idea of non-functional quality attributes in Chapter 4 and described them in Table 4.2. Figure 8.1 shows these software product quality attributes.

Quality attributes fall into three groups:

1. Reliability attributes: reliability, availability, security, and resilience. These all relate to the software's ability to deliver its functionality as expected by the user, without going wrong.

2. User experience attributes: responsiveness and usability. These relate to the user's interaction with your product.

3. Maintainability: a complex attribute related to how easy it is for developers to make changes to the program to correct bugs and add new features.

Sometimes these attributes are mutually supportive, and sometimes they are opposing. For example, if you improve the security of a program by validating all inputs, you also improve its reliability. Because validation involves additional checks, however, it can slow down your program and reduce its

Figure 8.1 Product quality attributes

responsiveness. Improving security by adding extra authentication levels also affects a program's usability because users have to remember and input more information before they can start doing useful work.

I focus here on techniques that help improve the overall reliability of a program, where I use the term "reliability" to cover reliability, availability, security and resilience. Usability and responsiveness are critical attributes in practice. However, they are subjective attributes that differ for every program, depending on its application domain and its market. It is therefore difficult to provide product-independent guidance on how best to achieve responsiveness and usability.

Maintainability depends on the understandability of a program and its structure. To be maintainable, a program has to be composed of well-written, replaceable, testable units. Most techniques that improve reliability also contribute to improving maintainability.

Specialized techniques have been developed for achieving reliability in critical software systems. These are systems whose failure may lead to human injury or death or to significant environmental or economic damage. These techniques include formal specification and verification of programs and the use of reliability architectures, which include redundant components. The system can automatically switch to a backup component in the event of failure.

These techniques are too expensive and time-consuming for software product development. However, three simpler, low-cost techniques for improving product reliability can be applied in any software company:

1. *Fault avoidance* You should program in such a way that you avoid introducing faults into your program.

2. *Input validation* You should define the expected format for user inputs and validate that all inputs conform to that format.

3. *Failure management* You should implement your software so that program failures have minimal impact on product users.

Programming for fault avoidance means that you use a programming style that reduces the chances of making mistakes that introduce faults into your program. Your programs should be easy to read so that readers can easily understand the code. You should minimize the use of programming language constructs that are error-prone. You should change and improve (refactor) your program to make it more readable and to remove obscure code. You should reuse trusted code and should program using well-understood, tried and tested concepts, such as design patterns.

In Chapter 7, I discussed the importance of input validation in avoiding several kinds of security threat to a system. Input validation, where you check that user inputs are as expected, is also important for reliability. By trapping invalid inputs, you ensure that incorrect data are not processed or entered into the system database.

However, you can't simply rely on fault avoidance. All programmers make mistakes, so you should assume that there will always be residual faults in your program. These faults may not cause problems for most users, but sometimes they lead to software failures. Most users now accept that things will go wrong and will tolerate failures so long as they do not have to redo work. Therefore, you should anticipate the possibility of failure in your program and include recovery features that allow users to restart with minimal disruption.

8.1 Fault avoidance

Faults in a program are a consequence of programming errors—when programmers make mistakes and introduce incorrect code. If the erroneous code is executed, the program fails in some way. An incorrect output may

Figure 8.2 Underlying causes of program errors

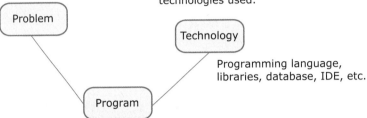

Programmers make mistakes because they don't properly understand the problem or the application domain.

Programmers make mistakes because they use unsuitable technology or they don't properly understand the technologies used.

Problem

Technology

Programming language, libraries, database, IDE, etc.

Program

Programmers make mistakes because they make simple slips or they do not completely understand how multiple program components work together and change the program's state.

be produced, the program may not terminate, or the program might crash and not continue execution. For example, a programmer may forget to increment a variable in a loop, with the consequence that the loop never terminates.

Therefore, to improve the reliability of your program, you should program in a way that minimizes the number of faults in the program. You can do this by testing your program to reveal faults and then changing the code to remove these faults. However, if you can, it is better to minimize programming errors that lead to program faults and subsequent execution failures. This is called fault avoidance.

Figure 8.2 shows three underlying causes of program errors. Let's look at examples of each of these types of error:

1. Imagine you are implementing a product to help businesses manage travel expenses. If you don't understand the tax laws that govern expenses payments, then you will inevitably make mistakes when implementing your product (Problem error).

2. Say you are implementing a cataloging system for museums and art galleries. Because you have experience with MySQL, you decide to use a relational database in this system. Because of the diversity of objects in museums, however, this involves creating a complex database schema. Because of the complexity, you are liable to make mistakes in fitting object descriptions into this schema. If you had chosen a NoSQL database, such as MongoDB, this could perhaps have been avoided (Technology error).

Figure 8.3 Software complexity

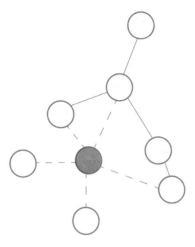

The shaded node interacts in some ways with
the linked nodes shown by the dotted lines.

3. We all make simple slips when programming, such as misspelling an
    identifier name. These can often be detected by a compiler or other tools.
    However, these tools can't pick up some types of slip, such as out-by-1
    errors in a for-loop. For example, in many languages, the characters in a
    string are addressed from 0, with the final character being at length (str)-1.
    If you write code that starts at position 1 rather than 0, then you will not
    process the first character in the string (Program error).

The underlying root cause of many program errors is complexity. As I
explained in Chapter 4, the more complex a program, the more difficult it is
to understand. If you don't completely understand a program, you are more
likely to make mistakes when changing it or adding new code. You should
therefore program in a way that minimizes complexity.

8.1.1 Program complexity

Complexity is related to the number of relationships between elements in
a program and the type and nature of these relationships (Figure 8.3). The
number of relationships between entities is called the coupling. The higher
the coupling, the more complex the system. The shaded node in Figure 8.3 has
a relatively high coupling because it has relationships with five other nodes.

Complexity is also affected by the type of relationship. A static relationship is one that is stable and does not depend on program execution. For example, whether or not one component is part of another component is a static relationship. Dynamic relationships, which change over time, are more complex than static relationships. An example of a dynamic relationship is the "calls" relationship between functions. This relationship changes depending on the pattern of program execution.

Complexity leads to programming errors because of the way our brains work. We use our short-term memory to work things out. We populate this with information from our senses and from longer-term memory, which we use to remember things for a longer time.

Short-term memory is limited in size, however, so it can only handle between four and seven discrete units of information. For more units, we need to transfer information between short-term memory and longer-term memory. This transfer slows down understanding and is potentially prone to errors. We may not transfer all of the necessary information, or we may transfer the wrong information. If we keep things simple, we can retain more information in short-term memory and so reduce the chances of errors.

Several metrics have been devised to measure program complexity, such as McCabe's cyclomatic complexity metric and SLOC, the number of lines of source code. Tools are available to analyze programs and compute these metrics. I am skeptical of these metrics, however, because code complexity also depends on how you organize your data. Code analysis tools do not take this into account. I don't think that trying to measure complexity using these metrics is worthwhile.

Program complexity is, to some extent, under the control of the programmer. However, the problem domain has its own complexity, and this may be difficult to simplify. For example, tax laws in all countries are complex, so this type of complexity is unavoidable if you are developing a product to help users with their tax returns. Similarly, if you are using complex tools, you may make mistakes because you don't understand the interactions between components of the tool.

Sometimes you can reduce problem complexity by redefining and simplifying the problem. This is impossible for some problems, however, and you have to deal with their inherent complexity. In those situations, you should write your program using structures and names that reflect how the problem is described and documented. As your understanding of the problem evolves, it is then easier to make changes to your program without introducing new faults.

This is one reason programming guidelines suggest that you use readable names in your program. For example, look at the following code segments that calculate the computation of a student's overall grade. The grades are computed from the grades allocated to three assignments and a final examination:

```
# Segment 1
G = A1\*0.1 + A2\*0.1 +A3\*0.2 + Ex \*0.6


#Segment 2
WrittenAssignmentWeight = 0.1
PracticalAssignmentWeight = 0.2
ExamWeight = 0.6


Grade = (Assignment1Mark + Assignment2Mark) * WrittenAssignmentWeight +
        ProjectMark * PracticalAssignmentWeight + ExamMark * ExamWeight
```

Segment 1 uses abbreviated names and is obviously faster to write. However, its meaning isn't clear. In contrast, it is immediately obvious from the code in Segment 2 what is being calculated and the elements that make up the final grade.

Readability and other programming guidelines, such as indentation guidelines, are important for fault avoidance because they reduce the "reading complexity" of a program. Reading complexity reflects how hard the program is to read and understand. There are various good practice guidelines, such as using readable names, indenting code, and naming constant values. I assume you already know about good programming practice, so I don't discuss these guidelines here.

In addition to reading complexity, you have to consider three other types of program complexity:

1. *Structural complexity* This reflects the number and types of relationships between the structures (classes, objects, methods, or functions) in your program.

2. *Data complexity* This reflects the representations of data used and the relationships between the data elements in your program.

3. *Decision complexity* This reflects the complexity of the decisions in your program.

To avoid introducing faults into your code, you should program so that, as far as possible, you minimize each of these types of complexity. There are no

Table 8.1   Complexity reduction guidelines

Type	Guideline
Structural complexity	Functions should do one thing and one thing only.
	Functions should never have side effects.
	Every class should have a single responsibility.
	Minimize the depth of inheritance hierarchies.
	Avoid multiple inheritance.
	Avoid threads (parallelism) unless absolutely necessary.
Data complexity	Define interfaces for all abstractions.
	Define abstract data types.
	Avoid using floating-point numbers.
	Never use data aliases.
Decision complexity	Avoid deeply nested conditional statements.
	Avoid complex conditional expressions.

hard and fast rules about how to do this, and sometimes reducing one type of complexity leads to an increase in some other type. However, following the good practice guidelines shown in Table 8.1 helps to reduce program complexity and the number of faults in a program. There's lots of information on these guidelines, as well as other good practice guidelines available on the web.

I don't have space here to describe all these guidelines in detail. To illustrate the general ideas, though, I discuss three guidelines that are relevant for most object-oriented programs:

- Ensure that every class has a single responsibility.

- Avoid deeply nested conditional statements.

- Avoid deep inheritance hierarchies.

Ensure that every class has a single responsibility   Since the advent of structured programming in the 1970s, it has been accepted that program units should do only one thing. Bob Martin, in his book *Clean Code*,[1] articulated this "single responsibility principle" for object-oriented development. He argued that you should design classes so that there is only a single reason to change a class. If you adopt this approach, your classes will be smaller and more cohesive. They will be less complex and easier to understand and change.

---

[1]Robert C. Martin, *Clean Code: A Handbook of Agile Software Craftsmanship* (Boston: Prentice Hall, 2008).

Figure 8.4 The DeviceInventory class

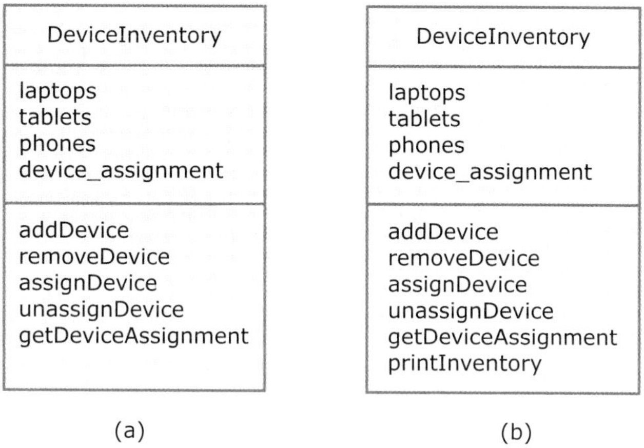

DeviceInventory
laptops tablets phones device_assignment
addDevice removeDevice assignDevice unassignDevice getDeviceAssignment

(a)

DeviceInventory
laptops tablets phones device_assignment
addDevice removeDevice assignDevice unassignDevice getDeviceAssignment printInventory

(b)

Martin's notion of "a single reason to change" is, I think, quite hard to understand. However, in a blog post[2] he explains the single responsibility principle in a much better way:

> *Gather together the things that change for the same reasons. Separate those things that change for different reasons.*

To illustrate this principle, Figure 8.4 shows two versions of a class diagram for a class called DeviceInventory, which could be part of a business product for inventory management. This class keeps track of who uses the business's laptops, tablets, and phones.

The original version of the class is shown in Figure 8.4(a), where there are methods to update the attributes of the class. Let's assume a product manager suggests that businesses should be able to print a report of device assignments. One way of doing this is to add a printInventory method, as shown in Figure 8.4(b).

This change breaks the single responsibility principle because it adds an additional "reason to change" the class. Without the printInventory method, the reason to change the class is that there has been some fundamental change in the inventory, such as recording who is using their personal phone for business purposes. If you add a print method, however,

---

[2]https://8thlight.com/blog/uncle-bob/2014/05/08/SingleReponsibilityPrinciple.html

Figure 8.5 The DeviceInventory and InventoryReport classes

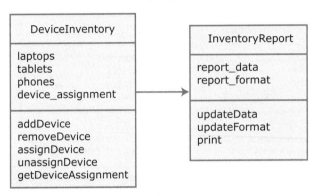

you are associating another data type (a report) with the class. Another reason for changing this class might then be to change the format of the printed report.

Instead of adding a printInventory method to DeviceInventory, it is better to add a new class to represent the printed report, as shown in Figure 8.5.

The benefits of following the single responsibility principle are not obvious in such a small illustrative example, but they are real when you have much larger classes. Unfortunately, modifying an existing class when a change is required is sometimes the quickest way of implementing that change. However, if you do so, your code becomes more and more complex. Consequently, as part of a refactoring process (discussed in Section 8.1.3) you should regularly reorganize your classes so that each has a single responsibility.

Avoid deeply nested conditional statements   Deeply nested conditional (if) statements are used when you need to identify which of a possible set of choices is to be made. For example, the function "agecheck" in Program 8.1 is a short Python function used to calculate an age multiplier for insurance premiums. The insurance company's data suggest that the age and experience of drivers affect the chances of them having an accident, so premiums are adjusted to take this into account. It is good practice to name constants rather than use absolute numbers, so Program 8.1 names all constants that are used.

Program 8.1 Deeply nested if-then-else statements

```
YOUNG_DRIVER_AGE_LIMIT = 25
OLDER_DRIVER_AGE = 70
ELDERLY_DRIVER_AGE = 80

YOUNG_DRIVER_PREMIUM_MULTIPLIER = 2
OLDER_DRIVER_PREMIUM_MULTIPLIER = 1.5
ELDERLY_DRIVER_PREMIUM_MULTIPLIER = 2
YOUNG_DRIVER_EXPERIENCE_MULTIPLIER = 2
NO_MULTIPLIER = 1

YOUNG_DRIVER_EXPERIENCE = 2
OLDER_DRIVER_EXPERIENCE = 5

def agecheck (age, experience):

    # Assigns a premium multiplier depending on the age and experience of the driver

    multiplier = NO_MULTIPLIER
    if age <= YOUNG_DRIVER_AGE_LIMIT:
        if experience <= YOUNG_DRIVER_EXPERIENCE:
            multiplier = YOUNG_DRIVER_PREMIUM_MULTIPLIER *
            YOUNG_DRIVER_EXPERIENCE_MULTIPLIER
        else:
            multiplier = YOUNG_DRIVER_PREMIUM_MULTIPLIER
    else:
        if age > OLDER_DRIVER_AGE and age <= ELDERLY_DRIVER_AGE:
            if experience <= OLDER_DRIVER_EXPERIENCE:
                multiplier = OLDER_DRIVER_PREMIUM_MULTIPLIER
            else:
                multiplier = NO_MULTIPLIER
            else:
                if age > ELDERLY_DRIVER_AGE:
                    multiplier = ELDERLY_DRIVER_PREMIUM_MULTIPLIER
    return multiplier
```

With deeply nested if statements, you have to trace the logic to see what the premium multiplier should be. However, if you use guards, with multiple returns, the conditions and their associated actions are clear (Program 8.2). A

Program 8.2 Using guards to make a selection

```
def agecheck_with_guards (age, experience):

    if age <= YOUNG_DRIVER_AGE_LIMIT and experience <=
        YOUNG_DRIVER_EXPERIENCE:
        return YOUNG_DRIVER_PREMIUM_MULTIPLIER *
        YOUNG_DRIVER_EXPERIENCE_MULTIPLIER
    if age <= YOUNG_DRIVER_AGE_LIMIT:
        return YOUNG_DRIVER_PREMIUM_MULTIPLIER
    if (age > OLDER_DRIVER_AGE and age <= ELDERLY_DRIVER_AGE) and experience <=
        OLDER_DRIVER_EXPERIENCE:
        return OLDER_DRIVER_PREMIUM_MULTIPLIER
    if age > ELDERLY_DRIVER_AGE:
        return ELDERLY_DRIVER_PREMIUM_MULTIPLIER
        return NO_MULTIPLIER
```

guard is a conditional expression placed in front of the code to be executed. It "guards" that code, as the expression must be true for the code to be executed. It is therefore easier to see the conditions under which the code segment will run.

You can implement guarded selections by using a switch statement (sometimes called a case statement) in Java or C++. Python does not have a switch statement, so you have to simulate it in some way. I think that a switch statement makes for more readable code and that Python's language designers have made a mistake in leaving this out.

Avoid deep inheritance hierarchies   One innovation in object-oriented programming was the idea of inheritance. The attributes and methods of a class, such as RoadVehicle, can be inherited by subclasses, such as Truck, Car, and MotorBike. This means there is no need to re-declare these attributes and methods in a subclass. When changes are made, they apply to all subclasses in the inheritance hierarchy.

Inheritance appears, in principle, to be an effective and efficient way of reusing code and making changes that affect all subclasses. However, inheritance increases the structural complexity of code, as it increases the coupling of subclasses. For example, Figure 8.6 shows part of a four-level inheritance hierarchy that could be defined for staff in a hospital.

The problem with deep inheritance is that if you want to make changes to a class, you have to look at all of its superclasses to see where it is best to make

Figure 8.6 Part of the inheritance hierarchy for hospital staff

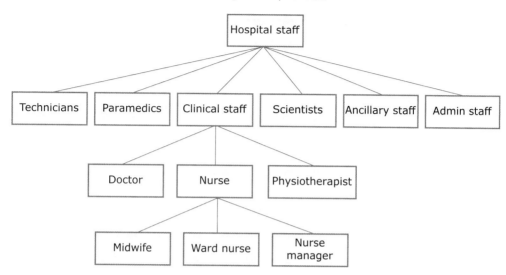

the change. You also have to look at all of the related subclasses to check that the change does not have unwanted consequences. It's easy to make mistakes when you are doing this analysis and introduce faults into your program.

A general problem with trying to reduce complexity in your program is that the complexity is sometimes "essential complexity" that comes from the application domain of your product. For example, hospitals have many different types of staff, as shown in Figure 8.6. If you simplify the inheritance hierarchy, this may involve introducing conditional statements within methods to distinguish between different types of staff. For example, you can remove the lowest level in the hierarchy in Figure 8.6 by having a single Nurse type, but you then have to introduce guards when programming. For example:

```
if NurseType = Midwife:
    do_something ()
elsif NurseType = WardNurse:
    do_something_else ()
else:
    do_another_thing ()
```

These guards increase the decision complexity, so you are trading off structural complexity for decision complexity. I think this is preferable, however, as decision complexity is localized (everything is in one place) and is usually easier to understand.

8.1.2 Design patterns

An effective way to avoid faults in your code is to reuse working software. Existing software, often in libraries, has usually been extensively tested and used in other applications, so many of the bugs have been discovered and fixed. However, you must also test the software you reuse in the context of your product to make sure that it really meets your needs. Your product may use the software in a different way from other applications. Although the reused code may have been extensively tested, you cannot be sure that the testing has covered your type of use.

Code reuse is not always possible as it may be too expensive to adapt code for use in your product. Another type of reuse, which avoids these problems, is to reuse concepts and ideas that have been tried and tested in other systems. Design patterns, first proposed in the 1980s, are an example of this type of reuse. Patterns are a way of describing good practice in object-oriented programming. Using design patterns contributes to fault avoidance because patterns describe reliable solutions to common problems. You don't have to discover your own solutions through a process of trial and error.

I think the definition of a design pattern in Wikipedia[3] is a good one:

> *A general reusable solution to a commonly occurring problem within a given context in software design.*

Design patterns are object-oriented and describe solutions in terms of objects and classes. They are not off-the-shelf solutions that can be directly expressed as code in an object-oriented language. They describe the structure of a problem solution that has to be adapted to suit your application and the programming language you are using.

Two fundamental programming principles are the basis for most design patterns:

1. *Separation of concerns* Each abstraction in the program (class, method, etc.) should address a separate concern, and all aspects of that concern should be covered there. For example, if authentication is a concern in your program, then everything to do with authentication should be in one place, rather than distributed throughout your code. This principle is closely related to the single responsibility guideline that I explained in the previous section.

---

[3]https://en.wikipedia.org/wiki/Software_design_pattern

2. *Separation of the "what" from the "how"* If a program component provides a particular service, you should make available only the information that is required to use that service (the "what"). The implementation of the service (the "how") should be of no interest to service users. This reflects the complexity reduction guideline, shown in Table 8.1, which suggests that you define separate interfaces for all abstractions.

If you follow these principles, then your code will be less complex and, consequently, contain fewer faults. Complexity increases the chances that you will make mistakes and introduce bugs into your program.

Patterns have been developed in several different areas, but the best-known patterns are those developed by the so-called Gang of Four in their book *Design Patterns: Elements of Reusable Object-Oriented Software.*[4] They classify patterns into three types:

1. *Creational patterns* are concerned with class and object creation. They define ways of instantiating and initializing objects and classes that are more abstract than the basic class and object creation mechanisms defined in a programming language.

2. *Structural patterns* are concerned with class and object composition. Structural design patterns are a description of how classes and objects may be combined to create larger structures.

3. *Behavioral patterns* are concerned with class and object communication. They show how objects interact by exchanging messages, the activities in a process, and how these are distributed among the participating objects.

Table 8.2 is a list of examples of creational, structural, and behavioral patterns.

Let's assume you are implementing a product in which you want to give the user the ability to create multiple views of some dynamic data object. Users can interact with any of the views, and the changes that are made should be immediately reflected in all other open views. For example, if you are implementing a product that's aimed at people interested in family history, you may provide both a list view and a family tree view of the user's ancestors (Figure 8.7).

---

[4]E. Gamma, R. Helm, R. Johnson, and J. Vlissides. *Design Patterns: Elements of Reusable Object-Oriented Software* (Reading, MA: Addison-Wesley, 1995).

Table 8.2 Examples of creational, structural, and behavioral patterns

Pattern name	Type	Description
Factory	Creational	Used to create objects when slightly-different variants of the object may be created.
Prototype	Creational	Used to create an object clone—that is, a new object with exactly the same attribute values as the object being cloned.
Facade	Structural	Used to match semantically compatible interfaces of different classes.
Facade	Structural	Used to provide a single interface to a group of classes in which each class implements some functionality accessed through the interface.
Mediator	Behavioral	Used to reduce the number of direct interactions between objects. All object communications are handled through the mediator.
State	Behavioral	Used to implement a state machine in which an object changes its behavior when its internal state changes.

The challenge when dealing with multiple data views is to make sure that all views are updated when changes are made. The Observer pattern shown in Table 8.3 documents a good way of solving this common problem.

The Observer pattern is an example of a behavioral design pattern. This pattern is the basis of the most widespread architecture for web-based systems: the model-view-controller (MVC) architecture that I introduced in Chapter 4.

Figure 8.7 List view and tree view of ancestors

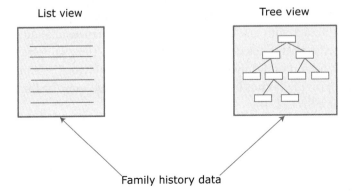

Table 8.3 The Observer pattern

Element	Description
Name	Observer
Description	This pattern separates the display of an object from the object itself. There may be multiple displays associated with the object. When one display is changed, all others are notified and take action to update themselves.
Problem	Many applications present multiple views (displays) of the same data with the requirement that all views must be updated when any one view is changed. You may also wish to add new views without the object whose state is being displayed knowing about the new view or how the information is presented.
Solution	The state to be displayed (sometimes called the Model) is maintained in a Subject class that includes methods to add and remove observers and to get and set the state of the Model. An observer is created for each display and registers with the Subject. When an observer uses the set method to change the state, the Subject notifies all other Observers. They then use the Subject's getState( ) method to update their local copy of the state and so change their display. Adding a new display simply involves notifying the Subject that a new display has been created.
Implementation	This pattern is implemented using abstract and concrete classes. The abstract Subject class includes methods to register and deregister observers and to notify all observers that a change has been made. The abstract Observer class includes a method to update the local state of each observer. Each Observer subclass implements these methods and is responsible for managing its own display. When notifications of a change are received, the Observer subclasses access the model using the getState( ) method to retrieve the changed information.
Things to consider	The Subject does not know how the Model is displayed so cannot organize its data to optimize the display performance. If a display update fails, the Subject does not know that the update has been unsuccessful.

This architecture separates the system state (the model) from its presentation (the views). The controller is responsible for managing the views as the state changes.

Design patterns are usually documented in the stylized way shown in Table 8.3, including:

■ a meaningful name for the pattern and a brief description of what it does;

■ a description of the problem it solves;

Table 8.4 The Prototype pattern

Element	Description
Name	Prototype
Description	Given an existing object, this pattern creates (clones) a new object, which is an exact copy of an existing object; that is, the attributes in both objects have the same values. It is used as an alternative to the normal method of object construction.
Problem	This pattern is used when you need to instantiate new classes at run time depending on some user input. It is also used when the instances of a class can have only one of several state variations.
Solution	The Prototype class includes a set of subclasses, with each of these subclasses encapsulating an object that is to be cloned. Each subclass provides an implementation of the clone method in the Prototype class. When a new clone is required, the clone method of the Prototype class is used to create an exact copy of the cloneable object.
Implementation	The Prototype class includes an abstract method clone() and maintains a registry of cloneable objects. Each of these must implement its own clone() method. When a clone is required, the client calls the clone() method of Prototype with a parameter indicating what type of object is to be cloned.
Things to consider	Every subclass of Prototype (i.e., the things being cloned) must implement a clone method. This can be difficult if the object being cloned includes other objects that don't support copying or that include complex cross-references.

■ a description of the solution and its implementation;

■ the consequences and trade-offs of using the pattern and other issues you should consider.

The implementation section is usually more detailed than in Table 8.3, with diagrams defining the abstract and concrete classes that implement the pattern. Abstract classes define the method names for accessing the model without an associated implementation. These methods are implemented in lower-level concrete classes. I leave out this detailed implementation information to save space.

Tables 8.4 and 8.5 are, respectively, brief descriptions of creational and structural design patterns. You might use the Prototype pattern when you need to initialize a group of objects in a similar way. For example, if you have recommender system, you may want to create similar objects to represent the things that you are recommending to users.

Table 8.5 The Facade pattern

Element	Description
Name	Facade
Description	A complex package or library might have many different objects and methods that are used in different ways. The Facade pattern provides a simple interface to the more complex underlying library or package.
Problem	As functionality is added to a system, the number of objects in that system grows, either directly or by including libraries in the system. Component functionality may be implemented by using several other objects, so that there is a tight coupling between the component functionality and the underlying objects. The resulting code is often complex and hard to understand and change.
Solution	A Facade class provides a simple interface to the set of classes used to implement an aspect of the system's functionality and so hides complexity from the user of that functionality. For example, say initializing a system involves using classes A, B, C, and D. Instead of accessing these objects directly, an initialization facade would provide a single initialize() method that hides classes A, B, C, and D and simplifies initialization. Multiple facades may be implemented as interfaces to subsets of the functionality provided by libraries or packages.
Implementation	A Facade class is created that includes the required interface methods. It accesses the underlying objects directly.
Things to consider	Implementing a facade hides the underlying complexity, but it does not prohibit clients from accessing that functionality directly. You could therefore end up with a system where the same functionality is accessed in different ways. Accessing functionality without going through the Facade should be discouraged, as it adds complexity to the software.

You use the Facade pattern when you have a set of objects that offer a range of related functionality, but you do not need to access all of that functionality. By defining a facade, you limit the possible interactions with these objects and so reduce the overall complexity of the interaction.

I don't have space to describe all the design patterns defined by the Gang of Four. Many pattern tutorials are available on the web, and I recommend that you look at them to understand the details of programming with patterns.

Once you have some experience using patterns, they can become abstract building blocks and you can use them as you are developing code. If you have a prototype implementation of your product, this can be used to identify code that can be encapsulated in patterns when you rewrite your system.

Figure 8.8 A refactoring process

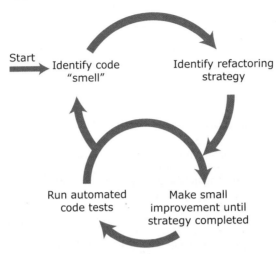

Sometimes it makes sense to start programming with patterns, but at other times a simpler, more direct implementation is a better initial solution. However, as you add more and more code to your system, the complexity of the implementation increases. This is an indication that you need to refactor and introduce design patterns, which make the code simpler and easier to change.

The general idea of patterns is applicable not only when an object-oriented approach is used. People have also suggested design patterns for microservices architecture. These define commonly occurring organizations of microservices. I do not cover these here, as they are still immature; however, I have included a link in the Recommended Reading section.

8.1.3 Refactoring

Refactoring means changing a program to reduce its complexity without changing the external behavior of that program. Refactoring makes a program more readable (so reducing the "reading complexity") and more understandable. It also makes the program easier to change, which means that you reduce the chances of making mistakes when you introduce new features.

You might think that if you follow good programming practice then you won't have to refactor your program. However, the reality of programming is that as you make changes and additions to existing code, you inevitably increase its complexity. The code becomes harder to understand and change. The abstractions and operations that you started with become more and

Table 8.6 Examples of code smells

Code smell	Refactoring action
Large classes	Large classes may mean that the single responsibility principle is being violated. Break down large classes into easier-to-understand, smaller classes.
Long methods/functions	Long methods or functions may indicate that the function is doing more than one thing. Split into smaller, more specific functions or methods.
Duplicated code	Duplicated code may mean that when changes are needed, these have to be made everywhere the code is duplicated. Rewrite to create a single instance of the duplicated code that is used as required.
Meaningless names	Meaningless names are a sign of programmer haste. They make the code harder to understand. Replace with meaningful names and check for other shortcuts that the programmer may have taken.
Unused code	This simply increases the reading complexity of the code. Delete it even if it has been commented out. If you find you need it later, you should be able to retrieve it from the code management system.

more complex because you modify them in ways that you did not originally anticipate.

Figure 8.8 shows a possible refactoring process. When planning product development, you should always include time for code refactoring. This can be a separate activity (Scrum sprint), or it can be an inherent part of your normal development process.

Martin Fowler, a refactoring pioneer, suggests that the starting point for refactoring should be to identify code "smells." Code smells are indicators in the code that there might be a deeper problem. For example, very large classes may indicate that the class is trying to do too much. This probably means that its structural complexity is high. Lots of lists of code smells are available on the web. Table 8.6 lists some common code smells you should look out for.

Code smells point you to code that needs to be refactored. There are many possible refactorings you may use, and most of these help reduce program complexity. Table 8.7 lists examples of refactoring that focus on reducing complexity. Fowler has a longer list of possible refactorings that I have included in the Recommended Reading section.

Refactoring involves changing a program without changing its functionality. As far as possible, you should not do "big bang" refactoring, which means

Table 8.7 Examples of refactoring for complexity reduction

Type of complexity	Possible refactoring
Reading complexity	You can rename variable, function, and class names throughout your program to make their purpose more obvious.
Structural complexity	You can break long classes or functions into shorter units that are likely to be more cohesive than the original large class.
Data complexity	You can simplify data by changing your database schema or reducing their complexity. For example, you can merge related tables in your database to remove duplicated data held in these tables.
Decision complexity	You can replace a series of deeply nested if-then-else statements with guard clauses, as I explained earlier in this chapter.

that you change a lot of code at the same time. Rather, you should make a series of small changes, each of which is a step toward the more significant changes that you're aiming for. I recommend that you use automated testing, discussed in Chapter 9, and run your suite of tests after every program change. This will check that you have not accidentally introduced new bugs into your program during refactoring.

To ensure that your program continues to work during refactoring, you may have to temporarily maintain duplicate code in your system. Part of the system may be refactored, but other parts may still use the old code. You should always aim to remove this duplicate code when you have completed refactoring.

Refactoring usually involves making changes at different places in a program. Refactoring tools are stand-alone tools or editor plug-ins that help with the refactoring process. They partially automate the process of making changes, such as renaming identifiers throughout a program or moving a method from one class to another. This reduces the chances of you missing changes to variables, objects, and functions that are required.

8.2 Input validation

Input validation involves checking that a user's input is in the correct format and that its value is within the range defined by input rules. Input validation is critical for security and reliability. In addition to catching inputs from attackers that are deliberately invalid, input validation detects accidentally invalid inputs that could crash your program or pollute your database. A database becomes polluted when incorrect information is added to it. User input errors are the most common cause of database pollution.

Without exception, you should define rules for every type of input field, and you should include code that applies these rules to check the field's validity. If the input does not conform to the rules, it should be rejected.

For example, say you have a field in a form where users input their family name. Although people can call themselves anything they wish, in practice there are rules of thumb that can be used for checking names in languages that use the Roman alphabet:[5]

1. The length of a name should be between 2 and 40 characters.

2. The characters in the name must be alphabetic or alphabetic characters with an accent plus a small number of special separator characters. Names must start with a letter.

3. The only non-alphabetic separator characters allowed are hyphen and apostrophe.

If you use rules like these, it becomes impossible to input very long strings that might lead to buffer overflow, or to embed SQL commands in a name field. Of course, if someone decides to call themselves something like Mark C-3PO, then they can't use your system, but such unusual cases are rare.

In addition to using input fields for code injection, an attacker may input an invalid but syntactically correct value in a field in an attempt to crash your system or to discover potential vulnerabilities. For example, say you have a field where a user is expected to input age in years. An attacker could input a very long number in that field—such as 2147483651—hoping that it will cause a numeric overflow or cause the system to crash in some other way. You can easily stop this by including the rule that ages have to be 0 (if babies can be included) or positive integers less than 120.[6]

Two approaches are commonly used for input security checks:

1. *Blacklisting* Filters are defined for known incorrect inputs. For example, inputs can be checked for the existence of the <script> tag, which might be used in a cross-site scripting attack.

---

[5]The Roman alphabet is used in languages such as English, Spanish, and German. Asian languages use different alphabets, so different rules may apply.

[6]According to Wikipedia, there has been only one person whose verified age was more than 120.

Table 8.8 Methods of implementing input validation

Validation method	Implementation
Built-in validation functions	You can use input validator functions provided by your web development framework. For example, most frameworks include a validator function that will check that an email address is of the correct format. Web development frameworks such as Django (Python), Rails (Ruby), and Spring (Java) all include an extensive set of validator functions.
Type coercion functions	You can use type coercion functions, such as int() in Python, that convert the input string into the desired type. If the input is not a sequence of digits, the conversion will fail.
Explicit comparisons	You can define a list of allowed values and possible abbreviations and check inputs against this list. For example, if a month is expected, you can check this against a list of all months and their recognized abbreviations.
Regular expressions	You can use regular expressions to define a pattern that the input should match and reject inputs that do not match that pattern. Regular expressions are a powerful technique that I cover in Section 8.2.1.

2. *Whitelisting* Filters are defined that identify the allowed inputs. For example, if an input is a zip code (post code), then the format of the zip code can be defined as a regular expression and the input checked against that.

Whitelisting is usually better than blacklisting because attackers can sometimes find ways to get around the defined filter. Furthermore, the blacklisting filter may sometimes reject legitimate input. For example, inputs that include SQL usually include 'characters, so you may define a blacklist to exclude inputs that contain '. However, some Irish names, such as O'Donnell, include apostrophes and so would be rejected by this filter.

Various methods of implementing input validation are shown in Table 8.8. You often need to use a combination of these approaches.

If possible, you should present users with a menu showing valid inputs. This means they can't input an incorrect value. Where there are a large number of choices, however, menus can be irritating. For example, asking a user to choose a birth year from a menu involves displaying a menu with almost 100 items.

One way to implement input checking is to use Javascript that runs in the user's browser or by using local code in a mobile app. This can be useful for providing immediate information to users about possible errors. You should not rely on this, however, as it is not difficult for a malicious user to bypass these checks. Client-side validation is helpful because it detects user errors and highlights them for correction. However, for security, you should also do validation checks on the server.

8.2.1   Regular expressions

Regular expressions (REs) are a way of defining patterns. They were invented in the 1950s but came into common use in the Unix operating system in the 1970s. A search can be defined as a pattern, and all items matching that pattern are returned. For example, the following Unix command will list all the JPEG files in a directory:

```
ls | grep ..*\.jpg$
```

grep is the UNIX regular expression matcher, and the regular expression in this case is

```
..*\.jpg$
```

A single dot means "match any character," and * means zero or more repetitions of the previous character. Therefore, ..* means "one or more characters." The file prefix is .jpg and the $ character means that it must occur at the end of a line.

There are many variants of REs, and most programming languages have a regular expression library that you can use to define and match regular expressions. I use the Python library (called re) in the examples here. There are usually several ways of writing a regular expression, some more concise than others. There is often a trade-off between conciseness and understandability, so that very concise representations are often obscure and difficult to understand. I prefer to write understandable REs, without concern for their conciseness.

To use regular expressions to check an input string, you write an expression that defines a pattern that will match all valid strings. You then check the input against this pattern and reject any inputs that do not match. For example, say that your input is a name, which should follow the rules that I have set out above.

The regular expression below defines a pattern that encodes these rules. For simplicity, I ignore the possibility that accented characters may be used in names.

$$\verb|^[a-zA-Z][a-zA-Z-']{1,39}$|$$

The ^ sign forces a match to begin at the start of a string, and the $ sign means it must match to the end. As you always want to check the whole of an input, you should always include these signs in your regular expression. Enclosing characters in square brackets means "match any of these characters," and a-z means all alphabetic characters. The subexpression [a-zA-Z-'] therefore matches all upper- and lowercase letters plus the symbols, <hyphen> and <apostrophe>.

The part of the expression in braces is used to implement the rule that a name should have at least 1 character and no more than 40 characters. The numbers specify the number of repetitions that should be matched; in this case, the expression will match 1 to 39 repetitions. Single-character names are not allowed.

This check will probably be effective for rejecting all invalid inputs, but for added security you can add more explicit checks. SQL poisoning requires quoted text to be included in a name and/or SQL comments that begin with a double hyphen. Program 8.3 is a short Python function that includes this check.

Program 8.3 A name-checking function

```python
def namecheck (s):

    # checks that a name only includes alphabetic characters, -, or single quote
    # names must be between 2 and 40 characters long
    # quoted strings and -- are disallowed

    namex = r"^[a-zA-Z][a-zA-Z-']{1,39}$"
    if re.match (namex, s):
        if re.search ("'.*'", s) or re.search ("--", s):
            return False
        else:
            return True
    else:
        return False
```

Different languages have different mechanisms for writing regular expressions that may use special characters. In Python, these are written as raw strings, which are indicated by preceding the string quotes with 'r'. The function re.match matches the RE from the beginning of the string being checked, and re.search matches anywhere in the string being checked. Therefore, to check for quoted strings, you can use the expression '.*', which matches any sequence of characters between the quotes.

Notice that the function here returns either True or False. If the input does not match the rules, it does not give any indication of why the validation failed. It is best not to provide any information to an attacker when an incorrect input is detected. Error information can help attackers figure out what checking is going on and how checking could be bypassed.

This kind of check is a syntactic check that is designed to catch inputs that could be code rather than a valid name. This type of check does not catch inputs that are syntactically valid but impossible names, such as "x--ugh." These have a nuisance value in that they will pollute your database so that you will end up with many entries that do not relate to real people. You can address this problem to some extent by insisting that names must always start with a letter, but in general you need to devise other rules to check that names are sensible. Because there are so many possible name variations, however, there are no universal semantic checks that can be applied to them.

One of the problems with regular expressions is that they can quickly become very complex. For example, say that you want to write a checker for UK postcodes (zip codes in the United States). An example of a postcode is ML10 6LT, and the general form of a postcode is

```
<area><district><sector><unit>
```

So, using ML10 6LT as an example, the area is ML, the district within the area is 10, the sector within the district is 6, and the unit is LT. Postcodes are fine-grained so that an address can be identified from a house number and postcode.

There are several variants of valid postcodes, and a general regular expression to represent them is complex. For example, the postcode-matching expression below has been taken from a regular expression library:[7]

```
" ^([A-PR-UWYZ0-9][A-HK-Y0-9][AEHMNPRTVXY0-9]?
[ABEHMNPRVWXY0-9]? {1,2}[0-9][ABD-HJLN-UW-Z]{2}|GIR 0AA)$
```

---

[7]Author Stuart Wade, http://regexlib.com/REDetails.aspx?regexp_id=260

I haven't tested this expression, but I suspect it misses some special cases of London postcodes that have a slightly different organization.

Because of the complexity of regular expressions where there are many special cases, it is often simpler to break a regular expression into simpler sub-expressions and check each of these individually. This makes it easier to test that your validation check is accurate and complete. Therefore, for postcodes you might check the individual elements of the postcode separately rather than try to encompass all variants in a single regular expression.

8.2.2 Number checking

Number checking is used with numeric inputs to check that these are not too large or too small and that they are sensible values for the type of input. For example, if the user is expected to input height in meters, then you should expect a value between 0.6 m (a very small adult) and 2.6 m (a very tall adult). If possible, you should define a range check for all numeric inputs and check that the values input fall within that range.

Number checking is important for two reasons:

1. If numbers are too large or too small to be represented, this may lead to unpredictable results and numeric overflow or underflow exceptions. If these exceptions are not properly handled, large or small inputs can cause a program to crash.

2. The information in a database may be used by several other programs, and these may make their own assumptions about the numeric values stored. If the numbers are not as expected, this may lead to unpredictable results.

In addition to checking the ranges of inputs, you may perform checks on these inputs to ensure that they represent sensible values. Not only do these protect your system from accidental input errors, but they also stop intruders who have gained access using a legitimate user's credentials from seriously damaging their account. For example, if a user is expected to enter the reading from an electricity meter, then you should check that it is (a) equal to or larger than the previous meter reading and (b) consistent with the user's normal consumption. Say that a user's recent meter readings are

```
20377, 20732, 21057, 21568
```

In this sequence, the difference between readings varies from 325 to 511. This is normal given that different amounts of electricity are used at different times of the year. If the user then enters 32043 (a difference greater than 10,000), this value is unlikely. It could be a mistake, where the user has typed a 3 instead of a 2 as the first digit, or it could be a malicious input designed to cause a very large bill to be generated for that user. You should reject the value and ask for it to be reentered. If the user continues to enter the same value, you should then flag it for manual checking.

8.3 Failure management

Software is so complex that, irrespective of how much effort you put into fault avoidance, you will make mistakes. You will introduce faults into your program that will sometimes cause it to fail. Program failures may also be a consequence of the failure of an external service or component that your software depends on. Whatever the cause, you have to plan for failure and make provisions in your software for that failure to be as graceful as possible.

Software failures fall into three general categories:

1. *Data failures* The outputs of a computation are incorrect. For example, if someone's year of birth is 1981 and you calculate their age by subtracting 1981 from the current year, you may get an incorrect result. This type of error, if unnoticed, can pollute a database, as the incorrect information is used in computations that generate more incorrect information. Finding this kind of error relies on users reporting data anomalies that they have noticed. It does not usually lead to immediate system crashes or more widespread data corruption.

2. *Program exceptions* The program enters a state where normal continuation is impossible. If these exceptions are not handled, then control is transferred to the run-time system, which halts execution. In short, the software crashes. For example, if a request is made to open a file that does not exist, then an IOexception has occurred. Programmer errors often lead to exceptions.

3. *Timing failures* Interacting components fail to respond on time or where the responses of concurrently executing components are not properly synchronized. For example, if service S1 depends on service S2, and S2 does not respond to the request, then S1 will fail.

As a product developer, your priority should be to manage failures and thus minimize the effects of software failure on product users. This means that in the event of failure:

▪ persistent data (i.e., data in a database or files) should not be lost or corrupted;

▪ the user should be able to recover work done before the failure occurred;

▪ your software should not hang or crash;

▪ you should always "fail secure" so that confidential data are not left in a state where an attacker can gain access to them.

Sometimes failures are so unexpected that you can't achieve all of these goals, but you should design your software so that, as far as possible, it will fail gracefully without losing users' work.

Transactions are a mechanism that can be used to avoid database inconsistency and data loss. A transaction ensures that the database is always left in a consistent state. Changes are grouped and applied to the database as a group rather than individually. The group of changes is called an ACID transaction. This is guaranteed either to be successful, with all changes applied to the database, or to fail so that no changes are applied. The database is never left in an inconsistent state.

Therefore, to avoid the problem of data corruption caused by failures, you may use a relational DBMS and organize updates using transactions. As I explained in Chapter 6, however, this may not always be possible if you use a microservices architecture for your product or if you need a NoSQL database.

To allow a user to recover work and to avoid a system crash, you can use the exception-handling mechanisms of the programming language that you use. Exceptions are events that disrupt the normal flow of processing in a program (Figure 8.9). When an exception occurs, control is automatically transferred to exception-handling code. Most modern programming languages include a mechanism for exception handling. In Python, you use **try-except** keywords to indicate exception-handling code; in Java, the equivalent keywords are **try-catch**.

In most programming languages, exceptions are detected by the language run-time system. They are then passed to an exception handler for processing. If the language does not support exceptions or if no exception handler has been defined, control is transferred to the language's run-time system. This notifies the user of the error and terminates execution of the program.

Figure 8.9 Exception handling

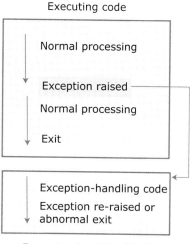

As part of this process, the run-time system usually does some tidying up; for example, it may close open files.

In languages with exceptions, the programmer can define exception handlers that are executed when an exception occurs. Program 8.4 is a Python example that illustrates some aspects of exception handling:

1. Normal processing is defined in a **try** block. If an exception of some kind occurs in a try block, control is passed to the exception block, defined after the **except** keyword.

2. The run-time system starts by looking for an exception handler in the method or function where the exception occurred. If it does not find a handler, it looks in the calling method or function until it finds one or concludes that there is no defined handler.

3. Once an exception has been processed in a method or function, it can be "raised." This means that exception processing is not finished. The run-time system will look for an exception handler in the calling method or function. If found, it will execute the code to handle the exception. You can see this in Program 8.4, where the exception is processed in do_normal_processing ( ) and in main ( ). The exception handler in main ( ) ensures that unencrypted workfiles are deleted before failure.

Program 8.4 Secure failure

```python
def do_normal_processing (wf, ef):
        # Normal processing here. Code below simulates exceptions
        # rather than normal processing
        try:
            wf.write ('line 1\n')
            ef.write ('encrypted line 1')
            wf.write ('line 2\n')
            wf.close()

            print ('Force exception by trying to open non-existent file')
            tst = open (test_root+'nofile')
        except IOError as e:
            print ('I/O exception has occurred')
            raise e


def main ():

    wf = open (test_root+'workfile.txt', 'w')
    ef = open(test_root+'encrypted.txt', 'w')

    try:
        do_normal_processing (wf, ef)

    except Exception:
        # If the modification time of the unencrypted work file (wf) is
        # later than the modification time of the encrypted file (ef)
        # then encrypt and write the workfile

        print ('Secure shutdown')

        wf_modtime = os.path.getmtime(test_root+'workfile.txt')
        ef_modtime = os.path.getmtime(test_root+'encrypted.txt')

        if wf_modtime > ef_modtime:
            encrypt_workfile (wf, ef)
        else:
            print ('Workfile modified before encrypted')
```

```
wf.close()
ef.close()
os.remove (test_root+'workfile.txt')

print ('Secure shutdown complete')
```

It is sometimes possible to define an exception handler that recovers from a problem that has arisen and allows execution to continue normally. This involves rolling back execution to a known correct state. More commonly, however, the exception is not a recoverable condition. The job of the exception handler is to tidy up before the system shuts down. As you can see in Program 8.4, this makes it possible for an application to "fail securely," so that no confidential information is exposed in the event of a system failure.

Two other mechanisms can reduce the probability of users losing work after a system failure (Figure 8.10):

1. *Activity logging* You keep a log of what the user has done and provide a way to replay that against their data. You don't need to keep a complete session record, simply a list of actions since the last time the data were saved to persistent store.

2. *Auto-save* You automatically save the user's data at set intervals—say, every 5 minutes. This means that, in the event of a failure, you can restore the saved data with the loss of only a small amount of work. In practice, you don't have to save all of the data but simply the changes made since the last explicit save.

If you are developing a system with a service-oriented architecture, you will probably use external services provided by some other provider. You have no control over these services, and the only information you have on service failure is whatever is provided in the service's API. As services may be written in different programming languages, these errors can't be returned as exception types but are usually returned as a numeric code. As I discussed in Chapter 6, RESTful services often use the standard HTTP error codes to return error information.

When you are calling an external service, you should always check that the return code of the called service indicates that it has operated successfully. You should also, if possible, check the validity of the result of the service call, as you cannot be certain that the external service has carried out its computation correctly. You can use an assert statement, which is available

Figure 8.10 Auto-save and activity logging

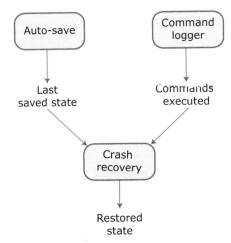

in languages such as Java and Python, to check the result of an external call. This raises an AssertionError exception if the call returns unexpected results.

Program 8.5 is a Python example of how to use assertions to check the results of an external service that checks credit ratings. I have simulated an external service with a call to a local function.

In addition to "normal" failures of service, where the service cannot deliver the result expected or the result is incorrect in some way, you have to deal with the situation where the service simply does not respond. If your program halts and waits for a reply, then your program will hang because of the unresponsive external service. The user will be unable to continue working.

The simplest way to get around this problem is to use a timeout mechanism where you start a timer when you call a service. If no response is received within some set time, the timer raises an exception and the service call is canceled.

As I explained in Chapter 6, however, the problem with using timeouts is that when you have several users of your service, the timeout mechanism kicks in for all of them and they all are delayed by the failed external service. It is better to access external services through a circuit breaker (see Figure 6.12). Using a timeout mechanism, the circuit breaker detects whether an external service is not responding and immediately rejects requests so that the calling service does not have to wait for a response. The circuit breaker can also periodically check whether the requested service has returned to normal operation.

When you are processing exceptions that will lead to a system failure, you have to decide what information you should give the user. Simply repeating a technical run-time system error message, such as "kernel panic," is not

Program 8.5 Using assertions to check results from an external service

```
def credit_checker (name, postcode, dob):

    # Assume that the function check_credit_rating calls an external service
    # to get a person's credit rating. It takes a name, postcode (zip code),
    # and date of birth as parameters and returns a sequence with the database
    # information (name, postcode, date of birth) plus a credit score between 0 and
    # 600. The final element in the sequence is an error_code that may
    # be 0 (successful completion), 1, or 2.


    NAME = 0
    POSTCODE = 1
    DOB = 2
    RATING = 3
    RETURNCODE = 4
    REQUEST_FAILURE = True
    ASSERTION_ERROR = False

    cr = ['', '', '', -1, 2]

    # Check credit rating simulates call to external service

    cr = check_credit_rating (name, postcode, dob)

    try:
        assert cr [NAME] == name and cr [POSTCODE] == postcode and cr [DOB] == dob
            and (cr [RATING] >= 0 and cr [RATING] <= 600) and
            (cr [RETURNCODE] >= 0 and cr [RETURNCODE] <= 2)

        if cr [RETURNCODE] == 0:
            do_normal_processing (cr)
        else:
            do_exception_processing (cr, name, postcode, dob, REQUEST_FAILURE)
    except AssertionError:
            do_exception_processing (cr, name, postcode, dob, ASSERTION_ERROR)
```

helpful. You should translate the error messages into a form that is under-standable and reassures users that they are not the cause of the problem. You may also send information to your servers for further analysis, although you must get the user's permission before you do this.

KEY POINTS

▪ The most important quality attributes for most software products are reliability, security, availability, usability, responsiveness, and maintainability.

▪ To avoid introducing faults into your program, you should use programming practices that reduce the probability that you will make mistakes.

▪ You should always aim to minimize complexity in your programs. Complexity makes programs harder to understand. It increases the chances of programmer errors and makes the program more difficult to change.

▪ Design patterns are tried and tested solutions to commonly occurring problems. Using patterns is an effective way to reduce program complexity.

▪ Refactoring is the process of reducing the complexity of an existing program without changing its functionality. It is good practice to refactor your program regularly to make it easier to read and understand.

▪ Input validation involves checking all user inputs to ensure that they are in the format that is expected by your program. Input validation helps avoid the introduction of malicious code into your system and traps user errors that can pollute your database.

▪ Regular expressions are a way of defining patterns that can match a range of possible input strings. Regular expression matching is a compact and fast way of checking that an input string conforms to the rules you have defined.

▪ You should check that numbers have sensible values depending on the type of input expected. You should also check number sequences for feasibility.

▪ You should assume that your program may fail and manage these failures so that they have minimal impact on the user.

▪ Exception management is supported in most modern programming languages. Control is transferred to your own exception handler to deal with the failure when a program exception is detected.

▪ You should log user updates and maintain user data snapshots as your program executes. In the event of a failure, you can use these to recover the work that the user has done. You should also include ways of recognizing and recovering from external service failures.

RECOMMENDED READING

"McCabe's Cyclomatic Complexity and Why We Don't Use It"

This post is a good explanation of the problems with the widely used cyclomatic complexity metric used to measure the decision complexity of code. As the author says, there is no simple measurement that can express complexity as a single number. (B. Hummel, 2014)
https://www.cqse.eu/en/blog/mccabe-cyclomatic-complexity/

"A Beginner's Guide to Design Patterns"

This readable introduction to design patterns includes examples of patterns that are different from the ones I've shown in the chapter. The accompanying code is in PHP but is fairly easy to understand. (N. Bautista, 2010)
https://code.tutsplus.com/articles/a-beginners-guide-to-design-patterns--net-12752

"A Pattern Language for Microservices"

This site includes a number of design patterns for microservices. I suspect there is quite a lot of overlap between these, and as we gain experience with microservices architectures, it will be possible to integrate some of these patterns. (C. Richardson, undated)
https://microservices.io/patterns/

"Catalog of Refactorings"

This is a comprehensive list of possible code refactorings that can be applied to reduce the complexity of your programs. (M. Fowler, 2013)
https://refactoring.com/catalog/index.html

"Input Validation Cheat Sheet"

This is a good summary of why you need to validate inputs and techniques you can use for this. (OWASP, 2017)
https://www.owasp.org/index.php/Input_Validation_Cheat_Sheet

"How to Handle Errors and Exceptions in Large Scale Software Projects"

This clearly written article discusses the difference between errors and exceptions and emphasizes the importance of managing these for reliable system operation. (F. Dimitreivski, 2017)
https://raygun.com/blog/errors-and-exceptions/

PRESENTATIONS, VIDEOS, AND LINKS

https://iansommerville.com/engineering-software-products/reliable-programming

EXERCISES

8.1. Describe, in your own words, each of the seven quality attributes shown in Figure 8.1.

8.2. Explain why reducing the complexity of a program is likely to reduce the number of faults in that program.

8.3. Explain why it is practically impossible to avoid introducing complexity into a software product.

8.4. Give two reasons why using design patterns in your code contributes to fault avoidance.

8.5. Based on your own programming experience, suggest three examples of code smells, apart from those listed in Table 8.6, that might suggest the need for program refactoring.

8.6. The Luhn algorithm is one of the checks applied to test whether a credit card number is valid. Assuming that credit card numbers are 16 digits long, look up and implement the Luhn algorithm to check that a valid credit card number has been input.

8.7. Using the regular expression library in a programming language that you know, write a short program to check whether a filename conforms to the Linux rules for filenames. Look up these rules if you don't know them.

8.8. An alternative to using regular expressions to check that an input string is valid is to write your own code to check the input. What are the advantages and disadvantages of using this approach?

8.9. Explain why the use of ACID transaction management in a database management system helps to avoid system failures.

8.10. Assume that you can save and restore the state of a program using functions called save_state ( ) and restore_state ( ). Show how these can be used in an exception handler to provide "non-stop" operation, where in the event of a failure, the system state is restored to the last saved state and execution is restarted from there.

9

Testing

Software testing is a process in which you execute your program using data that simulate user inputs. You observe your program's behavior to see whether or not it is doing what it's supposed to do. Tests pass if the behavior is what you expect; tests fail if the behavior differs from that expected.

If your program does what you expect, then for the inputs used, the program behaves correctly. If these inputs are representative of a larger set of inputs, you can infer that the program will behave correctly for all members of this larger input set. This is especially true if you test it with several inputs from this larger set and it behaves as you expect for all of them.

If the behavior of the program does not match the behavior that you expect, then this means your program has bugs that need to be fixed. There are two causes of program bugs:

1. *Programming errors* You have accidentally included faults in your program code. For example, a common programming error is an "off-by-1" error, in which you make a mistake with the upper bound of a sequence and fail to process the last element in that sequence.

2. *Understanding errors* You have misunderstood or have been unaware of some of the details of what the program is supposed to do. For example, if your program processes data from a file, you may not be aware that some of these data are in the wrong format, so your program doesn't include code to handle this.

In both cases, you have to change your code to fix the bug or bugs that the tests have identified. If your tests can isolate a bug to code within a single unit in your program, it is usually easy to find and fix that bug. However, if tests

Table 9.1 Types of testing

Test type	Testing goals
Functional testing	Test the functionality of the overall system. The goals of functional testing are to discover as many bugs as possible in the implementation of the system and to provide convincing evidence that the system is fit for its intended purpose.
User testing	Test that the software product is useful to and usable by end-users. You need to show that the features of the system help users do what they want to do with the software. You should also show that users understand how to access the software's features and can use these features effectively.
Performance and load testing	Test that the software works quickly and can handle the expected load placed on the system by its users. You need to show that the response and processing time of your system is acceptable to end-users. You also need to demonstrate that your system can handle different loads and scales gracefully as the load on the software increases.
Security testing	Test that the software maintains its integrity and can protect user information from theft and damage.

fail only when several program components are cooperating then it is often difficult to find and correct the bug or bugs.

Testing is the main technique used to convince software developers and product managers that a software product is fit for purpose and ready to be released for sale or general distribution. However, testing can never demonstrate that a program is fault-free and will never fail. There may be inputs or input combinations that have not been used in tests, and the program might fail if these inputs are used in practice.

Consequently, I think it is essential to use code reviews (covered in Section 9.5) as well as program testing. Reviews can find bugs that testing does not reveal. They involve the developer talking through the code with other developers, with the aim of finding bugs and suggesting ways in which the code can be improved.

In this chapter, I concentrate on functional testing. This means testing the software to find bugs and to demonstrate that the code works as expected. Other types of testing are also important for software product development, as shown in Table 9.1.

User testing focuses on testing what the software does and how users interact with the system (Figure 9.1), rather than testing the implementation to find

Figure 9.1 User testing

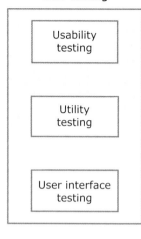

User testing

Usability testing	Test if users can learn to use the system quickly. Test if users can use the system without making mistakes.
Utility testing	Test if the system features allow users to do what they want to do with the system. Test if the system feature set offers enough coverage of users' work.
User interface testing	Test if users like the look and feel of the system's user interface.

bugs. Like functional testing, it identifies changes that need to be made to the software to make it more usable or responsive.

User testing may be organized into two phases:

1. *Alpha testing* Users work with developers to test the system. The aim of alpha testing is to answer the question "Do users really want the features that you've planned for your product?" Ideally, you should involve users in development from an early stage in the process so that you can get feedback on whether product features are likely to be useful. In practice, however, this is hard to organize, especially for new products.

2. *Beta testing* You distribute early versions of your product to users for comments. Beta testing also answers questions about the usefulness of features, but it is usually more concerned with the usability of the product and whether it works effectively in the user's operational environment.

Performance testing aims to check that the system responds quickly to requests for service. If the system processes transactions, you should test that transactions are processed without undue delays. We know that users have a low tolerance for delay when they use software. It is therefore important that when they activate a function, your product's response is fast. Performance can be adversely affected when a system is heavily loaded, so you need to test responses with different numbers of users and with different workloads.

Load testing usually involves preparing test scripts and using a simulator to mimic the actions of the system users. If you have designed your system for 100 simultaneous connections (say), you need to gradually increase the number of connections to this level and then go beyond the expected maximum load. In such cases, your system should degrade gracefully rather than fail abruptly. Load testing can help you identify bottlenecks in your code that need improvement. If your system is based on a microservices architecture, load testing can help you identify the services that you may need to auto-scale as the load on your software increases.

Security testing is a specialized process that involves testing the software to find vulnerabilities that attackers may exploit. I briefly discuss security testing in Section 9.4, but I don't have the expertise or experience to cover this topic in detail.

Major companies spend thousands of hours testing their products, yet bugs still reveal themselves after the software has been delivered and put into use. The reason is that modern software is incredibly complex. Not only are there thousands or hundreds of thousands of lines of code in the products themselves, but also the software interacts with a very complex environment (operating system, container, database, etc.) that may change in unexpected ways after a product has gone into use.

Consequently, you can never exhaustively test a system or be completely confident that it does not contain faults. You have to make a pragmatic decision about the cost effectiveness of testing and release your product when you think it is good enough. You may deliberately decide to release software with known bugs because the software meets a need. Users may be willing to accept some unreliability if the software saves them time and effort in other areas. You have to be very careful here, however. Many software companies have overestimated the usefulness of their product and have failed because users have rejected their buggy software.

9.1 Functional testing

Functional testing involves developing a large set of program tests so that, ideally, all of a program's code is executed at least once. The number of tests needed obviously depends on the size and the functionality of the application. For a business-focused web application, you may have to develop thousands of tests to convince yourself that your product is ready for release to customers.

Figure 9.2 Functional testing

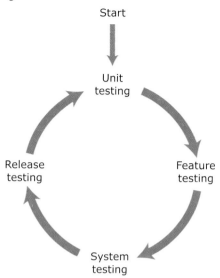

Software testing is a staged activity in which you initially test individual units of code (Figure 9.2 and Table 9.2). You integrate code units with other units to create larger units and then do more testing. The process continues until you have created a complete system ready for release.

You should not wait until you have a complete system before you start system testing. Testing should start on the day you start writing code. You should test as you implement code, so that even a minimal system with hardly any features is tested. As more features are added, the develop/test cycle continues until a finished system is available. This develop/test cycle is simplified if you develop automated tests so that you can rerun tests whenever you make code changes.

9.1.1 Unit testing

Unit testing is part of the normal process of program development. While you are developing a code unit, you should also develop tests for that code. A code unit is anything that has a clearly defined responsibility. It is usually a function or class method but can also be a module that includes a small number of other functions. It is normally possible to automate unit tests, as I explain in Section 9.2.

Table 9.2 Functional testing processes

Testing process	Description
Unit testing	The aim of unit testing is to test program units in isolation. Tests should be designed to execute all of the code in a unit at least once. Individual code units are tested by the programmer as they are developed.
Feature testing	Code units are integrated to create features. Feature tests should test all aspects of a feature. All of the programmers who contribute code units to a feature should be involved in its testing.
System testing	Code units are integrated to create a working (perhaps incomplete) version of a system. The aim of system testing is to check that there are no unexpected interactions between the features in the system. System testing may also involve checking the responsiveness, reliability, and security of the system. In large companies, a dedicated testing team may be responsible for system testing. In small companies, this is impractical, so product developers are also involved in system testing.
Release testing	The system is packaged for release to customers and the release is tested to check that it operates as expected. The software may be released as a cloud service or as a download to be installed on a customer's computer or mobile device. If DevOps is used, then the development team is responsible for release testing; otherwise, a separate team has that responsibility.

Unit testing is based on a simple general principle:

If a program unit behaves as expected for a set of inputs that have some shared characteristics, it will behave in the same way for a larger set whose members share these characteristics.

For example, say your program behaves correctly when presented with inputs from the set {1, 5, 17, 45, 99}. If you know that the intention of the unit is to process integer inputs in the range 1 to 99, you may conclude that it will also process all other integers in this range correctly.

To test a program efficiently, you should identify sets of inputs that will be treated in the same way in your code. These sets are called equivalence partitions (Figure 9.3). The equivalence partitions that you identify should not just include those containing inputs that produce the correct values. You should also identify "incorrectness partitions," where the inputs are deliberately incorrect. These test that your program detects and handles incorrect inputs in the expected way.

Figure 9.3 Equivalence partitions

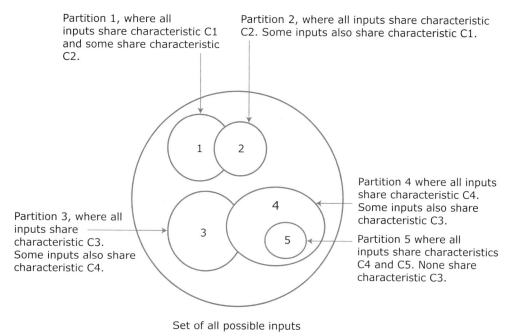

Partition 1, where all inputs share characteristic C1 and some share characteristic C2.

Partition 2, where all inputs share characteristic C2. Some inputs also share characteristic C1.

Partition 4 where all inputs share characteristic C4. Some inputs also share characteristic C3.

Partition 3, where all inputs share characteristic C3. Some inputs also share characteristic C4.

Partition 5 where all inputs share characteristics C4 and C5. None share characteristic C3.

Set of all possible inputs

You should test your program using several inputs from each equivalence partition. If possible, you should identify partition boundaries and choose inputs at these boundaries. The reason for this is that a very common programming mistake is an off-by-1 error, where either the first or the last element in a loop is not properly handled. You may also identify output equivalence partitions and create test inputs that generate results in these partitions.

I illustrate the idea of equivalence partitions using tests for the simple name-checking function that I used in Chapter 8 to demonstrate the use of regular expressions (see Program 8.3). I show the program again as Program 9.1. This function checks that its input parameter (a person's family name) conforms to a set of rules. Recall the rules for family names:

1. The length of a name should be between 2 and 40 characters.

2. The characters in the name must be alphabetic or alphabetic characters with an accent plus a small number of special separator characters.

3. The only nonalphabetic separator characters allowed are hyphen and apostrophe. Names must start with a letter.

Program 9.1 A name-checking function

```
def namecheck (s):

    # Checks that a name only includes alphabetic characters,-, or
    # a single quote. Names must be between 2 and 40 characters long.
    # Quoted strings and -- are disallowed.

    namex = r"^[a-zA-Z][a-zA-Z-']{1,39}$"
    if re.match (namex, s):
        if re.search ("'.*'", s) or re.search ("--", s):
            return False
        else:
            return True
    else:
        return False
```

From these rules, you can identify the equivalence partitions shown in Table 9.3. You can then go on to derive inputs from these equivalence partitions, such as Sommerville, O'Connell, Washington-Wilson, Z, and -Wesley. I return to this example in the test automation section and show the actual inputs that I used to test this function.

Table 9.3 Equivalence partitions for the name-checking function

Equivalence partition	Characteristic
Correct names 1	The inputs include only alphabetic characters and are between 2 and 40 characters long.
Correct names 2	The inputs include only alphabetic characters, hyphens, or apostrophes and are between 2 and 40 characters long.
Incorrect names 1	The inputs are between 2 and 40 characters long but include disallowed characters.
Incorrect names 2	The inputs include only allowed characters but are either a single character or more than 40 characters long.
Incorrect names 3	The inputs are between 2 and 40 characters long but the first character is a hyphen or an apostrophe.
Incorrect names 4	The inputs include only valid characters and are between 2 and 40 characters long but include a double hyphen, quoted text, or both.

Table 9.4   Unit testing guidelines

Guideline	Explanation
Test edge cases	If your partition has upper and lower bounds (e.g., length of strings, numbers, etc.), choose inputs at the edges of the range.
Force errors	Choose test inputs that force the system to generate all error messages. Choose test inputs that should generate invalid outputs.
Fill buffers	Choose test inputs that cause all input buffers to overflow.
Repeat yourself	Repeat the same test input or series of inputs several times.
Overflow and underflow	If your program does numeric calculations, choose test inputs that cause it to calculate very large or very small numbers.
Don't forget null and zero	If your program uses pointers or strings, always test with null pointers and strings. If you use sequences, test with an empty sequence. For numeric inputs, always test with zero.
Keep count	When dealing with lists and list transformations, keep count of the number of elements in each list and check that these are consistent after each transformation.
One is different	If your program deals with sequences, always test with sequences that have a single value.

Once you have identified equivalence partitions, the question is "What are the inputs from each partition that are most likely to uncover bugs?" Many proposals for unit testing guidelines are based around equivalence partitions and advise what test inputs to use. For example, Table 9.4 shows a number of testing guidelines based on those suggested by James Whittaker.[1]

These guidelines are not hard and fast rules but are based on extensive testing experience. A general observation that underlies these guidelines is that programmers make mistakes at boundaries. Consequently, test inputs at natural boundaries are the most likely to reveal program bugs. For example, for numeric inputs, you should always test using the highest and lowest possible values; for string inputs, you should always test with the empty string and single-character strings.

---

[1]James A. Whittaker, *How to Break Software: A Practical Guide to Testing* (Boston: Addison-Wesley, 2002).

9.1.2 Feature testing

A product feature implements some useful user functionality. Features have to be tested to show that the functionality is implemented as expected and that the functionality meets the real needs of users. For example, if your product has a feature that allows users to log in using their Google account, then you have to check that this feature registers the users correctly and informs them of what information will be shared with Google. You may want to check that users are given the option to sign up for email information about your product.

Normally, a feature that does several things is implemented by multiple interacting program units. These units may be implemented by different developers, and all of these developers should be involved in the feature-testing process. This process should involve two types of tests:

1. *Interaction tests* These test the interactions between the units that implement the feature. The developers of the units that are combined to make up the feature may have different understandings of what is required of that feature. These misunderstandings will not show up in unit tests; they may only come to light when the units are integrated. The integration may also reveal bugs in program units that were not exposed by unit testing.

2. *Usefulness tests* These test that the feature implements what users are likely to want. For example, the developers of a login with a Google feature may have implemented an opt-out default on registration so that users receive all emails from a company. Users must expressly choose what type of emails they don't want. They might prefer an opt-in default so they can choose what types of email they do want to receive. The product manager should be closely involved in designing usefulness tests, as they should have the most knowledge of user preferences.

A good way to organize feature testing is around a scenario or a set of user stories (see Chapter 3). For example, the "sign-in with Google" feature might be covered by three user stories, as shown in Table 9.5. Based on these user stories, you might develop a set of tests for the feature that carry out checks as shown in Table 9.6.

To develop feature tests, you need to understand the feature from the perspective of the user representatives and the product manager. You need to ask

Table 9.5 User stories for the sign-in with Google feature

Story title	User story
User registration	As a user, I want to be able to log in without creating a new account so that I don't have to remember another login ID and password.
Information sharing	As a user, I want to know what information you will share with other companies. I want to be able to cancel my registration if I don't want to share this information.
Email choice	As a user, I want to be able to choose the types of email that I'll get from you when I register for an account.

Table 9.6 Feature tests for sign-in with Google

Test	Description
Initial login screen	Test that the screen displaying a request for Google account credentials is correctly displayed when a user clicks on the "Sign-in with Google" link. Test that the login is completed if the user is already logged in to Google.
Incorrect credentials	Test that the error message and retry screen are displayed if the user inputs incorrect Google credentials.
Shared information	Test that the information shared with Google is displayed, along with a cancel or confirm option. Test that the registration is canceled if the cancel option is chosen.
Email opt-in	Test that the user is offered a menu of options for email information and can choose multiple items to opt in to emails. Test that the user is not registered for any emails if no options are selected.

them to explain what they expect from a feature and how they normally use it. There are published guidelines on how to develop feature tests, but I find these guidelines to be vague and generally unhelpful.

Feature testing is an integral part of behavior-driven development (BDD). In BDD, the behavior of a product is specified using a domain-specific language, and feature tests are automatically derived from this specification. Special-purpose tools are available to automate these tests. I include a link to information on BDD in the Recommended Reading section, but as I've never used this approach to software development, I can't comment on its effectiveness.

9.1.3 System and release testing

System testing involves testing the system as a whole rather than the individual system features. System testing starts at an early stage of the product development process—as soon as you have a workable, albeit incomplete, version of a system. System testing should focus on four issues:

1. Testing to discover if there are unexpected and unwanted interactions between the features in a system.

2. Testing to discover if the system features work together effectively to support what users really want to do with the system.

3. Testing the system to make sure it operates in the expected way in the different environments where it will be used.

4. Testing the responsiveness, throughput, security, and other quality attributes of the system.

Unexpected interactions between features can occur because feature designers may make different assumptions about how features operate. An example is a word processor that includes the ability to define multiple columns, with justified text in each column. The designer of the text justification feature may assume that it will always be possible to fit words into a column. The designer of a hyphenation feature may allow users to turn off hyphenation. However, if a user defines very narrow columns and turns hyphenation off, then it may be impossible to fit long words into the narrow column.

When you are testing for feature interaction, you should not just be looking for bugs or omissions in the feature implementation. Software products are intended to help users accomplish some task. You therefore need to design tests to check that a product is really effective in doing what users might want to do with it. It may be that all of the features they need are available but it is awkward to use them together, or some features may not really be well suited to supporting a user's tasks.

Environment testing involves testing that your system works in its intended operating environment and integrates properly with other software. If your product is accessed using a browser rather than a dedicated app, then you need to test it with the different browsers that are likely to be used. If you integrate with other software, you need to check that the integration works properly and information is seamlessly exchanged.

I think the best way to systematically test a system is to start with a set of scenarios that describe possible uses of the system and then work through these scenarios each time a new version of the system is created. You may have developed these scenarios as part of the process of understanding what the system has to do. If not, you should create scenarios so that you can have a repeatable testing process.

Table 9.7 Choosing a holiday destination

Andrew and Maria have a two-year-old son and a four-month-old daughter. They live in Scotland and they want to have a holiday in the sunshine. However, they are concerned about the hassle of flying with young children. They decide to try a family holiday-planning product to help them choose a destination that is easy to get to and that fits in with their children's routines.

Maria navigates to the holiday planner website and selects the "find a destination" page. This presents a screen with a number of options. She can choose a specific destination or a departure airport and find all destinations that have direct flights from that airport. She can also input the time band that she'd prefer for flights, holiday dates, and a maximum cost per person.

Edinburgh is their closest departure airport. She chooses "find direct flights." The system then presents a list of countries that have direct flights from Edinburgh and the days when these flights operate. She selects France, Italy, Portugal, and Spain and requests further information about these flights. She then sets a filter to display flights that leave on a Saturday or Sunday after 7.30 am and arrive before 6 pm. She also sets the maximum acceptable cost for a flight. The list of flights is pruned according to the filter and is redisplayed. Maria then clicks on the flight she wants. This opens a tab in her browser showing a booking form for this flight on the airline's website.

For example, say you are developing a holiday-planning product that's aimed at families traveling with children. For those families, direct flights are easier than changing at a hub airport. To fit in with children's sleep patterns, it is best for them to travel on daytime flights rather than on flights that leave very early or arrive late in the evening. Table 9.7 is an example of a scenario that describes parents with young children planning their holiday.

Using the scenario, you identify a set of end-to-end pathways that users might follow when using the system. An end-to-end pathway is a sequence of actions from starting to use the system for the task through to completion of the task. There are several completion states when using this system, and you should identify a pathway for all of them. Table 9.8 shows examples of pathways that could be used.

For each pathway, you need to check that the system's responses are correct and that appropriate information is provided to the user. For example, if Maria requests direct flights from Edinburgh Airport, you should check that the flights displayed match those that are shown on Edinburgh Airport's website. You should not just assume that the source used for flight information is correct. You also have to test that the system behaves sensibly if external services on which it depends, such as airline websites, are unavailable.

As with unit and feature testing, you should try to automate as many of the system tests as possible and run these tests each time a new version of the system is created. Because end-to-end pathways involve user interaction, however, it may be impractical to automate all system tests. As I explain in

Table 9.8 End-to-end pathways

1. User inputs departure airport and chooses to see only direct flights. User quits.

2. User inputs departure airport and chooses to see all flights. User quits.

3. User chooses destination country and chooses to see all flights. User quits.

4. User inputs departure airport and chooses to see direct flights. User sets filter specifying departure times and prices. User quits.

5. User inputs departure airport and chooses to see direct flights. User sets filter specifying departure times and prices. User selects a displayed flight and clicks through to airline website. User returns to holiday planner after booking flight.

Section 9.2, some testing tools can mimic interaction through a browser by capturing and replaying mouse clicks and selections. Sometimes, however, there are no real alternatives to manual testing based on a test script that describes the actions that a tester should take.

Release testing is a type of testing of a system that's intended for release to customers. There are two fundamental differences between release testing and system testing:

1. Release testing tests the system in its real operational environment rather than in a test environment. Although you obviously try to simulate the real environment when testing, there may be differences between it and the test environment. Problems commonly arise with real user data, which are sometimes more complex and less reliable than test data.

2. The aim of release testing is to decide if the system is good enough to release, not to detect bugs in the system. Therefore, you may ignore some tests that "fail" if these have minimal consequences for most users.

Preparing a system for release involves packaging that system for deployment (e.g., in a container if it is a cloud service) and installing software and libraries that are used by your product. You must define configuration parameters, such as the name of a root directory, the database size limit per user, and so on. However, you may make mistakes in this installation process. Therefore, you should rerun the system tests to check that you have not introduced new bugs that affect the functionality, performance, or usability of the system. Wherever possible, when testing the software release you should use real user data and other information collected from running the system.

As I discuss in Chapter 10, if your product is deployed in the cloud, you may use a continuous release process. This involves releasing a new version of your product whenever a change is made. This is practical only if you make frequent small changes and use automated tests to check that these changes have not introduced new bugs into your program.

Figure 9.4 Automated testing

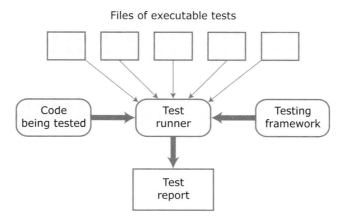

Files of executable tests

Code being tested → Test runner ← Testing framework

Test report

9.2 Test automation

One of the most significant innovations in agile software engineering is automated testing, which is now widely used in product development companies. Automated testing (Figure 9.4) is based on the idea that tests should be executable. An executable test includes the input data to the unit that is being tested, the expected result, and a check that the unit returns the expected result. You run the test and the test passes if the unit returns the expected result. Normally, you should develop hundreds or thousands of executable tests for a software product.

The development of automated testing frameworks, such as JUnit for Java in the 1990s, reduced the effort involved in developing executable tests. Testing frameworks are now available for all widely used programming languages. A suite of hundreds of unit tests, developed using a framework, can be run on a desktop computer in a few seconds. A test report shows the tests that have passed and failed.

Testing frameworks provide a base class, called something like "TestCase" that is used by the testing framework. To create an automated test, you define your own test class as a subclass of this TestCase class. Testing frameworks include a way of running all of the tests defined in the classes that are based on TestCase and reporting the results of the tests.

I illustrate this for Python in Program 9.2, which shows examples of simple automated tests for a function that's part of a financial planning product. The function calculates the interest due based on the amount of the loan and the period of the loan. The comments in the code explain the fundamental components of the test case.

Program 9.2 Test methods for an interest calculator

```
# TestInterestCalculator inherits attributes and methods from the class
# TestCase in the testing framework unittest

class TestInterestCalculator (unittest.TestCase):

        # Define a set of unit tests where each test tests one thing only
        # Tests should start with test_ and the name should explain
        # what is being tested

        def test_zeroprincipal (self):

                #Arrange - set up the test parameters
                p = 0
                r = 3
                n = 31
                result_should_be = 0

                #Action - Call the method to be tested
                interest = interest_calculator (p, r, n)

                #Assert - test what should be true
                self.assertEqual (result_should_be, interest)


        def test_yearly_interest (self):

                #Arrange - set up the test parameters
                p = 17000
                r = 3
                n = 365

                #Action - Call the method to be tested
                result_should_be = 270.36
                interest = interest_calculator (p, r, n)

                #Assert - test what should be true
                self.assertEqual (result_should_be, interest)
```

Program 9.2 shows two tests. In the first test (test_zeroprincipal), the sum involved (the principal) is zero, so no interest should be payable. In the second test (test_yearly_interest), the interest is calculated for a 365-day year. Obviously, you need more tests to test this unit properly, such as tests for leap years, tests to calculate the monthly interest that take the fact that months are of different lengths into account and tests that check the interest calculated is correct where the principal is partially or completely repaid during the year.

It is good practice to structure automated tests in three parts:

1. *Arrange* You set up the system to run the test. This involves defining the test parameters and, if necessary, mock objects that emulate the functionality of code that has not yet been developed.

2. *Action* You call the unit that is being tested with the test parameters.

3. *Assert* You make an assertion about what should hold if the unit being tested has executed successfully. In Program 9.2, I use assertEqual, which checks if its parameters are equal.

Once you set these up for one test, it is usually straightforward to reuse the setup code in other tests of the same unit. Ideally, you should have only one assertion in each test. If you have multiple assertions, you may not be able to tell which of them has failed. This is not an unbreakable rule, however. For example, if a function returns a composite value, then multiple assertions, with an assertion for each element of the composite, may be the simplest way to write the test. If you use multiple assertions in a test, you may include additional code that indicates which of the assertions has failed.

If you use equivalence partitions to identify test inputs, you should have several automated tests based on correct and incorrect inputs from each partition. I illustrate this in Program 9.3.

This program shows the tests that I developed for the name-checking function shown in Program 9.1. I deliberately include an extra test called test_thiswillfail to show the output produced from a test where the tested code does not behave as expected. To make the example program shorter, I do not use explicit arrange/action/assert sections.

Program 9.3 Executable tests for the namecheck function

```python
import unittest
from RE_checker import namecheck

class TestNameCheck (unittest.TestCase):

    def test_alphaname (self):
            self.assertTrue (namecheck ('Sommerville'))

    def test_doublequote (self):
            self.assertFalse (namecheck ("Thisis'maliciouscode'"))
    def test_namestartswithhyphen (self):
            self.assertFalse (namecheck ('-Sommerville'))

    def test_namestartswithquote (self):
            self.assertFalse (namecheck ("'Reilly"))

    def test_nametoolong (self):
            self.assertFalse (namecheck
            ('Thisisalongstringwithmorethan40charactersfrombeginningtoend'))

    def test_nametooshort (self):
            self.assertFalse (namecheck ('S'))

    def test_namewithdigit (self):
            self.assertFalse (namecheck('C-3PO'))

    def test_namewithdoublehyphen (self):
            self.assertFalse (namecheck ('--badcode'))

    def test_namewithhyphen (self):
            self.assertTrue (namecheck ('Washington-Wilson'))

    def test_namewithinvalidchar (self):
            self.assertFalse (namecheck('Sommer_ville'))

    def test_namewithquote (self):
            self.assertTrue (namecheck ("O'Reilly"))

    def test_namewithspaces (self):
            self.assertFalse (namecheck ('Washington Wilson'))

    def test_shortname (self):
            self.assertTrue ('Sx')

    def test_thiswillfail (self):
            self.assertTrue (namecheck ("O Reilly"))
```

Program 9.4 Code to run unit tests from files

```
import unittest

loader = unittest.TestLoader()

#Find the test files in the current directory

tests = loader.discover('.')

#Specify the level of information provided by the test runner

testRunner = unittest.runner.TextTestRunner(verbosity=2)
            testRunner.run(tests)
```

The testing framework provides a "test runner" that runs tests and reports results. To use a test runner, you set up your tests in files that start with a reserved name—in Python, the filename should start with 'test_'. The test runner finds all of the test files and runs them. I organize the unit tests by including the tests for each unit in a separate file.

Program 9.4 shows some simple code for running a set of tests. Program 9.5 shows the output produced by the test runner when the tests shown in Program 9.3 are executed.

You can see that the failed test (test_thiswillfail) provides information about the type of failure. Some test frameworks use visual indicators of success. A red light means some tests have failed; a green light means all tests have successfully executed.

When you are writing automated tests, you should keep them as simple as possible. This is important because test code, like any other program, inevitably includes bugs. You normally have thousands of tests for a product, so there will inevitably be some tests that are themselves incorrect.

As the point of automated testing is to avoid the manual checking of test outputs, you can't realistically discover test errors by running the tests. Therefore, you have to use two approaches to reduce the chances of test errors:

1. Make tests as simple as possible. The more complex the test, the more likely that it will be buggy. The test condition should be immediately obvious when reading the code.

2. Review all tests along with the code that they test. As part of the review process (Section 9.5), someone apart from the test programmer should check the tests for correctness.

Program 9.5 Unit test results

```
test_alphaname (test_alltests_namechecker.TestNameCheck) . . . ok
test_doublequote (test_alltests_namechecker.TestNameCheck) . . . ok
test_namestartswithhyphen (test_alltests_namechecker.TestNameCheck) . . . ok
test_namestartswithquote (test_alltests_namechecker.TestNameCheck) . . . ok
test_nametoolong (test_alltests_namechecker.TestNameCheck) . . . ok
test_nametooshort (test_alltests_namechecker.TestNameCheck) . . . ok
test_namewithdigit (test_alltests_namechecker.TestNameCheck) . . . ok
test_namewithdoublehyphen (test_alltests_namechecker.TestNameCheck) . . . ok
test_namewithhyphen (test_alltests_namechecker.TestNameCheck) . . . ok
test_namewithinvalidchar (test_alltests_namechecker.TestNameCheck) . . . ok
test_namewithquote (test_alltests_namechecker.TestNameCheck) . . . ok
test_namewithspaces (test_alltests_namechecker.TestNameCheck) . . . ok
test_shortname (test_alltests_namechecker.TestNameCheck) . . . ok
test_thiswillfail (test_alltests_namechecker.TestNameCheck) . . . FAIL


======================================================================
FAIL: test_thiswillfail (test_alltests_namechecker.TestNameCheck)
----------------------------------------------------------------------

Traceback (most recent call last):
    File "/Users/iansommerville/Dropbox/Python/Engineering Software
    Book/test_alltests_namechecker.py", line 46, in test_thiswillfail
        self.assertTrue (namecheck ("O Reilly"))
AssertionError: False is not true
----------------------------------------------------------------------

Ran 14 tests in 0.001s


FAILED (failures=1)
```

Regression testing is the process of re-running previous tests when you make a change to a system. This testing checks that the change has not had unexpected side effects. The code change may have inadvertently broken existing code, or it may reveal bugs that were undetected in earlier tests. If you use automated tests, regression testing takes very little time. Therefore, after you make any change to your code, even a very minor change, you should always re-run all tests to make sure that everything continues to work as expected.

Figure 9.5 The test pyramid

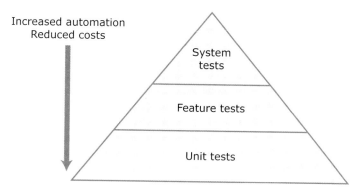

Unit tests are the easiest to automate, so the majority of your tests should be unit tests. Mike Cohn, who first proposed the test pyramid (Figure 9.5), suggests that 70% of automated tests should be unit tests, 20% feature tests (he called these service tests), and 10% system tests (UI tests).

The implementation of system features usually involves integrating functional units into components and then integrating these components to implement the feature. If you have good unit tests, you can be confident that the individual functional units and components that implement the feature will behave as you expect. However, as I explained, units may make different assumptions or may interact unexpectedly, so you still need feature tests.

Generally, users access features through the product's graphical user interface (GUI). However, GUI-based testing is expensive to automate so it is best to use an alternative feature testing strategy. This involves designing your product so that its features can be directly accessed through an API, not just from the user interface. The feature tests can then access features directly through the API without the need for direct user interaction through the system's GUI (Figure 9.6). Accessing features through an API has the additional benefit that it is possible to re-implement the GUI without changing the functional components of the software.

For example, a series of API calls may be required to implement a feature that allows a user to share a document with another user by specifying their email address. These calls collect the email address and the document identification information, check that the access permissions on the document allow sharing, check that the specified email address is valid and is a registered system user, and add the document to the sharing user's workspace.

Figure 9.6 Feature testing through an API

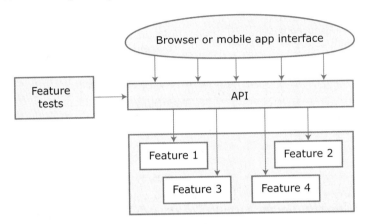

When these calls have been executed, a number of conditions should hold:

■ The status of the document is "shared."

■ The list of users sharing the document includes the specified email address.

■ There have been no deletions from the list of users sharing the document.

■ The shared document is visible to all users in the sharing list.

You can't usually implement automated feature tests using a single assertion. You need multiple assertions to check that the feature has executed as expected. Some feature test automation may be possible using a unit testing framework, but sometimes you have to use a specialized feature testing framework.

System testing, which should follow feature testing, involves testing the system as a surrogate user. You identify user activities, possibly from scenarios, and then use the system to work through these activities. As a system tester, you go through a process of selecting items from menus, making screen selections, inputting information from the keyboard, and so on. You have to make careful observations and notes of how the system responds and of unexpected system behavior. You are looking for interactions between features that cause problems, sequences of actions that lead to system crashes, and other issues.

Manual system testing, when testers have to repeat sequences of actions, is boring and prone to errors. In some cases, the timing of actions is important and is practically impossible to repeat consistently. To avoid these problems, testing tools have been developed to record a series of actions and automatically replay them when a system is retested (Figure 9.7).

Figure 9.7 Interaction recording and playback

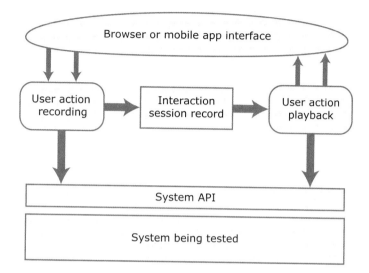

Interaction recording tools record mouse movements and clicks, menu selections, keyboard inputs, and so on. They save the interaction session and can replay it, sending commands to the application and replicating them in the user's browser interface. These tools also provide scripting support so that you can write and execute scenarios expressed as test scripts. This is particularly useful for cross-browser testing, where you need to check that your software works in the same way with different browsers.

As I said, automated testing is one of the most important developments in software engineering, and I believe it has led to significant improvements in program quality. The danger with automated testing, however, is automation bias. Automation bias means that you choose tests because they can be automated, not because they are the best tests for the system. In reality, not all tests can be automated. Subtle problems, such as timing problems and issues caused by incorrect data dependencies, may only be detectable using manual testing. Consequently, you should always plan to do some manual product testing, where you simulate user sessions, before your product is released.

9.3 Test-driven development

Test-driven development (TDD) is an approach to program development that is based on the general idea that you should write an executable test or tests for code that you are writing before you write the code. TDD was introduced by early users of the Extreme Programming agile method, but it can be used

Figure 9.8 Test-driven development

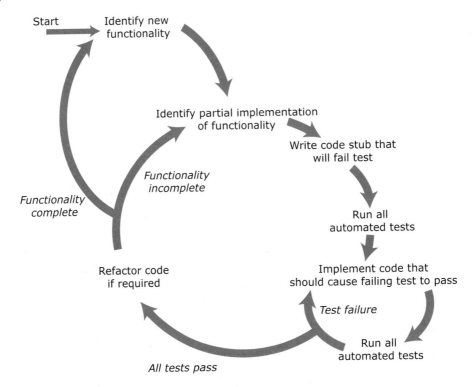

with any incremental development approach. Figure 9.8 is a model of the test-driven development process.

Assume that you have identified some increment of functionality to be implemented. The stages of the test-driven development process are shown in Table 9.9.

Test-driven development relies on automated testing. Every time you add some functionality, you develop a new test and add it to the test suite. All of the tests in the test suite must pass before you move on to developing the next increment.

The benefits of test-driven development are:

1. It is a systematic approach to testing in which tests are clearly linked to sections of the program code. This means you can be confident that your tests cover all of the code that has been developed and that there are no untested code sections in the delivered code. In my view, this is the most significant benefit of TDD.

Table 9.9 Stages of test-driven development

Activity	Description
Identify partial implementation	Break down the implementation of the functionality required into smaller mini-units. Choose one of these mini-units for implementation.
Write mini-unit tests	Write one or more automated tests for the mini-unit that you have chosen for implementation. The mini-unit should pass these tests if it is properly implemented.
Write a code stub that will fail test	Write incomplete code that will be called to implement the mini-unit. You know this will fail.
Run all automated tests	Run all existing automated tests. All previous tests should pass. The test for the incomplete code should fail.
Implement code that should cause the failing test to pass	Write code to implement the mini-unit, which should cause it to operate correctly.
Rerun all automated tests	If any tests fail, your code is incorrect. Keep working on it until all tests pass.
Refactor code if required	If all tests pass, you can move on to implementing the next mini-unit. If you see ways of improving your code, you should do this before the next stage of implementation.

2. The tests act as a written specification for the program code. In principle at least, it should be possible to understand what the program does by reading the tests. I'm not convinced that test code is all you need for a specification, but there is no doubt that tests help you understand the code being tested.

3. Debugging is simplified because, when a program failure is observed, you can immediately link this to the last increment of code that you added to the system.

4. It is argued that TDD leads to simpler code, as programmers only write code that's necessary to pass tests. They don't overengineer their code with complex features that aren't needed.

Test-driven development and automated testing using executable tests were developed around the same time. Some people who write about the benefits of TDD conflate it and automated testing. Consequently, you may see regression testing suggested as a benefit of TDD, whereas this is actually a benefit of automated testing, whether or not these tests were developed before or after the code. The same is true for refactoring tests that check that code refactoring has not introduced new bugs into the code.

Test-driven development works best for the development of individual program units; it is more difficult to apply to system testing. Even the strongest advocates of TDD accept that it is challenging to use this approach when you are developing and testing systems with graphical user interfaces.

Many programmers have enthusiastically adopted TDD and are happy with this approach. They claim that it is a more productive way to develop software and that the resulting software has fewer bugs than it would have without TDD. They also claim that the developed code is better structured and easier to understand. There have been several experiments to test whether this is actually the case. These experiments were inconclusive.

However, there are divided opinions in the software engineering community about the value of TDD. After experimenting with the approach for some time, I wrote a blog post about why I had decided to give up on it.[2] TDD didn't work for me because I spent more time thinking about the tests than about the program, and I didn't think that was a good thing.

My post received a huge number of comments, which were roughly evenly split. Adherents of TDD, as I anticipated, simply told me that I wasn't doing it right. Others strongly agreed with what I said about the problems with the approach. I've summarized my reasons for not using TDD in Table 9.10. My view is that TDD suits some people psychologically better than others. It didn't really work for me, but it might work for you.

As I say in my blog post, I think it is sensible to be pragmatic about TDD. Sometimes it is very helpful to write tests first, as it helps you clarify your understanding of what the program should do. On other occasions, it is faster and easier to develop that understanding by writing code first.

---

[2]http://iansommerville.com/systems-software-and-technology/giving-up-on-test-first-development/

Table 9.10 My reasons for not using TDD

Reason	Explanation
TDD discourages radical program change.	I found that I was reluctant to make refactoring decisions that I knew would cause many tests to fail. I tended to avoid radical program change for this reason.
I focused on the tests rather than the problem I was trying to solve.	A basic principle of TDD is that your design should be driven by the tests you have written. I found that I was unconsciously redefining the problem I was trying to solve to make it easier to write tests. This meant that I sometimes didn't implement important checks, because it was difficult to write tests in advance of their implementation.
I spent too much time thinking about the implementation details rather than the programming problem.	Sometimes when programming, it is best to step back and look at the program as a whole rather than focusing on implementation details. TDD encourages a focus on details that might cause tests to pass or fail rather than the overall structure of the program.
It is hard to write "bad data" tests.	Many problems involve dealing with messy and incomplete data. It is practically impossible to anticipate all of the data problems that might arise and write tests for these in advance. You might argue that you should simply reject bad data, but this is sometimes impractical.

9.4 Security testing

The goals of program testing are to find bugs and to provide convincing evidence that the program being tested does what it is supposed to do. Security testing has comparable goals. It aims to find vulnerabilities that an attacker may exploit and to provide convincing evidence that the system is sufficiently secure. The tests should demonstrate that the system can resist attacks on its availability, attacks that try to inject malware, and attacks that try to corrupt or steal users' data and identity.

Discovering vulnerabilities is much harder than finding bugs. Functional tests to discover bugs are driven by an understanding of what the software should do. Your tests only have to show that your software is operating as expected. However, you face three challenges in vulnerability testing:

Table 9.11 Examples of security risks

Unauthorized attacker gains access to a system using authorized credentials.

Authorized individual accesses resources that are forbidden to that person.

Authentication system fails to detect unauthorized attacker.

Attacker gains access to database using SQL poisoning attack.

Improper management of HTTP sessions.

HTTP session cookies are revealed to an attacker.

Confidential data are unencrypted.

Encryption keys are leaked to potential attackers.

1. When you are testing for vulnerabilities, you are testing for something that the software should not do, so there are an infinite number of possible tests.

2. Vulbenerabilities are often obscure and lurk in rarely used code, so they may not be revealed by normal functional tests.

3. Software products depend on a software stack that includes operating systems, libraries, databases, browsers, and so on. These may contain vulnerabilities that affect your software. These vulnerabilities may change as new versions of software in the stack are released.

Comprehensive security testing requires specialist knowledge of software vulnerabilities and approaches to testing that can find these vulnerabilities. Product development teams don't normally have the experience required for this security testing, so ideally you should involve external specialists in security testing. Many companies offer penetration testing (pen testing) services, where they simulate attacks on your software and use their ingenuity to find ways to break its security. Independent security testing is expensive, however, and may not be affordable by startup product companies.

One practical way to organize security testing is to adopt a risk-based approach, where you identify the common risks and then develop tests to demonstrate that the system protects itself from these risks. You may also use automated tools that scan your system to check for known vulnerabilities, such as unused HTTP ports being left open.

In a risk-based approach, you start by identifying the main security risks to your product. To identify these risks, you use knowledge of possible attacks, known vulnerabilities, and security problems. Table 9.11 shows examples of the risks that you might test for.

Based on the risks that have been identified, you then design tests and checks to see if the system is vulnerable. It may be possible to construct automated tests for some of these checks, but others inevitably involve manual checking of the system's behavior and its files.

Once you have identified security risks, you then analyze them to assess how they might arise. For example, for the first risk in Table 9.11 (unauthorized attacker) there are several possibilities:

1. The user has set weak passwords that an attacker can guess.

2. The system's password file has been stolen and an attacker has discovered the passwords.

3. The user has not set up two-factor authentication.

4. An attacker has discovered the credentials of a legitimate user through social engineering techniques.

You can then develop tests to check some of these possibilities. For example, you might run a test to check that the code that allows users to set their passwords always checks the strength of the passwords. It should not allow users to set passwords that are easy to crack. You may also test that users are always prompted to set up two-factor authentication.

The reliable programming techniques that I explained in Chapter 8 provide some protection against these risks. However, this does not mean that you do not need security testing. Developers might have made mistakes. For example, they might have forgotten to check the validity of some inputs or forgotten to implement a password strength check when a password is changed.

As well as adopting a risk-based approach to security testing, you can use basic tests that check whether or not common programming mistakes have occurred. These might test that sessions are properly closed or that inputs have been validated. An example of a basic test that checks for incorrect session management is a simple login test:

1. Log into a web application.

2. Navigate to a different website.

3. Click the BACK button of the browser

When you navigate away from a secure application, the software should automatically log you out so that you have to re-authenticate if you go back to that application. Otherwise, if someone gets access to your computer, they could use the BACK button to get into your supposedly secure account. Most types of security testing involve complex steps and outside-the-box thinking, but sometimes simple tests, like this one, help to expose the most severe security risks.

You need to think differently if you are to be a successful security tester. When you are testing the features of a system, it is sensible to focus on those features that are most used and to test the "normal" usage of these features. However, when you are testing the security of a system, you need to think like an attacker rather than a normal end-user.

This means that you deliberately try to do the wrong thing because system vulnerabilities often lurk in rarely used code that handles exceptional situations. You may repeat actions several times because sometimes this leads to different behavior. A widely publicized Apple security bug was revealed when a tester tried logging in with no password several times. On the fifth or sixth attempt, access was allowed. My guess is that there was some code included to make it easier to test the system without remembering passwords and then the developers forgot to remove this code before they shipped the system.

9.5 Code reviews

Testing is the most widely used technique for finding bugs in programs. However, it suffers from three fundamental problems:

1. You can only test code against your understanding of what that code should do. If you have misunderstood the purpose of the code, then this will be reflected in both the code and the tests.

2. Tests are sometimes difficult to design, with the consequence that the tests you write may not provide coverage of all the code you have written. This is most often a problem with code that handles rarely occurring errors and exceptions. One of the arguments for TDD is that it avoids this problem. You always have code associated with each test. However, TDD simply changes this problem. Instead of test incompleteness, you may have code incompleteness because you don't think about rare exceptions.

3. Testing doesn't really tell you anything about other attributes of a program, such as its readability, structure, or evolvability or whether it is interacting efficiently with its environment.

To reduce the effects of these problems, many software companies insist that all code has to go through a process of code review before it is integrated into the product codebase. Code reviews complement testing. They are

Figure 9.9 Code reviews

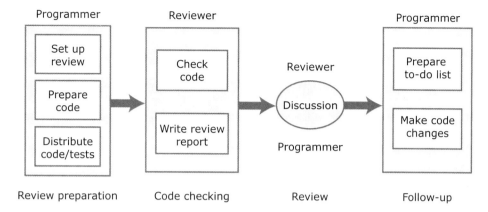

effective in finding bugs that arise through misunderstandings and bugs that may arise only when unusual sequences of code are executed.

Figure 9.9 shows the activities involved in the code review process. Details of the process vary across companies, depending on their culture (more or less formal) and their normal way of working. Table 9.12 describes each of these activities in more detail.

Table 9.12 Code review activities

Activity	Description
Set up review	The programmer contacts a reviewer and arranges a review date.
Prepare code	The programmer collects the code and tests for review and annotates them with information for the reviewer about the intended purpose of the code and tests.
Distribute code/tests	The programmer sends code and tests to the reviewer.
Check code	The reviewer systematically checks the code and tests against their understanding of what they are supposed to do.
Write review report	The reviewer annotates the code and tests with a report of the issues to be discussed at the review meeting.
Discussion	The reviewer and programmer discuss the issues and agree on the actions to resolve these.
Make to-do list	The programmer documents the outcome of the review as a to-do list and shares this with the reviewer.
Make code changes	The programmer modifies the code and tests to address the issues raised in the review.

Code reviews involve one or more people examining the code to check for errors and anomalies and discussing issues with the developer. If problems are identified, it is the developer's responsibility to change the code to fix the problems.

The general idea of code reviews was first publicized in the 1970s under the name "program inspections." Program inspections involved a team of four to six people examining the code and preparing a formal report on the problems they discovered. Inspections are very effective in discovering programming errors, but because so many people are involved, they are expensive and time-consuming to organize.

Consequently, a lightweight approach is now the norm for code reviews. A single code reviewer is used, who may be part of the same development team or may work in a related area. As well as checking the code under review, the reviewer should also look at the automated tests that have been developed. The reviewer should check that the test set is complete and that the tests are consistent with their understanding of the purpose of the code.

Code reviews should be approached positively by both the programmer and the reviewer. The reviewer should not implicitly or explicitly criticize the programmer's ability and should not see the review as a way to show how clever they are. You may collect metrics, such as the number of discovered defects, from code reviews. These should be used to improve the review process rather than to evaluate the developers involved.

Apart from the obvious benefit of finding bugs, code reviews are important for sharing knowledge of a codebase. If all members of the team are involved in reviewing and programming, this means that if people leave or are unavailable, then it is easier for others to pick up their work and continue its development.

Along with looking for bugs and misunderstandings in the code, the reviewer may comment on the readability and understandability of the code. If your company has a coding standard, then the review should check conformance to this standard. However, I think it is best to use an automated tool for standards checking and to use it before submitting code for review.

Program inspections and code reviews usually involve a meeting between the developer and the code reviewers. I think this is the most effective way to organize a review. Face-to-face discussions are the quickest way to resolve misunderstandings. In companies where teams may not all work in the same place, however, the review may involve a phone discussion about the code.

As a general rule, you should not attempt to do too much in a review. It should last around an hour, so that between 200 and 400 lines of code can

Table 9.13 Part of a checklist for a Python code review

Review check	Rationale
Are meaningful variables and function names used? (General)	Meaningful names make a program easier to read and understand.
Have all data errors been considered and tests developed for these? (General)	It is easy to write tests for the most common cases, but it is equally important to check that the program won't fail when presented with incorrect data.
Are all exceptions explicitly handled? (General)	Unhandled exceptions may cause a system to crash.
Are default function parameters used? (Python)	Python allows default values to be set for function parameters when the function is defined. This often leads to errors when programmers forget about or misuse them.
Are types used consistently? (Python)	Python does not have compile-time type checking, so it is possible to assign values of different types to the same variable. This is best avoided, but if used, it should be justified.
Is the indentation level correct? (Python)	Python uses indentation rather than explicit brackets after conditional statements to indicate the code to be executed if the condition is true or false. If the code is not properly indented in nested conditionals, this may mean that incorrect code is executed.

be reviewed in a single session. Because people make similar mistakes, it is usually effective to prepare a checklist for reviewers to use while checking the code. Checklists may contain a mix of general items and specific items based on characteristic errors that can occur in the programming language that is used. You can find checklists for most programming languages on the web. Table 9.13 shows part of a checklist for reviewing Python code.

Several code review tools are now available to support the process. Using these tools, both the programmer and the reviewer can annotate the code being reviewed and document the review process by creating to-do lists. These review tools can be set up so that whenever a programmer submits code to a repository such as Github, a code review is automatically set up. Review tools may also integrate with an issue tracking system, messaging systems such as Slack, and voice communication systems such as Skype.

KEY POINTS

- The aim of program testing is to find bugs and to show that a program does what its developers expect it to do.

- Four types of testing that are relevant to software products are functional testing, user testing, load and performance testing, and security testing.

- Unit testing involves testing program units, such as functions or class methods, that have a single responsibility. Feature testing focuses on testing individual system features. System testing tests the system as a whole to check for unwanted interactions between features and between the system and its environment.

- Identifying equivalence partitions, in which all inputs have the same characteristics, and choosing test inputs at the boundaries of these partitions are an effective way of finding bugs in a program.

- User stories may be used as a basis for deriving feature tests.

- Test automation is based on the idea that tests should be executable. You develop a set of executable tests and run these each time you make a change to a system.

- The structure of an automated unit test should be arrange-action-assert. You set up the test parameters, call the function or method being tested, and make an assertion about what should be true after the action has been completed.

- Test-driven development is an approach in which executable tests are written before the code. Code is then developed to pass the tests.

- A disadvantage of test-driven development is that programmers focus on the details of passing tests rather than considering the broader structure of their code and algorithms used.

- Security testing may be risk-driven, with a list of security risks used to identify tests that may reveal system vulnerabilities.

- Program reviews are an effective supplement to testing. They involve people checking the code to comment on its quality and to look for bugs.

RECOMMENDED READING

"An Overview of Software Testing" This good article goes into more detail about different types of software testing. (M. Parker, 2015)

http://openconcept.ca/blog/mparker/overview-software-testing

"How to Perform Software Product Testing" My coverage of testing focuses on testing during the initial development of a product. This interesting article discusses the broader issues of testing over a product's life cycle, from introduction to product retirement. (Software Testing Help, 2017)

http://www.softwaretestinghelp.com/how-perform-software-product-testing/

"Why Most Unit Testing Is Waste" This view is contrary to the conventional wisdom that most tests should be automated unit tests. It is written by an author who was one of the original authors of the *Design Patterns* book. He argues that integration and system tests deliver real value, whereas a big proportion of unit tests tell us nothing that we don't know about the code. I don't agree with everything the author says, but I do agree with his general premise that thinking is more valuable than testing. (J. O. Coplien, 2014)

https://rbcs-us.com/documents/Why-Most-Unit-Testing-is-Waste.pdf

"The Art of Agile Development: Test-Driven Development" This is an online version of a chapter from the book *The Art of Agile Development*, a good description of test-driven development that goes into much more detail than I do here. Examples are in Java. (J. Shore, 2010)

http://www.jamesshore.com/Agile-Book/test_driven_development.html

"Introducing BDD" Behavior-driven design is an evolution of test-driven design where the focus of the testing process is the expected behavior of the software being tested. A stylized language can be used to describe behavior and tests derived from this description. I have never tried this approach, but it seems to get around some of the problems with TDD. (D. North, 2006)

https://dannorth.net/introducing-bdd/

"Best Practices for Code Review" This is a nice summary of good review practice from a vendor of Collaborator, a code review tool. The same site has a number of blog posts that expand on these practices and provide review checklists. (SmartBear, 2018)

https://smartbear.com/learn/code-review/best-practices-for-peer-code-review/

PRESENTATIONS, VIDEOS, AND LINKS

https://iansommerville.com/engineering-software-products/testing

EXERCISES

9.1. Explain why you can never be completely confident that program testing has revealed all the faults in a software product.

9.2. What are the important distinctions between unit testing and feature testing?

Table 9.14 Setting up a group email

Emma is a history teacher who is arranging a school trip to the historic battlefields in northern France. She wants to set up a "battlefields group" where the students who are attending the trip can share their research about the places they are visiting as well as their pictures and thoughts about the visit.

Emma logs in to a "group management" app, which recognizes her role and school from her identity information and creates a new group. The system prompts her for her year (S3) and subject (history) and automatically populates the new group with all S3 students who are studying history. She selects the students going on the trip and adds her teacher colleagues, Jamie and Claire, to the group.

She names the group and confirms the group creation. This sets up an icon on her iLearn screen to represent the group, creates an email alias for the group, and asks Emma if she wishes to share the group. She shares access to the group with everyone in the group, which means that they also see the icon on their screen. To avoid getting too many emails from students, she restricts sharing of the email alias to Jamie and Claire.

9.3. Imagine that your software includes a feature that can automatically create a contents list for a document or book. Suggest tests that you might develop to test this feature. It is described by the following user stories:

(a) As a user, I want to automatically create a contents list for my document that includes all of the headings that I have marked up in my text.

(b) As a user, I want to be able to identify elements of a contents list and mark these up at different levels.

For simplicity, I have left out stories concerned with formatting the contents list.

9.4. Table 9.14 is a simplified version of the scenario I used in Chapter 3 for the iLearn system (see Table 3.6). Suggest six end-to-end tests that could be used to test the features of the system in this scenario.

9.5. Explain why it is easier to develop automated unit tests than automated feature tests.

9.6. Using any programming language that you know, write a function/method that accepts a list of integers as a parameter and returns the sum of the numbers in that list. Using an appropriate test framework, write automated tests to test that function. Make sure you test with both incorrect and correct data.

9.7. What is regression testing, and why is it important? Explain why automated testing makes regression testing straightforward.

9.8. Explain why it is essential to have a refactoring stage in the test-driven development process.

9.9. Explain why software security testing is more difficult than functional testing.

9.10. Give three reasons why you should use code reviews as well as testing when you are developing software.

10

DevOps and Code Management

The ultimate goal of software product development is to release a product to customers. Mobile products are usually released through an app store; products for computers and servers may be made available for downloading from the vendor's website or an app store. Increasingly, however, software products are made available as a cloud-based service, so there is no need for customer downloads.

After you have released your product, you have to provide some customer support. This may be as little as a list of FAQs on a web page or as much as a dedicated help desk that users may contact. You may also collect problem reports from customers to help you decide what changes to make in later releases of your product.

Traditionally, separate teams were responsible for software development, software release, and software support (Figure 10.1). The development team passed a "final" version of the software to a release team. That team then built a release version, tested it, and prepared release documentation before releasing the software to customers. A third team provided customer support. The original development team was sometimes responsible for implementing software changes. Alternatively, the software may have been maintained by a separate maintenance team.

In these processes, communication delays between the groups were inevitable. Development and operations engineers used different tools, had different skill sets, and often didn't understand the other's problems. Even when an urgent bug or security vulnerability was identified, it could take several days for a new release to be prepared and pushed to customers.

Many companies still use this traditional model of development, release, and support. However, more and more companies are using an alternative

Figure 10.1 Development, release, and support

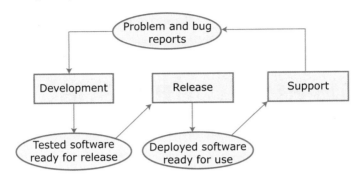

approach called DevOps. DevOps (development + operations) integrates development, deployment, and support, with a single team responsible for all of these activities (Figure 10.2). Three factors led to the development and widespread adoption of DevOps:

1. Agile software engineering reduced the development time for software, but the traditional release process introduced a bottleneck between development and deployment. Agile enthusiasts started looking for a way around this problem.

2. Amazon re-engineered their software around services and introduced an approach in which a service was both developed and supported by the

Figure 10.2 DevOps

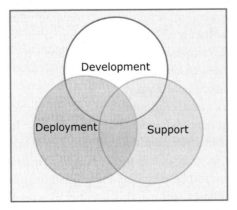

Multi-skilled DevOps team

Table 10.1 DevOps principles

Principle	Explanation
Everyone is responsible for everything.	All team members have joint responsibility for developing, delivering, and supporting the software.
Everything that can be automated should be automated.	All activities involved in testing, deployment, and support should be automated if it is possible to do so. There should be mimimal manual involvement in deploying software.
Measure first, change later.	DevOps should be driven by a measurement program where you collect data about the system and its operation. You then use the collected data to inform decisions about changing DevOps processes and tools.

same team. Amazon's claim that this led to significant improvements in reliability was widely publicized.

3. It became possible to release software as a service, running on a public or private cloud. Software products did not have to be released to users on physical media or downloads.

There is no simple definition of DevOps. Companies interpret the integration of development and operations differently, depending on their culture and the type of software they are developing. However, the three fundamental principles listed in Table 10.1 are the basis for effective DevOps.

Likewise, the specific benefits of using DevOps depend on a company's technology, organization, and culture. However, almost all adopters of DevOps report that important benefits to them are a faster deployment cycle for their software, reduced risk of major failures or outages, faster problem resolution, and more stable and productive teams. I explain why these are universal benefits of DevOps in Table 10.2.

For software product companies, all aspects of DevOps are relevant if your product is delivered as a cloud-based service. If your product is released through an app store or through your website, DevOps is still relevant. Some processes, however, such as continuous delivery, have to be modified for downloaded software.

In this chapter, I focus on automation and measurement, the technical aspects of DevOps. However, many people argue that without the right culture, the full potential of DevOps cannot be realized. Historically, there has often been a culture of mistrust between development and operations engineers.

Table 10.2   Benefits of DevOps

Benefit	Explanation
Faster deployment	Software can be deployed to production more quickly because communication delays between the people involved in the process are dramatically reduced.
Reduced risk	The increment of functionality in each release is small so there is less chance of feature interactions and other changes that cause system failures and outages.
Faster repair	DevOps teams work together to get the software up and running again as soon as possible. There is no need to discover which team was responsible for the problem and to wait for them to fix it.
More productive teams	DevOps teams are happier and more productive than the teams involved in the separate activities. Because team members are happier, they are less likely to leave to find jobs elsewhere.

DevOps aims to change this by creating a single team that is responsible for both development and operations. Developers also take responsibility for installing and maintaining their software.

Creating a DevOps team means bringing together a number of different skill sets, which may include software engineering, UX design, security engineering, infrastructure engineering, and customer interaction. Unfortunately, some software engineers consider their work to be more challenging and important than the work of others. They don't try to understand what team members with different skills do or the problems they face. This leads to tensions as members try to establish a "pecking order" of importance.

A successful DevOps team has a culture of mutual respect and sharing. Everyone on the team should be involved in Scrums and other team meetings. Team members should be encouraged to share their expertise with others and to learn new skills. Developers should support the software services that they have developed. If a service fails over a weekend, that developer is responsible for getting it up and running again. If that person is unavailable, however, other team members should take over rather than wait for their return. The team priority should be to fix failures as quickly as possible, rather than to assign blame to a team member or subgroup.

Table 10.3   A code management problem

Alice and Bob worked for a company called FinanceMadeSimple and were team members involved in developing a personal finance product. Alice discovered a bug in a module called TaxReturnPreparation. The bug was that a tax return was reported as filed but sometimes it was not actually sent to the tax office. She edited the module to fix the bug. Bob was working on the user interface for the system and was also working on TaxReturnPreparation. Unfortunately, he took a copy before Alice had fixed the bug and, after making his changes, he saved the module. This overwrote Alice's changes, but she was not aware of this.

The product tests did not reveal the bug, as it was an intermittent failure that depended on the sections of the tax return form that had been completed. The product was launched with the bug. For most users, everything worked OK. However, for a small number of users, their tax returns were not filed and they were fined by the revenue service. The subsequent investigation showed the software company was negligent. This was widely publicized and, as well as a fine from the tax authorities, users lost confidence in the software. Many switched to a rival product. FinanceMadeSimple failed and both Bob and Alice lost their jobs.

10.1 Code management

DevOps depends on the source code management system that is used by the entire team. However, source code management predates DevOps by almost 40 years. The need to manage an evolving codebase was recognized in the early 1970s. Whether or not your team adopts DevOps, managing source code is essential for all types of software engineering.

During the development of a software product, the development team will probably create tens of thousands of lines of code and automated tests. These will be organized into hundreds of files. Dozens of libraries may be used, and several different programs may be involved in creating and running the code. Without automated support, it is impossible for developers to keep track of the changes made to the software.

Code management[1] is a set of software-supported practices used to manage an evolving codebase. You need code management to ensure that changes made by different developers do not interfere with each other and to create different product versions. Code management tools make it easy to create an executable product from its source code files and to run automated tests on that product.

To illustrate why code management is important, consider the scenario shown in Table 10.3. If a code management system had been used, it would

---

[1]Code management was originally called "software configuration management" and this term is still widely used. However, "configuration management" is now commonly used to refer to the management of a server infrastructure.

Figure 10.3 Code management and DevOps

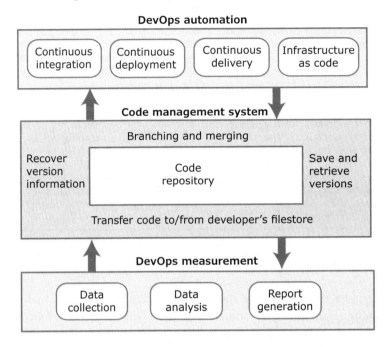

have detected the conflict between Bob's and Alice's changes, the bug would have been fixed, and the company could have continued in business.

Source code management, combined with automated system building, is critical for professional software engineering. In companies that use DevOps, a modern code management system is a fundamental requirement for "automating everything." Not only does it store the project code that is ultimately deployed, but it also stores all other information that is used in DevOps processes. DevOps automation and measurement tools all interact with the code management system (Figure 10.3).

I cover DevOps automation and measurement tools in more detail in Sections 10.2 and 10.3.

10.1.1 Fundamentals of source code management

Source code management systems are designed to manage an evolving project codebase to allow different versions of components and entire systems to be stored and retrieved. Developers can work in parallel without interfering with each other and they can integrate their work with that from other developers.

The code management system provides a set of features that support four general areas:

1. *Code transfer* Developers take code into their personal file store to work on it; then they return it to the shared code management system.

2. *Version storage and retrieval* Files may be stored in several different versions, and specific versions of these files can be retrieved.

3. *Merging and branching* Parallel development branches may be created for concurrent working. Changes made by developers in different branches may be merged.

4. *Version information* Information about the different versions maintained in the system may be stored and retrieved.

All source code management systems have the general form shown in Figure 10.3, with a shared repository and a set of features to manage the files in that repository:

1. All source code files and file versions are stored in the repository, as are other artifacts such as configuration files, build scripts, shared libraries, and versions of tools used. The repository includes a database of information about the stored files, such as version information, information about who has changed the files, what changes were made at what times, and so on.

2. The source code management features transfer files to and from the repository and update the information about the different versions of files and their relationships. Specific versions of files and information about these versions can always be retrieved from the repository.

Several open-source and proprietary-source code management systems are currently used. All of them provide the features shown in Table 10.4.

When files are added, the source code management system assigns a unique identifier to each file. This is used to name stored files; the unique name means that managed files can never be overwritten. Other identifying attributes may be added to the controlled file so that it can be retrieved by name or by using these attributes. Any version of a file can be retrieved from the system. When a change is made to a file and it is submitted to the system, the submitter must add an identifying string that explains the changes made. This helps developers understand why the new version of the file was created.

Table 10.4   Features of source code management systems

Feature	Description
Version and release identification	Managed versions of a code file are uniquely identified when they are submitted to the system and can be retrieved using their identifier and other file attributes.
Change history recording	The reasons changes to a code file have been made are recorded and maintained.
Independent development	Several developers can work on the same code file at the same time. When this is submitted to the code management system, a new version is created so that files are never overwritten by later changes.
Project support	All of the files associated with a project may be checked out at the same time. There is no need to check out files one at a time.
Storage management	The code management system includes efficient storage mechanisms so that it doesn't keep multiple copies of files that have only small differences.

Code management systems support independent development when several developers work on the same file simultaneously. They submit changes to the code management system, which creates a new version of the file for each submission. This avoids the file overwriting problem that I described in Table 10.3. It is common for different projects to share components, so code management systems also provide some form of project support. Project support features allow users to retrieve all the versions of files that are relevant to the project that they are working on.

High storage costs were an important driver for the development of code management systems in the 1970s. Rather than storing every version of a file, storage compaction reduced the space required for the set of files being managed. These systems stored a version as a list of changes from a master version of a file. The version file could be recreated by applying these changes to the master file. If several versions of a file had been created, it was relatively slow to recreate a specific version, as this involved retrieving and applying several sets of code edits.

As storage is now cheap and plentiful, modern code management systems are less concerned with optimizing storage. They use faster mechanisms for version storage and retrieval.

Early source code management systems had a centralized repository architecture that requires users to check in and check out files (Figure 10.4). If a user checks out a file, anyone else who tries to check out that file is warned

Figure 10.4 Centralized source code management

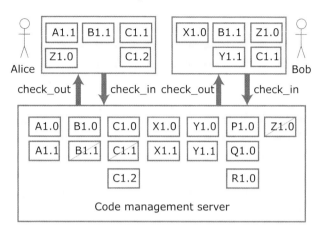

that it is already in use. When the edited file is checked in, a new version of that file is created.

In Figure 10.4, both Alice and Bob have checked out the files they need from the repository. Both have checked out B1.1, C1.1, and Z1.0. These are marked in the repository as shared. When Alice and Bob check in these files, the source code management system ensures that file copies do not conflict.

This centralized architecture was the dominant model for code management systems for more than 30 years and is still used in some code management systems. Subversion is the best-known, open-source code management product that is based around a centralized repository. However, distributed code management systems are now the most commonly used code management systems for software product development. In these systems, the repository is replicated on each developer's computer.

In 2005, Linus Torvalds, the developer of Linux, revolutionized source code management by developing a distributed version control system (DVCS) called Git to manage the code of the Linux kernel. Git was geared to supporting large-scale open-source development. It took advantage of the fact that storage costs had fallen to such an extent that most users did not have to be concerned with local storage management. Instead of only keeping the copies of the files that users are working on, Git maintains a clone of the repository on every user's computer (Figure 10.5).

A fundamental concept in Git is the "master branch," which is the current master version of the software that the team is working on. You create new versions by creating a new branch, as I explain below. In Figure 10.5, you can

Figure 10.5 Repository cloning in Git

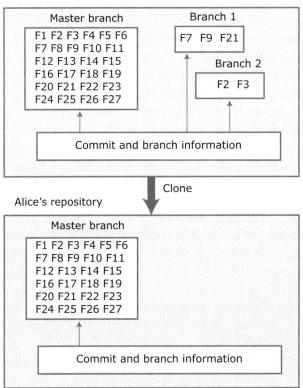

see that two branches have been created in addition to the master branch. When users request a repository clone, they get a copy of the master branch that they can work on independently.

Git and other distributed code management systems have several advantages over centralized systems:

1. *Resilience* Everyone working on a project has their own copy of the repository. If the shared repository is damaged or subjected to a cyberattack, work can continue, and the clones can be used to restore the shared repository. People can work offline if they don't have a network connection.

2. *Speed* Committing changes to the repository is a fast, local operation and does not need data to be transferred over the network.

Figure 10.6 Git repositories

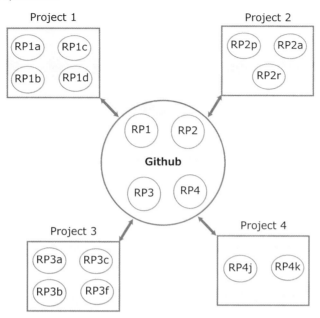

3. *Flexibility* Local experimentation is much simpler. Developers can safely try different approaches without exposing their experiments to other project members. With a centralized system, this may only be possible by working outside the code management system.

Most software product companies now use Git for code management. For teamwork, Git is organized around the notion of a shared project repository and private clones of that repository held on each developer's computer (Figure 10.6). A company may use its own server to run the project repository. However, many companies and individual developers use an external Git repository provider. Several Git repository hosting companies, such as Github and Gitlab, host thousands of repositories on the cloud. In the examples here, I use Github as the shared repository.

Figure 10.6 shows four project repositories on Github, RP1–RP4. RP1 is the repository for project 1, RP2 is the repository for project 2, and so on. Each of the developers on each project is identified by a letter (a, b, c, etc.) and has an individual copy of the project repository. Developers may work on more than one project at a time, so they may have copies of several Git repositories on their computer. For example, developer a works on Project 1, Project 2, and Project 3, so has clones of RP1, RP2, and RP3.

10.1.2   Using Git

When you join a project, you set up a project directory on your computer that acts as your workspace for that project. If necessary, you install the same versions of tools (including Git) that your team uses. As you work in the project directory, the following sequence of commands sets up a local Git repository, often called a repo, in that directory. The local project directory is then cloned from a remote repo.

```
cd myproject
git init #Sets up the local repo in the project directory called myproject
git clone <URL of external repository>
```

The clone command copies the master files from the remote repository to the working directory. These are usually the most recent versions of the project files. It also copies the repository information from the external repository so that you can see what other developers have done. You can query this information and download other branches from the project repo if you need them.

You can then start to work on the files in your project directory, adding new files and making changes as required. To update your local repo, you use the add and commit commands. The list of files in the add command are those files that you want to manage. The commit command adds these files to the local repo after you have made changes to them.

```
git add <list of files to be controlled>
git commit
```

To work with Git, you need to understand the concepts of branching and merging, which are the features that allow developers to work on the same files without interference.

Branching and merging are fundamental ideas that are supported by all code management systems. A branch is an independent, stand-alone version that is created when a developer wishes to change a file. The changes made by developers in their own branches may be merged to create a new shared branch. The repository ensures that branch files that have been changed cannot overwrite repository files without a merge operation.

Let's assume that Alice and Bob are working on the same file in the Git repo. To make their changes, each creates a branch for working on a copy of

Figure 10.7 Branching and merging

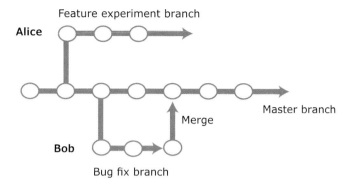

that file (Figure 10.7). Alice is working on a new experimental feature, and Bob is working on a bug fix.

If Alice or Bob make mistakes on the branch they are working on, they can easily revert to the master file. If they commit changes while working, they can revert to earlier versions of the work they have done. When they have finished and tested their code, they can replace the master file by merging the work they have done with the master branch. Figure 10.7 shows that Bob has merged his bug fix with the master branch.

Bob and Alice work with their local repos and there are no conflicts between them. At some stage, however, both of them may try to update the external repository with their changed files. Let's assume Bob is first to update the external repo. He merges the changed files and pushes the changes to the shared repo. His update is accepted. Alice then tries to push her changes to the repo, but they are rejected because of the possible conflict with Bob's changes.

Git compares versions of files on a line-by-line basis. There is no conflict if developers have changed different lines in the file. If they have made changes to the same lines, however, then a merge conflict is signaled. Git highlights the lines where the conflict occurs, and it is up to the developers to resolve these conflicts. In this example, Alice should talk with Bob about his changes and then make changes to the files to resolve the conflict.

Git is very efficient in managing branches, so it makes sense to use this mechanism even when you are making small changes to your code. To create a new branch based on the files in your working directory, you use the checkout command with a -b flag. The command below creates a new branch called fix-header-format

```
git checkout -b fix-header-format
```

Let's assume this involves editing two files: report_printer.py and generate_header.py. You make the edits to these files, add them, and commit.

```
git add report_printer.py generate_header.py
git commit
```

The commit command defaults to committing the changes to the current branch, which is fix-header-format. You then decide that you are happy with the changes that you have made and want to merge them with the master branch in your directory. You check out the master branch from the project repo to make sure that you have the most recent version of all master files and then issue a merge command:

```
git checkout master
git merge fix-header-format
```

At this stage, you have updated the master branch in your local repository but not the external repository. To incorporate the changes that you have made in the master branch of the external repository, you use a push command:

```
git push
```

Git then examines your repo and the external repo, works out what files have changed, and pushes the changes to the external repo. Although I do not shown this here, you can push to specific branches on the external repo.

In the Alice and Bob scenario, Bob issues a push command to push his changed files to the external repo. Alice tries to push her changes, but Git rejects them because it knows that Bob has already issued a push command with possible conflicts. Alice must then update her repository with Bob's changes using a pull command:

```
git pull
```

The pull command fetches a copy of the files that includes Bob's changes from the master in the external repo. It updates Alice's local repo with these files. Alice then works on fixing the potential conflict and then pushes the updated branch to the external repo.

Git was originally developed to support open-source software development. In the open-source model, many different people can work independently on the code without any knowledge of what others are doing. The master version of the open-source software is managed by an individual or

Figure 10.8 Using Github for open-source development

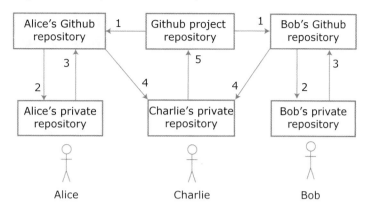

small group that decides what changes should be incorporated. Figure 10.8 shows how Git and GitHub can support this way of working.

Alice and Bob are both making their own changes to the open-source software. Each has a repository on Github as well as a private repository on their own computer. The master repository for the open-source project is held on Github and is managed by Charlie. Charlie is responsible for deciding whether changes made by developers should be incorporated into the master.

This is the sequence of actions involved in updating the master version of an open-source project:

1. Alice and Bob copy the master branch from the project repository on Github into their personal Github repositories.

2. They pull their shared public repo to their private repos and complete their changes to the code.

3. They push these changes to their public repos and tell Charlie about the changes they have made.

4. Charlie pulls the changes from Alice's and Bob's repos into his private repo. He examines and checks the work, runs tests if necessary, and decides whether it should be included in the open-source system.

5. If the software changes are acceptable, Charlie pushes these changes from his private repo to the definitive project repo.

Github uses a very general mechanism called Webhooks to trigger actions in response to an update to the project repository. Webhooks sends data, using an HTTP POST request, to a URL when some action occurs. Therefore, you can configure Github to send messages to developers about changes and to trigger a system build and test when new code is added. This feature is used to communicate with external tools such as the DevOps automation tools that I cover in the next section.

10.2 DevOps automation

Historically, the processes of integrating a system from independently developed parts, deploying that system in a realistic testing environment, and releasing it were time-consuming and expensive. By using DevOps with automated support, however, you can dramatically reduce the time and costs for integration, deployment, and delivery.

"Everything that can be should be automated" is a fundamental principle of DevOps. In addition to reducing the costs and time required for integration, deployment, and delivery, automation makes these processes more reliable and reproducible. Automation information is encoded in scripts and system models that can be checked, reviewed, versioned, and stored in the project repository. Deployment does not depend on a system manager who knows the server configurations. A specific server configuration can be quickly and reliably reproduced using the system model.

Figure 10.3 showed the four aspects of DevOps automation. I explain these in Table 10.5.

Another area of automation that I think is important is the automation of issue tracking. Issue and bug tracking involves recording observed problems and the development team's responses to these problems. If you use Scrum or a Scrum-like process, these issues should be automatically added to the product backlog.

Several open-source and proprietary issue-tracking tools are widely used, such as Bugzilla, FogBugz, and JIRA. These systems include the following features:

1. *Issue reporting* Users and testers can report an issue or a bug and provide further information about the context where the problem was discovered. These reports can be sent automatically to developers. Developers can comment on the report and indicate if and when the issue has been resolved. Reports are stored in an issue database.

Table 10.5 Aspects of DevOps automation

Aspect	Description
Continuous integration	Each time a developer commits a change to the project's master branch, an executable version of the system is built and tested.
Continuous delivery	A simulation of the product's operating environment is created and the executable software version is tested.
Continuous deployment	A new release of the system is made available to users every time a change is made to the master branch of the software.
Infrastructure as code	Machine-readable models of the infrastructure (network, servers, routers, etc.) on which the product executes are used by configuration management tools to build the software's execution platform. The software to be installed, such as compilers and libraries and a DBMS, are included in the infastructure model.

2. *Searching and querying* The issue database may be searched and queried. This is important to discover whether issues have already been raised, to discover unresolved issues, and to find out if related issues have been reported.

3. *Data analysis* The issue database can be analyzed and information extracted, such as the number of unresolved issues, the rate of issue resolution, and so on. This is often presented graphically in a system dashboard.

4. *Integration with source code management* Issue reports can be linked to versions of software components stored in the code management system.

I do not go into any more details about issue-tracking tools, but it is essential for DevOps to use automated issue tracking. The issue-tracking system captures data about the use of a software product that can be analyzed in conjunction with other data in a DevOps measurement system.

10.2.1 Continuous integration

System integration (system building) is the process of gathering all of the elements required in a working system, moving them into the right directories, and putting them together to create an operational system. This involves more

Figure 10.9 Continuous integration

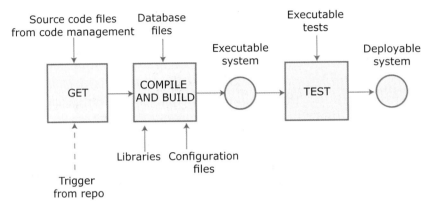

than compiling the system. You usually have to complete several other steps to create a working system. Although every product is different, the following typical activities are part of the system integration process:

- installing database software and setting up the database with the appropriate schema;

- loading test data into the database;

- compiling the files that make up the product;

- linking the compiled code with the libraries and other components used;

- checking that the external services used are operational;

- deleting old configuration files and moving configuration files to the correct locations;

- running a set of system tests to check that the integration has been successful.

If a system is infrequently integrated, many of the system's components are changed, sometimes significantly, between integrations. When problems are discovered, they are often difficult to isolate, and fixing them slows down the system development. To avoid this problem, the developers of the Extreme Programming method suggested that continuous integration should be used.

Continuous integration simply means that an integrated version of the system is created and tested every time a change is pushed to the system's shared code repository. On completion of the push operation, the repository sends a message to an integration server to build a new version of the product (Figure 10.9).

Figure 10.10 Local integration

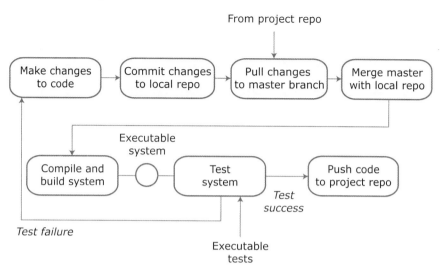

The squares in Figure 10.9 are the elements of a continuous integration pipeline that is triggered by a repository notification that a change has been made to the master branch of the system.

In a continuous integration environment, developers have to make sure that they don't "break the build." Breaking the build means pushing code to the project repository, which when integrated, causes some of the system tests to fail. This holds up other developers. If this happens to you, your priority is to discover and fix the problem so that normal development can continue. To avoid breaking the build, you should always adopt an "integrate twice" approach to system integration. You should integrate and test on your own computer before pushing code to the project repository to trigger the integration server (Figure 10.10).

The advantage of continuous integration compared to less frequent integration is that it is faster to find and fix bugs in the system. If you make a small change and some system tests then fail, the problem almost certainly lies in the new code that you have pushed to the project repo. You can focus on this code to find the bug that's causing the problem.

If you continuously integrate, then a working system is always available to the whole team. This can be used to test ideas and to demonstrate the features of the system to management and customers. Furthermore, continuous integration creates a "quality culture" in a development team. Team members want to avoid the stigma and disruption of breaking the build. They are likely to check their work carefully before pushing it to the project repo.

Figure 10.11 A dependency model

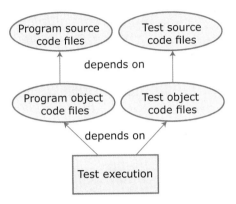

Continuous integration is effective only if the integration process is fast and developers do not have to wait for the results of their tests of the integrated system. However, some activities in the build process, such as populating a database or compiling hundreds of system files, are inherently slow. It is therefore essential to have an automated build process that minimizes the time spent on these activities.

Fast automated building is possible because, in a continuous integration system, the changes made to the system between one integration and another are usually relatively small. Usually this means that only a few source code files have been changed. Code integration tools use an incremental build process so that they only have to repeat actions, such as compilation, if the dependent files have been changed.

To understand incremental system building, you need to understand the concept of dependencies. Figure 10.11 is a dependency model that shows the dependencies for test execution. An upward-pointing arrow means "depends on" and shows the information required to complete the task shown in the rectangle at the base of the model. Figure 10.11 therefore shows that running a set of system tests depends on the existence of executable object code for both the program being tested and the system tests. In turn, these depend on the source code for the system and the tests that are compiled to create the object code.

The first time you integrate a system, the incremental build system compiles all the source code files and executable test files. It creates their object code equivalents, and the executable tests are run. Subsequently, however, object code files are created only for new and modified tests and for source code files that have been modified.

Figure 10.12 File dependencies

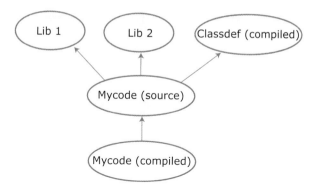

Figure 10.12 is a lower-level dependency model that shows the dependencies involved in creating the object code for a source code file called Mycode. Source code files are rarely independent but rely on other information such as libraries. Mycode depends on two libraries (Lib 1 and Lib 2) and an externally defined class definition.

An automated build system uses the specification of dependencies to work out what needs to be done. It uses the file modification timestamp to decide whether a source code file has been changed after the associated object code file was created. If so, the source code must be recompiled. To illustrate this, consider three scenarios based on Figure 10.12:

1. The modification date of the compiled code is later than the modification date of the source code. The build system infers that no changes have been made to the source code and does nothing.

2. The modification date of the compiled code is earlier than the modification date of the compiled code. The build system recompiles the source and replaces the existing file of compiled code with an updated version.

3. The modification date of the compiled code is later than the modification date of the source code. However, the modification date of Classdef is later than the modification date of the source code of Mycode. Therefore, Mycode has to be recompiled to incorporate these changes.

Manually recording file dependencies is a tedious and time-consuming task. For most programming languages, however, either the compiler or a separate tool can automatically create a dependency model that can be used for system building. The system building software uses the model when it builds the system to optimize the build process.

The oldest and perhaps best known system building tool is make, which was originally developed in the 1970s for Unix. System building commands are written as a shell script. Other tools such as Ant and Maven, which are Java oriented, and Rake, which is Ruby oriented, use different approaches to specify dependencies, but all basically do the same thing.

Tools that support the entire continuous integration process allow you to define an activity pipeline, such as that shown in Figure 10.9, and execute that pipeline. In addition to building the system, they can populate the database, run automated tests, and so on. Examples of continuous integration tools include Jenkins, a widely used open-source system, and proprietary products such as Travis and Bamboo.

10.2.2 Continuous delivery and deployment

Continuous integration (CI) means creating an executable version of a software system whenever a change is made to the repository. The CI tool is triggered when a file is pushed to the repo. It builds the system and runs tests on your development computer or project integration server. However, the real environment in which software runs will inevitably be different from your development system. The production server may have a different filesystem organization, different access permissions, and different installed applications. Consequently, when your software runs in its real operational environment, bugs may be revealed that did not show up in the test environment.

Continuous delivery means that, after making changes to a system, you ensure that the changed system is ready for delivery to customers. This means that you have to test it in a production environment to make sure that environmental factors do not cause system failures or slow down its performance. As well as feature tests, you should run load tests that show how the software behaves as the number of users increases. You may also run tests to check the throughput of transactions and your system's response time.

The simplest way to create a replica of a production environment is to run your software in a container, as I explained in Chapter 5. Your production environment is defined as a container, so to create a test environment, you simply create another container using the same image. This ensures that changes made to the production environment are always reflected in the test environment.

Continuous delivery does not mean that the software will necessarily be released immediately to users for deployment. When to do this is a business decision, and there may be good reasons to delay, as I explain later in this section.

Figure 10.13 Continuous delivery and deployment

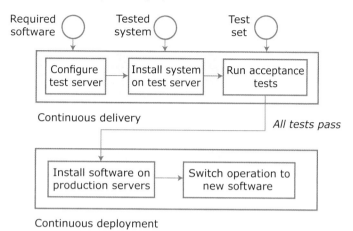

Continuous deployment

In the last few years, however, more and more companies have adopted continuous deployment, where a system is deployed as a cloud service after every change is made. I explained the continuous deployment process for microservices in Chapter 6 and showed the continuous deployment pipeline in Figure 6.16.

Figure 10.13 illustrates a summarized version of this deployment pipeline, showing the stages involved in continuous delivery and deployment.

After initial integration testing, a staged test environment is created. This is a replica of the actual production environment in which the system will run. The system acceptance tests, which include functionality, load, and performance tests, are then run to check that the software works as expected. If all of these tests pass, the changed software is installed on the production servers.

To deploy the system, you transfer the software and required data to the production servers. You then momentarily stop all new requests for service and leave the older version to process the outstanding transactions. Once these have been completed, you switch to the new version of the system and restart processing.

Table 10.6 shows the benefits of using continuous deployment for product companies.

Continuous deployment is obviously only practical for cloud-based systems. If your product is sold through an app store or downloaded from your website, continuous integration and delivery make sense. A working version is always available for release. If you update the downloadable version

Table 10.6 Benefits of continuous deployment

Benefit	Explanation
Reduced costs	If you use continuous deployment, you have no option but to invest in a completely automated deployment pipeline. Manual deployment is a time-consuming and error-prone process. Setting up an automated system is expensive and takes time, but you can recover these costs quickly if you make regular updates to your product.
Faster problem solving	If a problem occurs, it will probably affect only a small part of the system and the source of that problem will be obvious. If you bundle many changes into a single release, finding and fixing problems are more difficult.
Faster customer feedback	You can deploy new features when they are ready for customer use. You can ask them for feedback on these features and use this feedback to identify improvements that you need to make.
A/B testing	This is an option if you have a large customer base and use several servers for deployment. You can deploy a new version of the software on some servers and leave the older version running on others. You then use the load balancer to divert some customers to the new version while others use the older version. You can measure and assess how new features are used to see if they do what you expect.

regularly, your customers can decide when to update the software on their computers or mobile devices. It is sometimes helpful to provide an auto-update feature, so that users don't have to do anything. Many users dislike this, however, and you should always allow this feature to be disabled.

There are three business reasons you may not want to deploy every software change to customers:

1. You may have incomplete features available that could be deployed, but you want to avoid giving competitors information about these features until their implementation is complete.

2. Customers may be irritated by software that is continually changing, especially if this affects the user interface. They don't want to spend time continually learning about new features. Rather, they prefer to have a number of new features available before learning about them.

3. You may wish to synchronize releases of your software with known business cycles. For example, if your product is aimed at the education

market, your customers want stability at the start of their academic year when they are registering new students, setting up courses, and other start-of-year tasks. They are unlikely to try new features at that time. It makes more sense to release features to these customers when they have time to experiment with the new system.

CI tools such as Jenkins and Travis may also be used to support continuous delivery and deployment. These tools can integrate with infrastructure configuration management tools such as Chef and Puppet to implement software deployment. However, for cloud-based software, it is often simpler to use containers in conjunction with CI tools rather than use infrastructure configuration management software.

10.2.3   Infrastructure as code

In an enterprise environment, there are usually many different physical or virtual servers (web servers, database servers, file servers, etc.) that do different things. These have different configurations and run different software packages. Some may have to be updated when new versions of software become available; others may have to be kept stable because legacy software depends on older versions of installed software.

It is difficult to keep track of the software installed on each machine. Emergency changes, such as security updates, may have to be made, and the system administrators don't always have time to document these changes. Server documentation is often out of date. Consequently, manually maintaining a computing infrastructure with tens or hundreds of servers is expensive and error-prone.

The idea of infrastructure as code was proposed as a way to address this problem. Rather than manually updating the software on a company's servers, the process can be automated using a model of the infrastructure written in a machine-processable language. Configuration management (CM) tools, such as Puppet and Chef, can automatically install software and services on servers according to the infrastructure definition. The CM tool accesses a master copy of the software to be installed and pushes this to the servers being provisioned (Figure 10.14). When changes have to be made, the infrastructure model is updated and the CM tool makes the change to all servers.

Defining your software infrastructure as code is obviously relevant to products that are delivered as services. The product provider has to manage the infrastructure of their services on the cloud. However, it is also relevant if software is delivered through downloads. In this case, you have to test the

Figure 10.14 Infrastructure as code

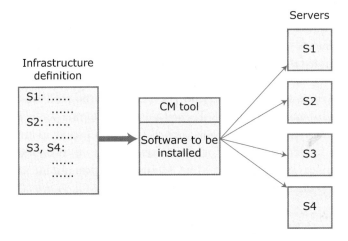

software in several contexts to ensure that it does not react adversely with the buyer's infrastructure. You can do this by defining several test infrastructures and defining each of them.

Defining your infrastructure as code and using a configuration management system solve two key problems of continuous deployment:

1. Your testing environment must be exactly the same as your deployment environment. If you change the deployment environment, you have to mirror those changes in your testing environment.

2. When you change a service, you have to be able to roll that change out to all of your servers quickly and reliably. If there is a bug in your changed code that affects the system's reliability, you have to be able to seamlessly roll back to the older system.

The business benefits of defining your infrastructure as code are lower costs of system management and lower risks of unexpected problems arising when infrastructure changes are implemented. These benefits stem from four fundamental characteristics of infrastructure as code, shown in Table 10.7.

As I explained in Chapter 5, the best way to deploy many cloud-based services is to use containers. A container provides a stand-alone execution environment that runs on top of an operating system such as Linux. The software installed in a Docker container is specified using a Dockerfile, which is essentially a definition of your software infrastructure as code. You build an executable container image by processing the Dockerfile.

Table 10.7 Characteristics of infrastructure as code

Characteristic	Explanation
Visibility	Your infrastructure is defined as a stand-alone model that can be read, discussed, understood, and reviewed by the whole DevOps team.
Reproducibility	Using a configuration management tool means that the installation tasks will always be run in the same sequence so that the same environment is always created. You are not reliant on people remembering the order that they need to do things.
Reliability	In managing a complex infrastructure, system administrators often make simple mistakes, especially when the same changes have to be made to several servers. Automating the process avoids these mistakes.
Recovery	Like any other code, your infrastructure model can be versioned and stored in a code management system. If infrastructure changes cause problems, you can easily revert to an older version and reinstall the environment that you know works.

Using containers makes it very simple to provide identical execution environments. For each type of server you use, you define the environment that you need and build an image for execution. You can run an application container as a test system or as an operational system; there is no distinction between them. When you update your software, you rerun the image creation process to create a new image that includes the modified software. You can then start these images alongside the existing system and divert service requests to them.

Cloud-based products usually have fewer server types (e.g., web servers, database servers, application servers) than enterprise systems. However, you may have to provision new servers in response to increasing demand and then shut down servers at quieter times. You can define containers for each type of server and use a container management system, such as Kubernetes, to deploy and manage these containers.

10.3 DevOps measurement

After you have adopted DevOps, you should try to continuously improve your DevOps process to achieve faster deployment of better-quality software. This means you need to have a measurement program in place in which you collect and analyze product and process data. By making measurements over time, you can judge whether or not you have an effective and improving process.

Measurements about software development and use fall into four categories:

1. *Process measurements* You collect and analyze data about your development, testing, and deployment processes.

2. *Service measurements* You collect and analyze data about the software's performance, reliability, and acceptability to customers.

3. *Usage measurements* You collect and analyze data about how customers use your product.

4. *Business success measurements* You collect and analyze data about how your product contributes to the overall success of the business.

Process measurements and service measurements are the most relevant types for DevOps. Usage measurements help you identify issues and problems with the software itself. Some people think that business success measurements should also be defined and measured. However, as I explain later, I think these are unreliable and I am not convinced that they are worthwhile.

Measurement of software and its development is a complex process. You have to identify the metrics that are likely to give you useful insights and find reliable ways of collecting and analyzing metrics data. It is sometimes impossible to measure what you really want to measure directly (such as customer satisfaction). You therefore have to make inferences from other metrics (such as the number of returning customers) that you can collect.

As far as possible, the DevOps principle of automating everything should be applied to software measurement. You should instrument your software to collect data about itself, and you should use a monitoring system, as I explained in Chapter 6, to collect data about your software's performance and availability. Some process measurements can also be automated. There are problems in process measurement, however, because people are involved. Different people work in different ways, may record information differently, and are affected by outside influences on the way they work.

For example, it may seem simple to record the lead time from the start of development of a change proposal to the deployment of the code implementing that change. However, what does "lead time" mean? Does it mean elapsed time or the time spent by the developer working on the problem? What assumptions are made about normal working hours? Do some changes have higher priority than others so that work on one change is stopped to implement another? There are no simple answers to these questions, which means that process metrics are never simple to collect and analyze.

Many articles on DevOps measurement make the point that you should link process and product measurements to business success measurements. They suggest that improvement to your DevOps process leads to a more successful business. This sounds fine in principle, but I think that linking DevOps measurements to business performance indicators is idealistic and impractical. Many factors contribute to business success, and it is practically impossible to isolate the contribution of DevOps. For example, a business may be more successful because it has introduced DevOps. Alternatively, the success may be due to better managers who have introduced changes, including the use of DevOps.

I believe you should accept that DevOps is worth doing and then focus on collecting process and performance metrics that you can use to improve your software delivery and deployment process. Payal Chakravarty from IBM suggests a very practical approach to DevOps measurement.[2]

Based on a goal of shipping code frequently without causing customer outages, she suggests the use of a metrics scorecard based on nine metrics that are fairly easy to collect. These are relevant to software that is delivered as a cloud service. They include process metrics and service metrics, as shown in Figure 10.15.

For the process metrics, you would like to see decreases in the number of failed deployments, the mean time to recovery after a service failure, and the lead time from development to deployment. You would hope to see increases in the deployment frequency and the number of lines of changed code that are shipped. For the service metrics, availability and performance should be stable or improving, the number of customer complaints should be decreasing, and the number of new customers should be increasing.

Chakravarty suggests that the collected data should be analyzed weekly and presented in a single screen that shows performance in the current and previous weeks. You can also use a graphical presentation that is better for seeing long-term trends. Figure 10.16 shows examples of this trend analysis.

---

[2]Payal Chakravarty, "The DevOps Scorecard," 2014, https://devops.com/devops-scorecard/

Figure 10.15 Metrics used in the DevOps scorecard

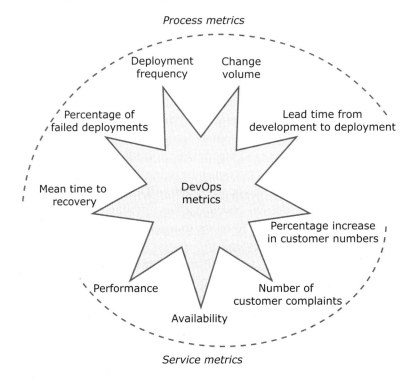

Figure 10.16 Metrics trends

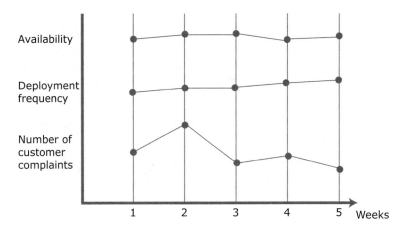

Figure 10.17 Logging and analysis

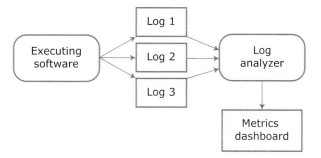

You can see from Figure 10.16 that the availability is roughly stable over time and the deployment frequency is increasing. The number of customer complaints is more variable. The jump in week 2 suggests that there were problems with one of the system releases that week. However, the overall trend indicates a small improvement over time.

To collect these data, you may use several different tools. Continuous integration tools such as Jenkins can collect data about deployments, successful tests, and so on. Cloud providers often have monitoring software, such as Cloudwatch from Amazon, that can provide data on availability and performance. You can collect customer-supplied data from an issue management system.

As well as using these tools, you may add instrumentation to your product to gather data on its performance and how it is used by customers. By analyzing these data, you gain insights into what customers really do, rather than what you expect them to do, and you identify parts of your software that need improvement. The most practical way of doing this is to use log files, where the entries in the log are timestamped events reflecting customer actions and/or software responses (Figure 10.17).

To be useful, you have to log as many events as possible, which means that the logging software may be recording hundreds of events per second. Various log analysis tools are available to manage these data in the cloud and analyze them to create useful information about how your software is used. These may present information using a metrics dashboard that shows the data that have been analyzed and how they are changing over time.

KEY POINTS

- DevOps is the integration of software development and the management of that software once it has been deployed for use. The same team is responsible for development, deployment, and software support.

- The benefits of DevOps are faster deployment, reduced risk, faster repair of buggy code, and more productive teams.

- Source code management is essential to avoid changes made by different developers interfering with each other.

- All code management systems are based around a shared code repository with a set of features that support code transfer, version storage and retrieval, branching and merging, and maintaining version information.

- Git is a distributed code management system that is the most widely used system for software product development. Each developer works with their own copy of the repository, which may be merged with the shared project repository.

- Continuous integration means that as soon as a change is committed to a project repository, it is integrated with existing code and a new version of the system is created for testing.

- Automated system building tools reduce the time needed to compile and integrate the system by recompiling only those components and their dependents that have changed.

- Continuous deployment means that as soon as a change is made, the deployed version of the system is automatically updated. This is only possible when the software product is delivered as a cloud-based service.

- Infrastructure as code means that the infrastructure (network, installed software, etc.) on which software executes is defined as a machine-readable model. Automated tools, such as Chef and Puppet, can provision servers based on the infrastructure model.

- Measurement is a fundamental principle of DevOps. You may make both process and product measurements. Important process metrics are deployment frequency, percentage of failed deployments, and mean time to recovery from failure.

RECOMMENDED READING

"What Is DevOps?" This blog post, written as DevOps was just starting to be used, is a thoughtful explanation of what DevOps means. It does not go into detail but encapsulates the essence of DevOps. (E. Mueller, 2010)

https://theagileadmin.com/what-is-dev/

"Why Git for Your Organization" This blog post discusses how Git is not just a system that benefits developers but also has wider organizational applicability with benefits for marketing, product management, customer support, and so on. (Atlassian, undated)

https://www.atlassian.com/git/tutorials/why-git

"Continuous Integration" This is quite an old post by one of the pioneers of continuous integration, but I think it is one of the best overviews of the topic. It's clear and easy to read. (M. Fowler, 2006)

https://www.martinfowler.com/articles/continuousIntegration.html

"Continuous Integration: The answer to life, the universe, and everything?" It is always useful to read a viewpoint contrary to the conventional wisdom that continuous integration is a good thing. This article points out some of the problems of introducing CI and suggests that the benefits may not always be as great as expected. (M. Heller, undated)

https://techbeacon.com/continuous-integration-answer-life-universe-everything

"Building and Deploying Software through Continuous Delivery" This is a good summary of the principles of continuous delivery, with useful links to other resources on the topic. (K. Brown, undated)

https://www.ibm.com/cloud/garage/content/deliver/practice_continuous_delivery/

"Infrastructure as Code: A Reason to Smile" This is a clear explanation of the benefits of defining your computing infrastructure as code. (J. Sitakange, 2016)

https://www.thoughtworks.com/insights/blog/infrastructure-code-reason-smile

PRESENTATIONS, VIDEOS, AND LINKS

https://iansommerville.com/engineering-software-products/dev-and-code-management

EXERCISES

10.1. Explain why adopting DevOps provides a basis for more efficient and effective software deployment and operation.

10.2. Briefly explain why it is essential to use a code management system when several developers are involved in creating a software system. What are the benefits of using a code management system if only a single developer is involved?

10.3. What is the fundamental difference between distributed and centralized code management systems? How does this difference lead to the most significant benefits of distributed code management systems?

10.4. What does creating a new branch in a code management system mean? What problems can arise when more than one developer is working on the same code and they try to merge their changes with the project master branch?

10.5. Explain how the use of Git and a shared public Git repository simplifies the process of managing open-source development when many developers may be working on the same code.

10.6. What is issue management, and why is it important for software product development?

10.7. Explain why there is more to system integration than simply recompiling the code of the software.

10.8. Why does the use of continuous integration make it easier to find bugs in the software that you are developing?

10.9. What are the differences between continuous integration, continuous delivery, and continuous deployment?

10.10. What are process metrics and service metrics? Explain why service metrics are easier to collect and potentially more accurate than process metrics.

Index

X

Y